Front of the CLASS

GRADE 1

Thinking Kids®
An imprint of Carson-Dellosa Publishing LLC
P.O. Box 35665
Greensboro, NC 27425 USA

Thinking Kids®
An imprint of Carson-Dellosa Publishing LLC
P.O. Box 35665
Greensboro, NC 27425 USA

ISBN 978-1-4838-2712-4
03-086171151

Table of Contents

READING

Name ______________________________

Name, Address, Phone

This book belongs to ______________________________

______________________________.

I live at ______________________________

______________________________.

The city I live in is ______________________________

______________________________.

The state I live in is ______________________________

______________________________.

My phone number is ______________________________

______________________________.

Name ______________________________

Review the Alphabet

Directions: Practice writing the letters.

Aa

Bb

Cc

Dd

Ee

Ff

Gg

Hh

Ii

Name ____________________

Review the Alphabet

Directions: Practice writing the letters.

Jj

Kk

Ll

Mm

Nn

Oo

Pp

Qq

Rr

Name ____________________

Review the Alphabet

Directions: Practice writing the letters.

Ss

Tt

Uu

Vv

Ww

Xx

Yy

Zz

Name ____________________

Letter Recognition

Directions: In each set, match the lower-case letter to the upper-case letter.

a	C
f	H
c	J
h	E
e	A
j	F
g	D
b	B
i	M
d	G
k	I
l	L
m	K

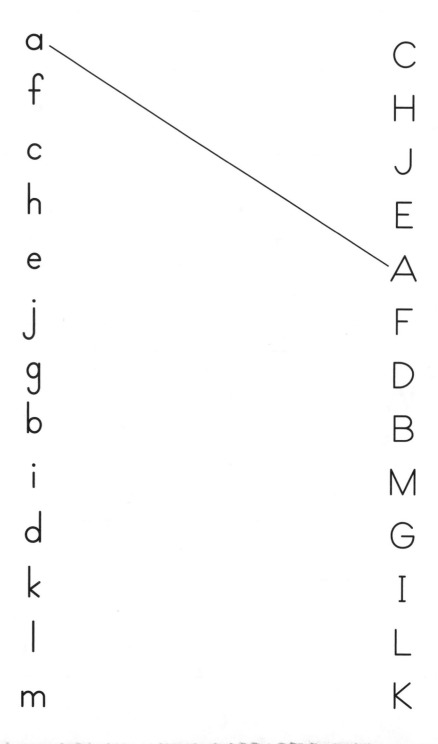

Name ______________________________

Letter Recognition

Directions: In each set, match the lower-case letter to the upper-case letter.

n	U
s	P
p	R
u	Q
r	N
q	S
t	V
y	O
v	T
o	W
x	Z
w	Y
z	X

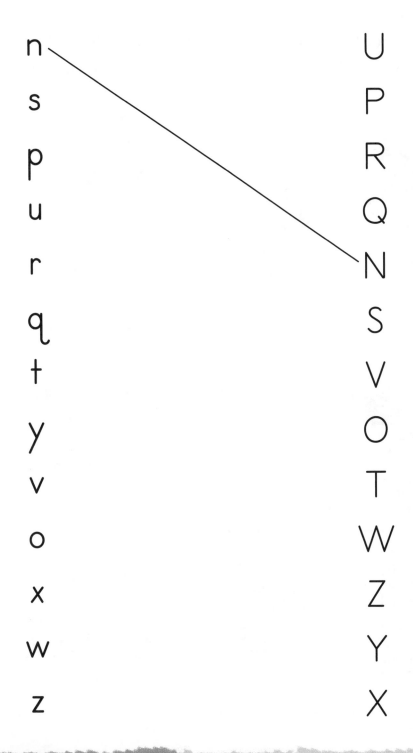

Name ______________________________

Beginning Consonants: Bb, Cc, Dd, Ff

Beginning consonants are the sounds that come at the beginning of words. Consonants are the letters b, c, d, f, g, h, j, k, l, m, n, p, q, r, s, t, v, w, x, y and z.

Directions: Say the name of each letter. Say the sound each letter makes. Circle the letters that make the beginning sound for each picture.

Bb

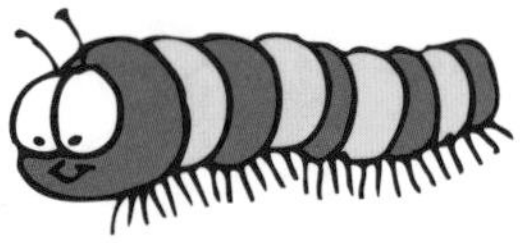
Cc

Dd

Ff

Bb Dd

Ff Cc

Cc Dd

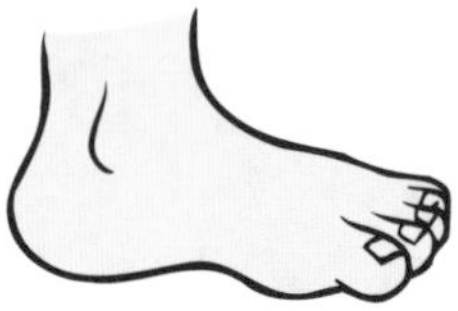
Ff Bb

Bb Dd

Ff Cc

Cc Dd

Ff Bb

Name ______________________________

Beginning Consonants: Bb, Cc, Dd, Ff

Directions: Say the name of each letter. Say the sound each letter makes. Draw a line from each letter to the picture which begins with that sound.

Ff 

Dd 

Cc 

Bb 

Dd 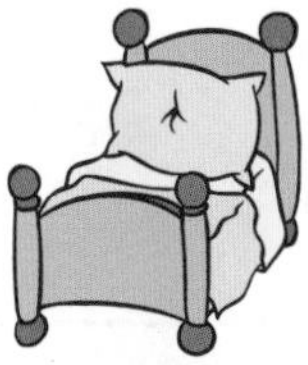

Ff 

Cc 

Bb 

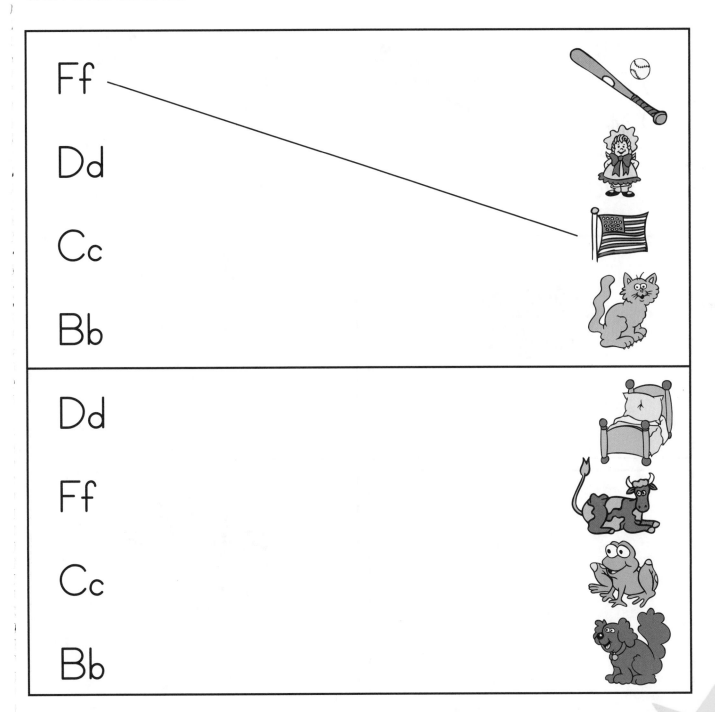

Name ______________________________

Beginning Consonants: Gg, Hh, Jj, Kk

Directions: Say the name of each letter. Say the sound each letter makes. Trace the letter pair that makes the beginning sound in each picture.

Gg

Hh

Jj

Kk

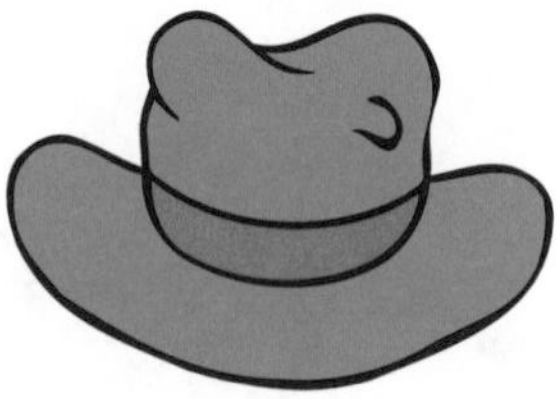

Kk Hh

Gg Kk

Gg Hh

Jj Gg

Name ________________________________

Beginning Consonants: Gg, Hh, Jj, Kk

Directions: Say the name of each letter. Say the sound each letter makes. Draw a line from each letter pair to the picture which begins with that sound.

Gg 

Kk 

Hh 

Jj 

Kk 

Hh 

Jj 

Gg 

Name ______________________________

Beginning Consonants: Ll, Mm, Nn, Pp

Directions: Say the name of each letter. Say the sound each letter makes. Trace the letters. Then draw a line from each letter pair to the picture which begins with that sound.

Ll

Mm

Nn

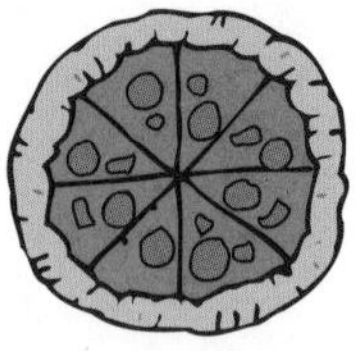

Pp

Ll

Mm

Nn

Pp

Name ______________________________

Beginning Consonants: Ll, Mm, Nn, Pp

Directions: Say the name of each letter. Say the sound each letter makes. Trace the letter pair that makes the beginning sound in each picture.

Ll

Mm

Nn

Pp

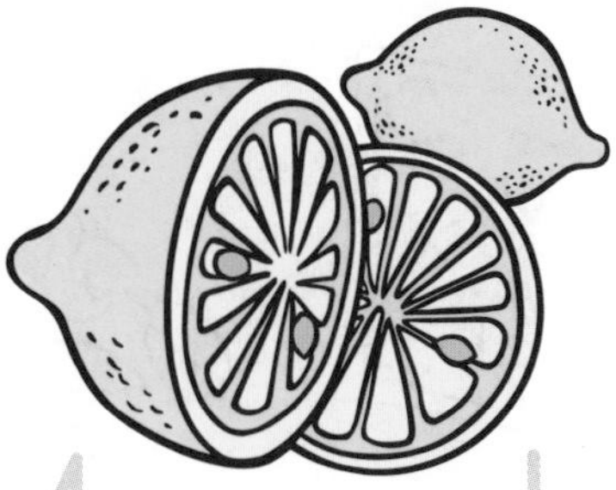

Mm Ll

Mm Pp

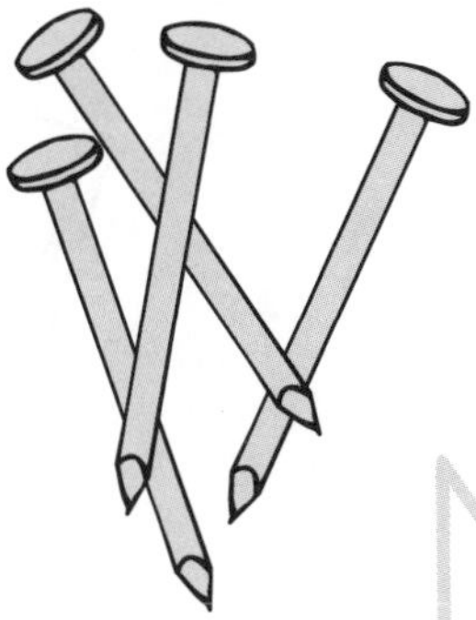

Ll Nn

Pp Mm

Name ____________________

Beginning Consonants: Qq, Rr, Ss, Tt

Directions: Say the name of each letter. Say the sound each letter makes. Trace the letter pair in the boxes. Then color the picture which begins with that sound.

Qq

Rr

Ss

Tt

Tt

Qq

Rr

Ss

Name ______________________________

Beginning Consonants: Qq, Rr, Ss, Tt

Directions: Say the name of each letter. Say the sound each letter makes. Draw a line from each letter pair to the picture which begins with that sound.

Qq 

Ss 

Rr 

Tt 

Tt 

Ss 

Rr 

Qq 

Name ______________________________

Beginning Consonants: Vv, Ww, Xx, Yy, Zz

Directions: Say the name of each letter. Say the sound each letter makes. Trace the letters. Then draw a line from each letter pair to the picture which begins with that sound.

Vv

Ww

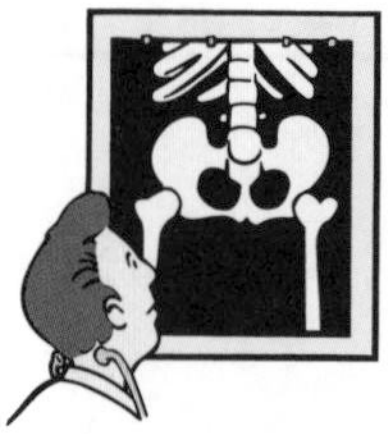
Xx

Yy

Zz

Vv 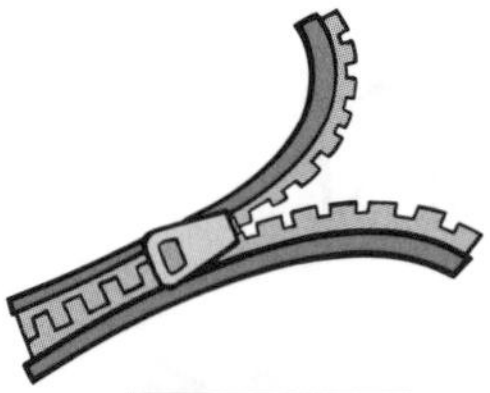

Ww 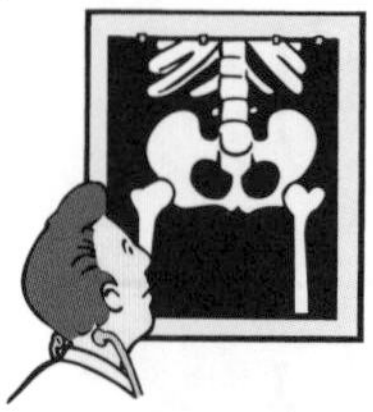

Xx 

Yy 

Zz 

Name ________________________________

Beginning Consonants: Vv, Ww, Xx, Yy, Zz

Directions: Say the name of each letter. Say the sound each letter makes. Then draw a line from each letter pair to the picture which begins with that sound.

Vv

Zz

Xx

Yy

Ww

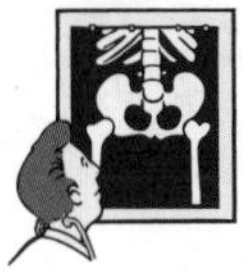

Vv

Zz

Yy

Ww

Xx

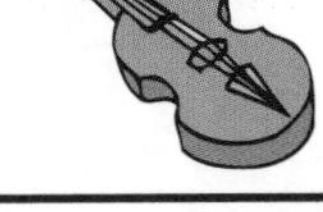

Name ____

Ending Consonants: b, d, f

Ending consonants are the sounds that come at the end of words.

Directions: Say the name of each picture. Then write the letter which makes the **ending** sound for each picture.

 ______	 ______	 ______
 ______	 ______	 ______
 ______	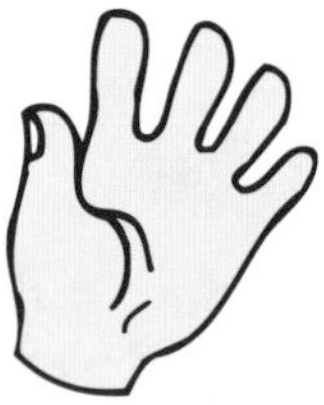 ______	 ______
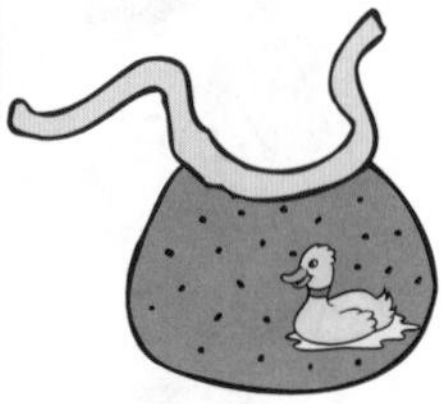 ______	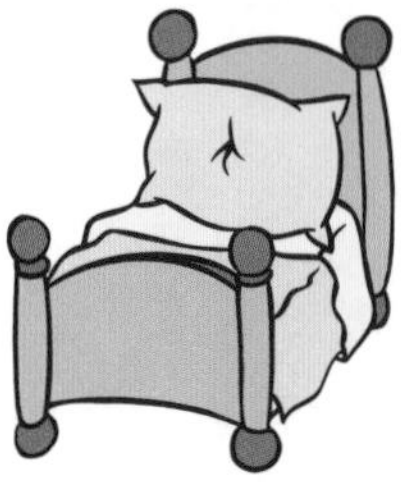 ______	 ______

Name ______________________________

Ending Consonants: g, m, n

Directions: Say the name of each picture. Draw a line from each letter to the pictures which end with that sound.

g m n

g

m

n

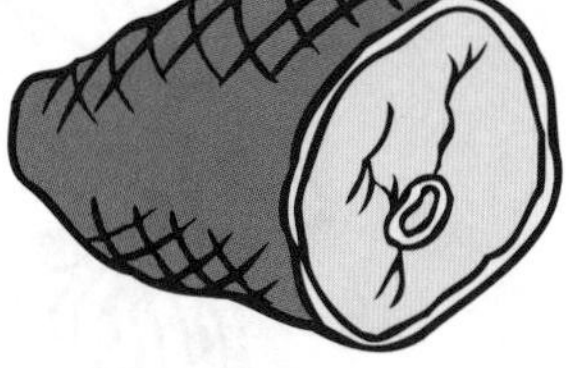

Name ______________________________________

Ending Consonants: k, l, p

Directions: Trace the letters in each row. Say the name of each picture. Then color the pictures in each row which end with that sound.

k

l

p

Name ______________________________

Ending Consonants: r, s, t, x

Directions: Say the name of each picture. Then circle the ending sound for each picture.

r s t x

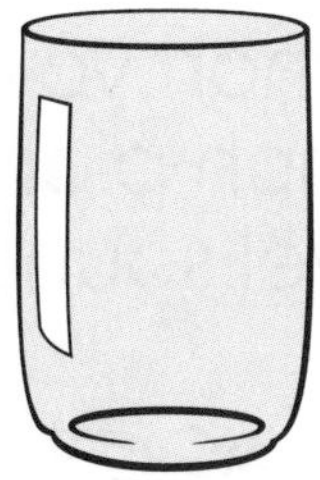

r s t x

r s t x

r s t x

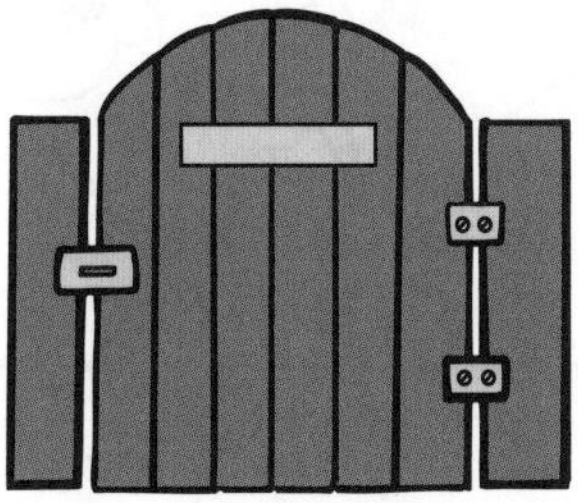

r s t x

r s t x

r s t x

r s t x

Name ______________________________

Short Vowels

Vowels are the letters **a**, **e**, **i**, **o** and **u**. Short **a** is the sound you hear in **ant**. Short **e** is the sound you hear in **elephant**. Short **i** is the sound you hear in **igloo**. Short **o** is the sound you hear in **octopus**. Short **u** is the sound you hear in **umbrella**.

Directions: Say the short vowel sound at the beginning of each row. Say the name of each picture. Then color the pictures which have the same short vowel sounds as that letter.

ă

ĕ

ĭ

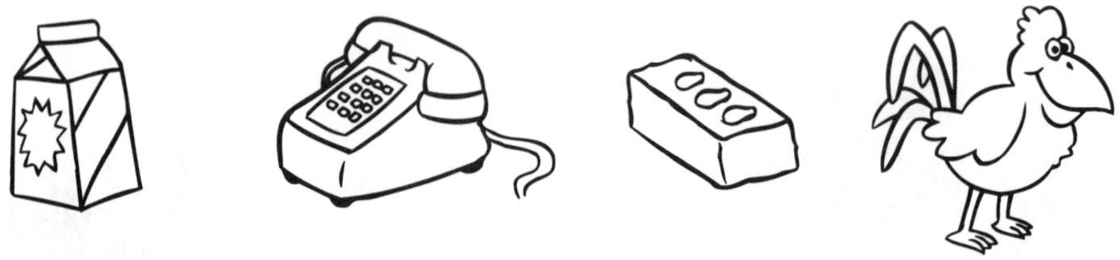

ŏ

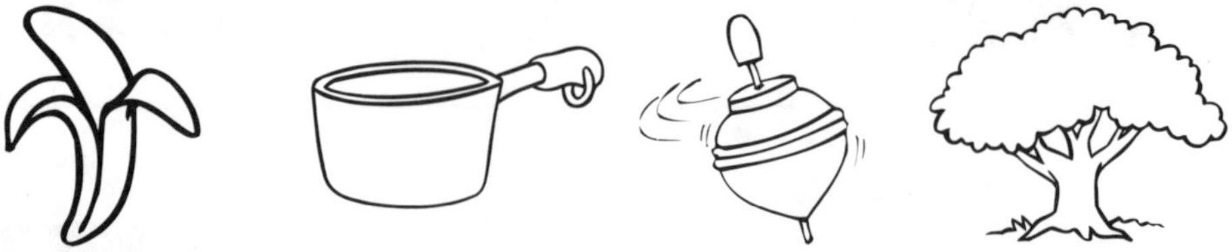

ŭ

Name ______________________________

Short Vowel Sounds

Directions: In each box are three pictures. The words that name the pictures have missing letters. Write **a, e, i, o** or **u** to finish the words.

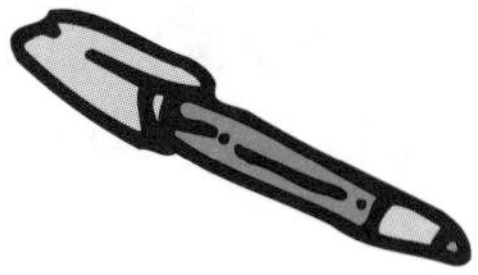
p ____ n

p ____ n

p ____ n

b ____ g

b ____ g

b ____ g

c ____ t

c ____ t

c ____ t

h ____ t

h ____ t

h ____ t

Name ____________________________________

Long Vowels

Vowels are the letters **a**, **e**, **i**, **o** and **u**. Long vowel sounds say their own names. Long **a** is the sound you hear in **hay**. Long **e** is the sound you hear in **me**. Long **i** is the sound you hear in **pie**. Long **o** is the sound you hear in **no**. Long **u** is the sound you hear in **cute**.

Directions: Say the long vowel sound at the beginning of each row. Say the name of each picture. Color the pictures in each row that have the same long vowel sound as that letter.

ā

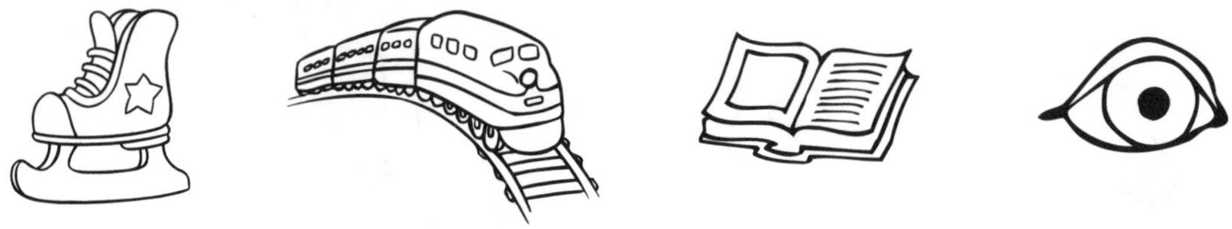

ē

ī

ō

ū

Long Vowel Sounds

Directions: Write **a, e, i, o** or **u** in each blank to finish the word. Draw a line from the word to the picture.

c ___ ke

r ___ se

k ___ te

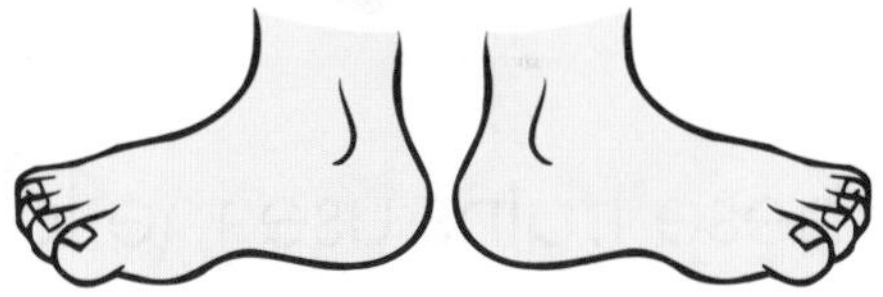

f ___ t

m ___ le

Name ______________________________

Words With a

Directions: Each train has a group of pictures. Write the word that names the pictures. Read your rhyming words.

These trains use the short **a** sound like in the word cat:

These trains use the long **a** sound like in the word lake:

Name ______________________________

Short and Long Aa

Directions: Say the name of each picture. If it has the short **a** sound, color it **red**. If it has the long **a** sound, color it **yellow**.

ă ā

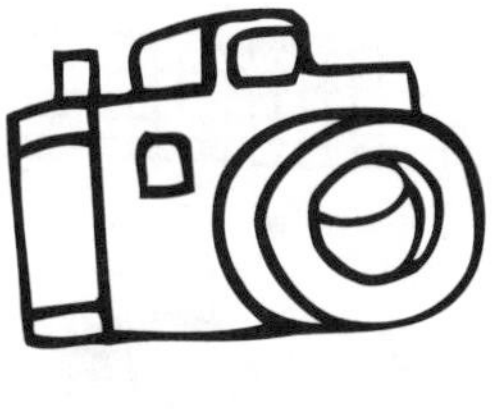

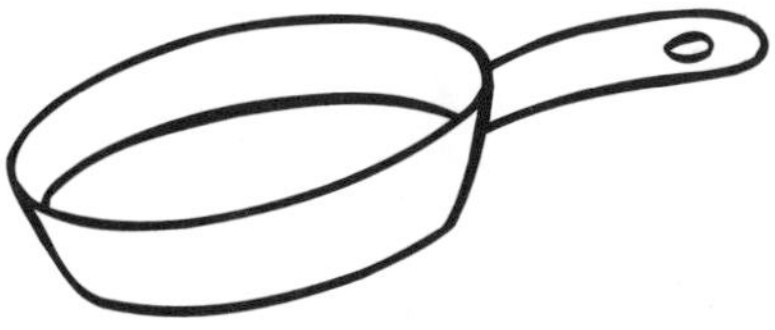

Name ______________________________

Words with e

Directions: Short **e** sounds like the **e** in hen. Long **e** sounds like the **e** in bee. Look at the pictures. If the word has a short **e** sound, draw a line to the **hen**. If the word has a long **e** sound, draw a line to the bee.

hen

bee

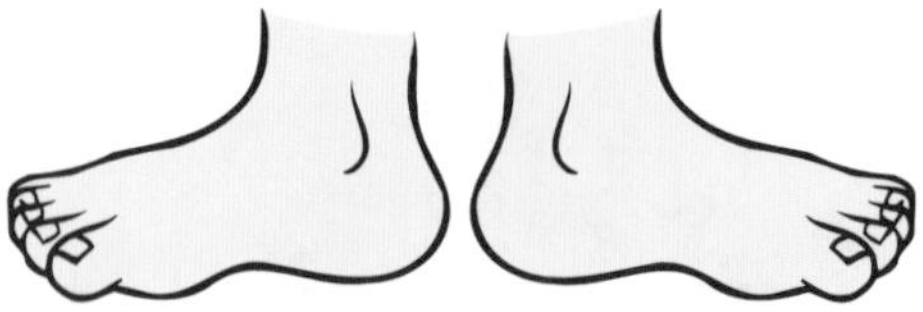

Name ________________________________

Short and Long Ee

Directions: Say the name of each picture. Circle the pictures which have the short **e** sound. Draw a triangle around the pictures which have the long **e** sound.

ĕ

ē

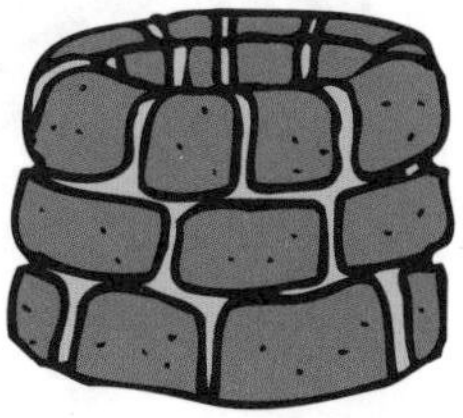

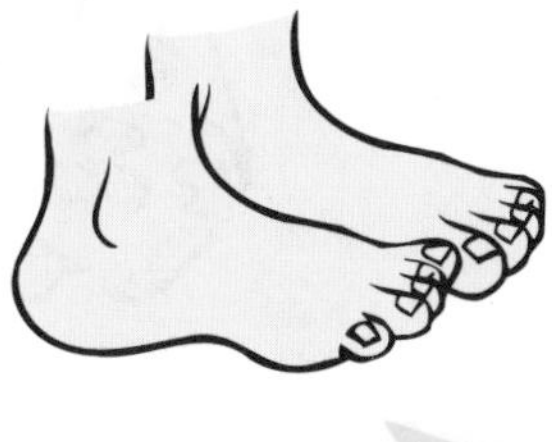

Name ______________________________

Words With i

Directions: Short **i** sounds like the **i** in pig. Long **i** sounds like the **i** in kite. Draw a circle around the words with the short **i** sound. Draw an **X** on the words with the long **i** sound.

pin

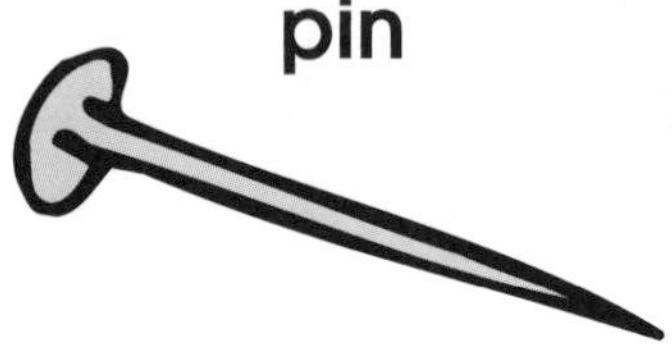

five

pig

slide

kite

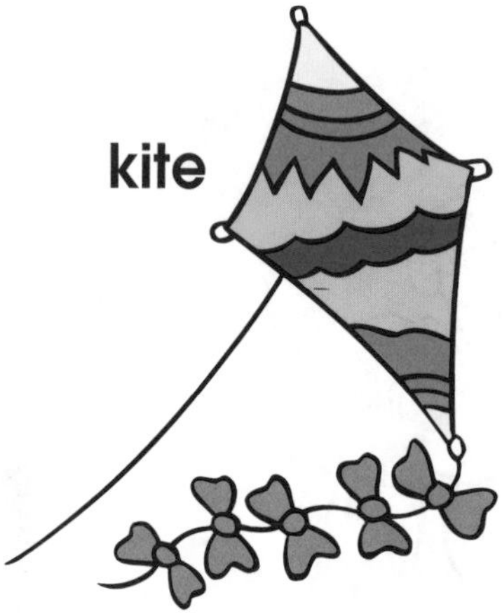

lid

tie

bib

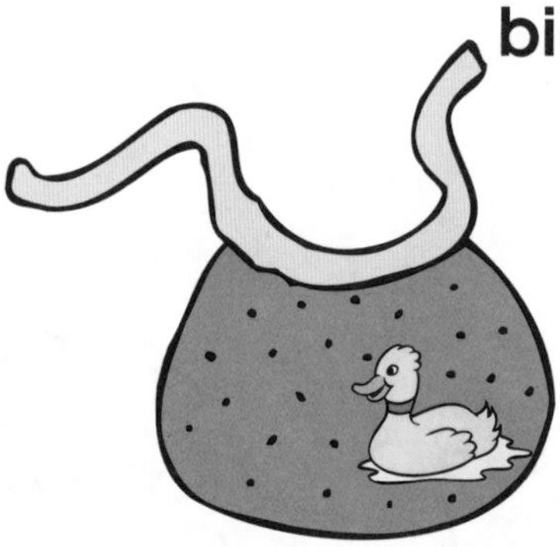

pie

Name ______________________________

Short and Long Ii

Directions: Say the name of each picture. If it has the short **i** sound, color it **yellow**. If it has the long **i** sound, color it **red**.

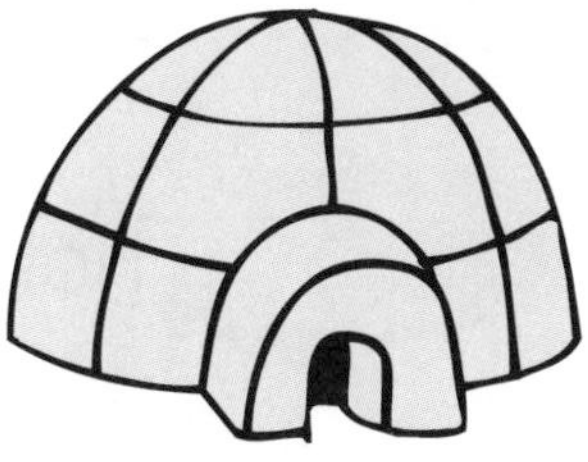

ĭ

ī

Name ______________________________

Words With o

Directions: The short **o** sounds like the **o** in dog. Long **o** sounds like the **o** in rope. Draw a line from the picture to the word that names it. Draw a circle around the word if it has a short **o** sound.

hot dog

fox

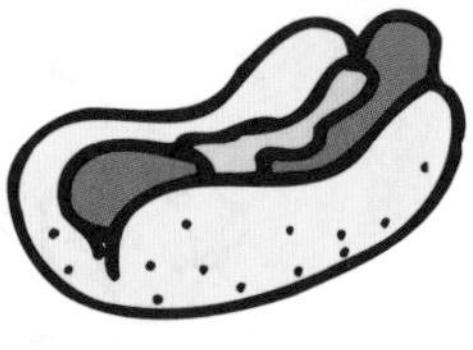

blocks

rose

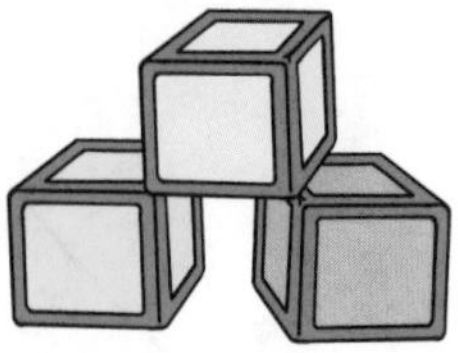

boat

Name ______________________________

Short and Long Oo

Directions: Say the name of each picture. If the picture has the long **o** sound write an **L** on the blank. If the picture has the short **o** sound, write an **S** on the blank.

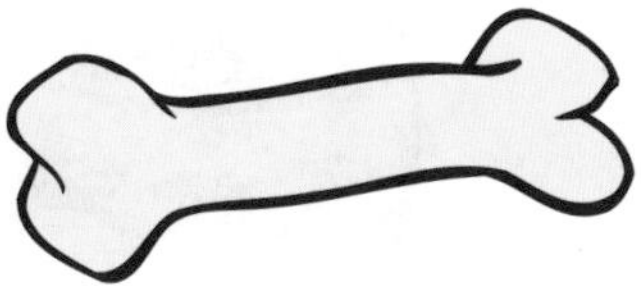

____

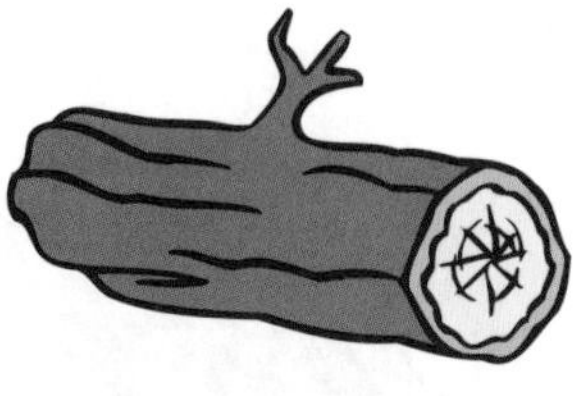

____

____

____

____

____

____

____

Name ______________________________

Words With u

Directions: The short **u** sounds like the **u** in bug. The long **u** sounds like the **u** in blue. Draw a circle around the words with short **u**. Draw an **X** on the words with long **u**.

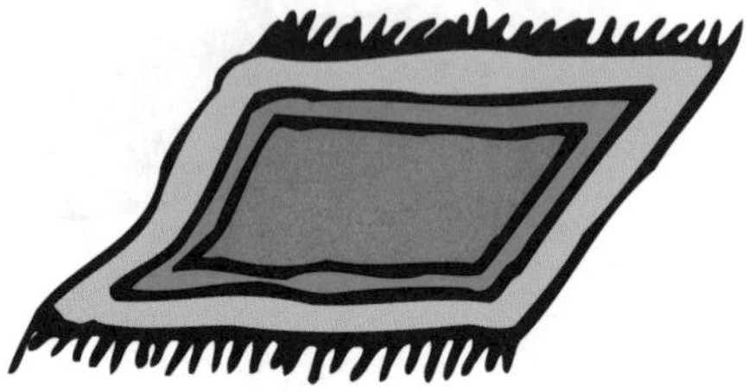

rug

cup

music

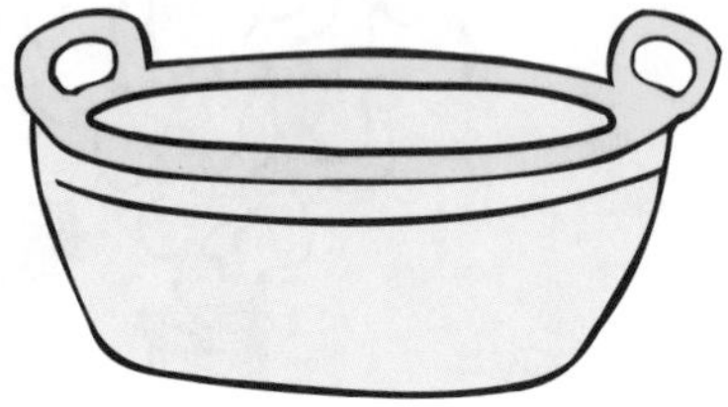

tub

suit

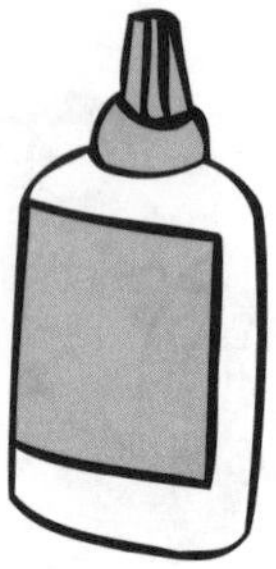

glue

bug

puppy

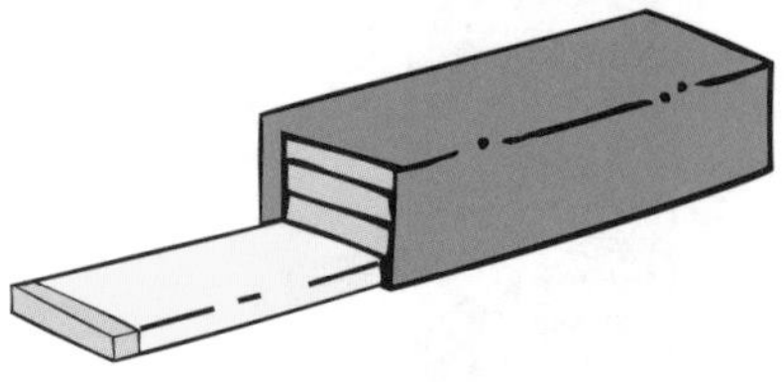

gum

Name ______________________________

Short and Long Uu

Directions: Say the name of each picture. If it has the long **u** sound, write a **u** in the **unicorn** column. If it has the short **u** sound, write a **u** in the **umbrella** column.

	ū	ŭ
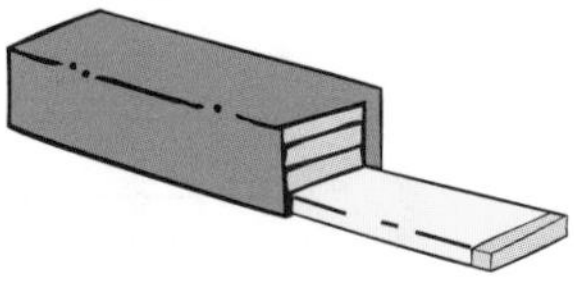	______	______
	______	______
	______	______
	______	______
	______	______

Name ______________________________

Super Silent E

When you add an **e** to the end of some words, the vowel changes from a short vowel sound to a long vowel sound. The **e** is silent.

Example: rip + **e** = ripe.

Directions: Say the word under the first picture in each pair. Then add an **e** to the word under the next picture. Say the new word.

pet

____

tub

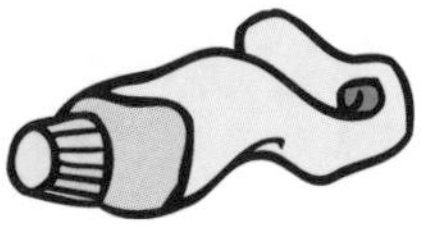

____

man

____

kit

____

pin

____

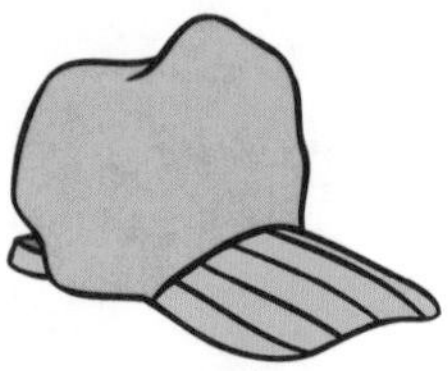

cap

____

Name ______________________________

Consonant Blends

Consonant blends are two or more consonant sounds together in a word. The blend is made by combining the consonant sounds.

Example: **fl**oor

Directions: The name of each picture begins with a **blend**. Circle the beginning blend for each picture.

bl fl cl

cl fl gl

fl bl pl

fl cl gl

pl gl cl

gl fl sl

gl fl cl

sl fl cl

cl gl sl

Name ____________________

Consonant Blends

Directions: The beginning blend for each word is missing. Fill in the correct blend to finish the word. Draw a line from the word to the picture.

______ ain

______ og

______ ab

______ um

______ ush

______ esent

Consonant Blends

Directions: Draw a line from the picture to the blend that begins its word.

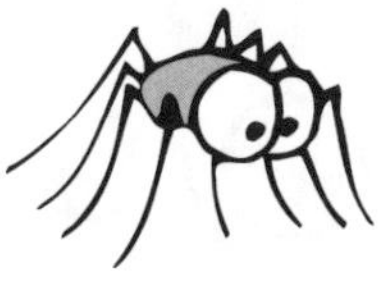

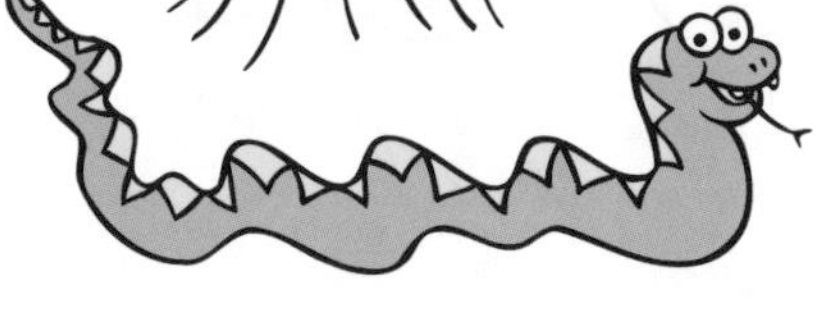

sk

sl

sm

sn

sp

st

sw

Name ____________________

Consonant Teams

Consonant teams are two or more consonants that work together to make a single sound. **Example: sh**ow

Directions: Look at the first picture in each row. Circle the pictures in the row that begin with the same sound.

Name ______________________________

Beginning Blends and Teams

Directions: Say the blend or team for each word as you search for it.

b	l	o	s	l	e	d	a	b	f	t	k	a	i	n
l	b	r	e	a	d	x	s	t	o	p	i	x	a	p
o	l	g	u	f	e	n	p	s	p	i	d	e	r	i
c	l	o	w	n	a	w	l	p	z	j	c	r	a	b
k	t	c	e	n	t	h	s	t	e	g	l	q	c	r
d	h	b	r	e	a	e	j	w	k	x	o	w	h	y
h	u	s	n	a	k	e	m	d	j	l	c	m	a	j
v	m	i	u	k	l	l	s	k	u	n	k	c	i	f
i	b	g	l	o	b	e	m	h	n	o	q	t	r	r
b	f	l	j	x	s	y	a	z	s	l	e	d	o	o
s	h	e	l	l	w	k	l	f	s	s	v	u	p	g
h	a	r	l	c	a	d	l	l	v	w	k	z	s	n
o	z	y	q	s	n	l	t	a	h	n	r	u	m	q
e	f	l	o	w	e	r	a	g	l	o	v	e	e	r
w	g	m	b	c	e	n	m	o	p	d	o	f	l	g
p	r	e	s	e	n	t	r	a	i	n	b	p	l	i

Words to find:

block	sled	globe	crab
clock	frog	present	flower
train	glove	skunk	snake
swan	flag	smell	spider
bread	small	chair	shell
stop	sled	shoe	
thumb	wheel	clown	

Name ____________________

Ending Consonant Blends

Directions: Write **lt** or **ft** to complete the words.

be ____

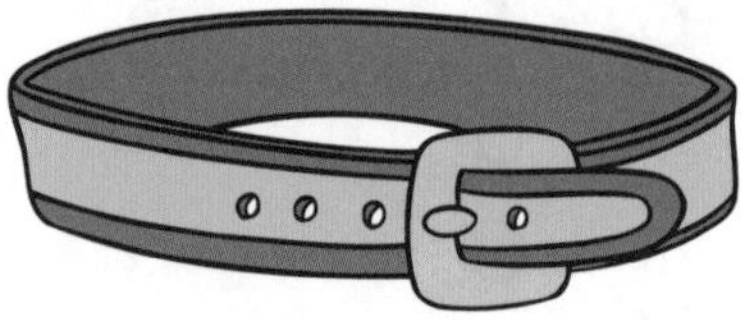

ra ____

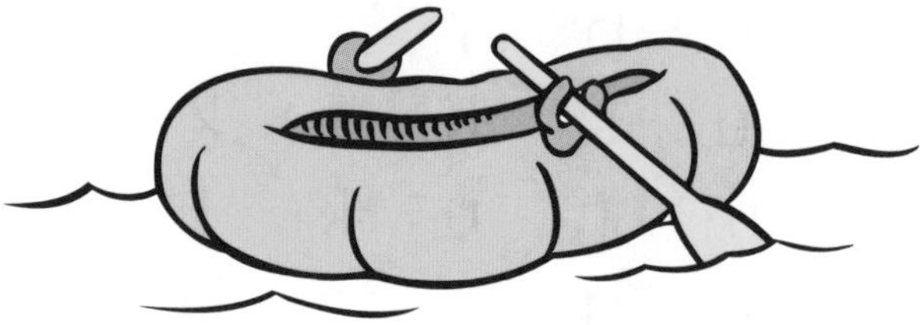

sa ____

qui ____

le ____

Name ______________________________

Ending Consonant Blends

Directions: Draw a line from the picture to the blend that ends the word.

lf

lk

sk

st

Name ____________________

Ending Consonant Blends

Directions: Every juke box has a word ending and a list of letters. Add each of the letters to the word ending to make rhyming words.

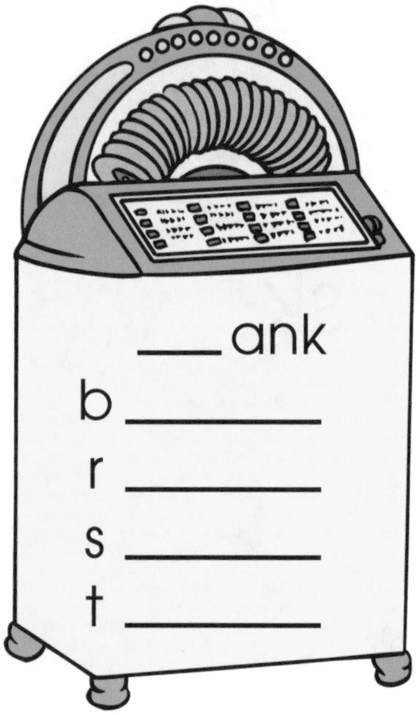

Name ______________________________

Rhyming Words

Rhyming words are words that sound alike at the end of the word. **Cat** and **hat** rhyme.

Directions: Draw a circle around each word pair that rhymes. Draw an **X** on each pair that does not rhyme.

Example:

soap rope	red dog	book hook
cold rock	cat hat	yellow black
one two	rock sock	rat flat
good nice	you to	meet toy
old sold	sale whale	word letter

Name ______________________________

Rhyming Words

Rhyming words are words that sound alike at the end of the word.

Directions: Draw a line to match the pictures that rhyme. Write two of your rhyming word pairs below.

______________________________ ______________________________

______________________________ ______________________________

Name ______________________

ABC Order

Directions: Circle the first letter of each word. Then put each pair of words in abc order.

car bird | moon two | nest fan

bird

car

card dog | pig bike | sun pie

Name ______________________________

ABC Order

Directions: Look at the words in each box. Circle the word that comes first in abc order.

duck four rock	chair apple yellow	peach this walk
game boy pink	light come one	mouse ten orange
angel table hair	zebra watch five	foot boat mine
look blue rope	who dog black	book tan six

Name ______________________________

Compound Words

Compound words are two words that are put together to make one new word.

Directions: Look at the pictures and the two words that are next to each other. Put the words together to make a new word. Write the new word.

Example:

house + boat = houseboat

side + walk = ______________________

lip + stick = ______________________

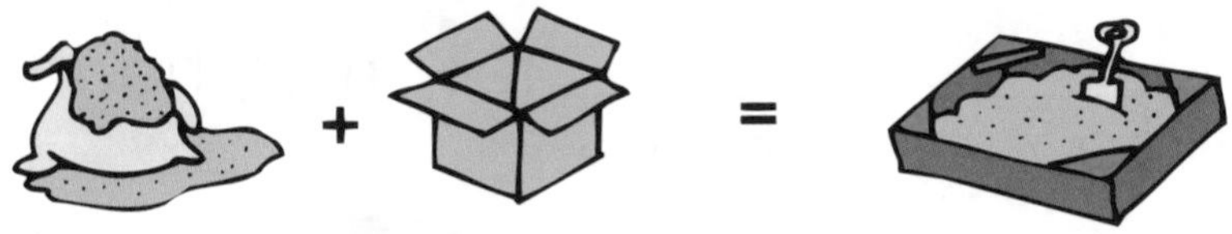

sand + box = ______________________

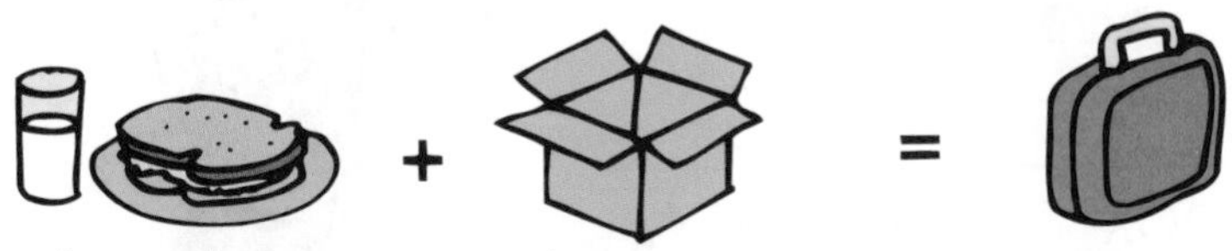

lunch + box = ______________________

Name ______________________________

Compound Words

Directions: Circle the compound word which completes each sentence. Write each word on the lines.

1. The ______________ brings us letters.
   mailman   snowman

2. A ______________ grows tall.
   sunlight   sunflower

3. The snow falls ______________.
   outside   inside

4. A ______________ fell on my head.
   raindrop   rainbow

5. I put the letter in a ______________.
   mailbox   shoebox

Name ______________________________

Names

You are a special person. Your name begins with a capital letter. We put a capital letter at the beginning of people's names because they are special.

Directions: Write your name. Did you remember to use a capital letter?

____

Directions: Write each person's name. Use a capital letter at the beginning.

Ted ______________________________

Katie ______________________________

Mike ______________________________

Tim ______________________________

Write a friend's name. Use a capital letter at the beginning. ______________________________

Name ______________________________

Names: Days of the Week

The days of the week begin with capital letters.

Directions: Write the days of the week in the spaces below. Put them in order. Be sure to start with capital letters.

Tuesday	
Saturday	
Monday	
Friday	
Thursday	
Sunday	
Wednesday	

Name ____________________

Names: Months of the Year

The months of the year begin with capital letters.

Directions: Write the months of the year in order on the calendar below. Be sure to use capital letters.

January	December	April	May	October	June
September	February	July	March	November	August

____________ 	____________ 
____________ 	____________ 
____________ 	____________ 
____________ 	____________ 
____________ 	____________ 
____________ 	____________ 

More Than One

Directions: An **s** at the end of a word often means there is more than one. Look at each picture. Circle the correct word. Write the word on the line.

two
dog dogs

four
flower flowers

one
bikes bike

three
toys toy

a
lamb lambs

two
cat cats

READING COMPREHENSION

Name ______________________________

More Than One

Directions: Choose the word which completes each sentence. Write each word on the line.

1. I have a ______________ .
   dog   dogs

2. Four ________________ are on the tree.
   apple   apples

3. I read two ______________ today.
   book   books

4. My ______________ is blue.
   bike   bikes

5. We saw lots of ________________ at the zoo.
   monkey   monkeys

6. I have five __________________ .
   balloon   balloons

Name ______________________

Riddles

Directions: Read the word. Trace and write it on the line. Then draw a line from the riddle to the animal it tells about.

long long ______________

giraffe

I am very big.
I lived a long, long time ago.
What am I?

rabbit

My neck is very long.
I eat leaves from trees.
What am I?

dinosaur

I have long ears.
I hop very fast.
What am I?

Name ______________________

Riddles

Directions: Read the word and write it on the line. Then read each riddle and draw a line to the picture and word that tells about it.

house

I like to play.
I am little. I am soft.
What am I?

house

kitten

I am big.
You live in me.
What am I?

kitten

flower

I am pretty.
I have petals and a stem.
What am I?

flower

pony

I can jump. I can run.
I have a mane.
What am I?

pony

Name ______________________________

Riddles

Directions: Write a word from the box to answer each riddle.

ice cream	book	chair	sun

There are many words in me.
I am fun to read.
What am I?

____

I am soft.
You can sit on me.
What am I?

____

I am in the sky.
I am hot. I am yellow.
What am I?

____

I am cold. I am sweet.
You like to eat me.
What am I?

____

Name ______________________

Comprehension

Directions: Look at the picture. Write the words from the box to finish the sentences.

frog	log	bird	fish	ducks

The ______________ can jump.

The turtle is on a ______________.

A ______________ is in the tree.

The boy wants a ______________.

I see three ______________.

Name ______________________________

Comprehension

Directions: Read the poem. Write the correct words in the blanks.

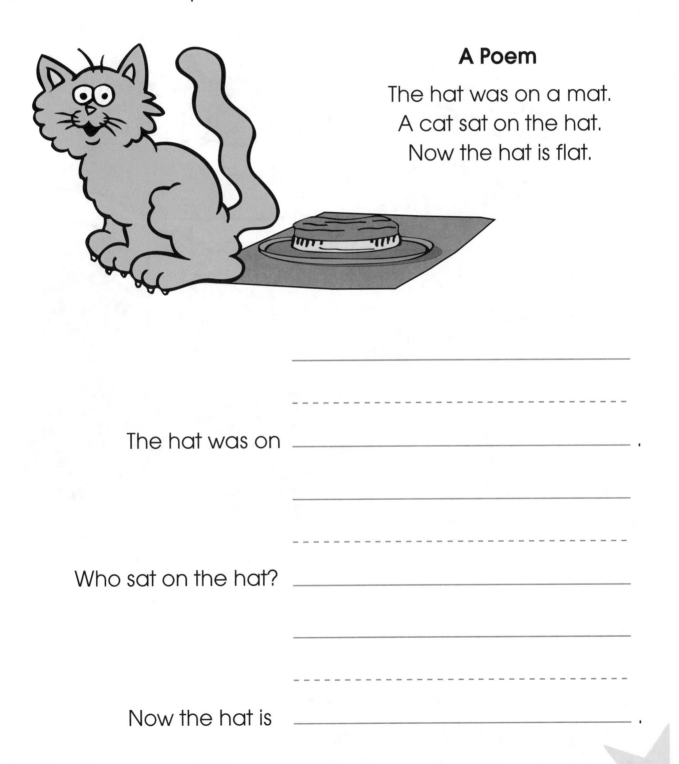

A Poem

The hat was on a mat.
A cat sat on the hat.
Now the hat is flat.

The hat was on ______________________.

Who sat on the hat? ______________________

Now the hat is ______________________.

Following Directions: Color the Path

Directions: Color the path the girl should take to go home. Use the sentences to help you.

1. Go to the school and turn left.
2. At the end of the street, turn right.
3. Walk past the park and turn right.
4. After you pass the pool, turn right.

Name ______________________________________

Following Directions

Directions: Look at the pictures. Follow the directions in each box.

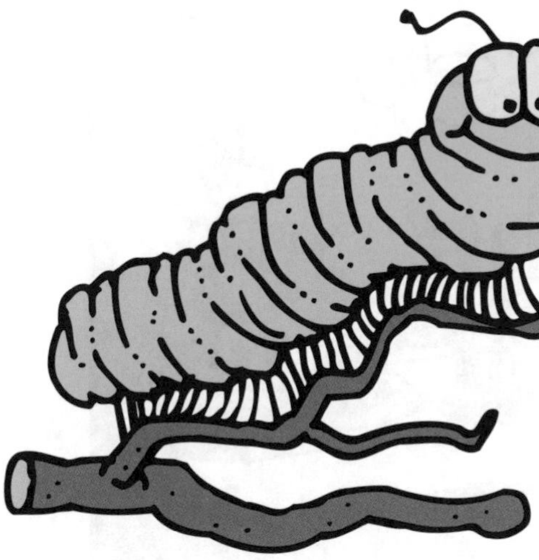

Draw a circle around the caterpillar.
Draw a line under the stick.

Draw an **X** on the mother bird.
Draw a triangle around the baby birds.

Draw a box around the rabbit.

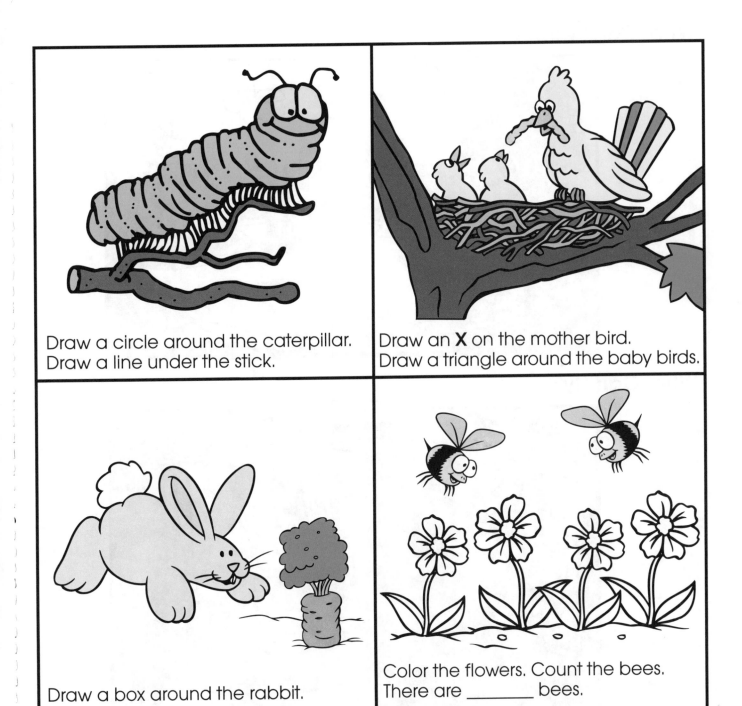

Color the flowers. Count the bees.
There are ________ bees.

Name ________________________

Classifying

Directions: Classifying is sorting things into groups. Draw a circle around the pictures that answer the question.

What Can Swim?

What Can Fly?

Name ______________________________

Classifying: These Keep Me Warm

Directions: Color the things that keep you warm.

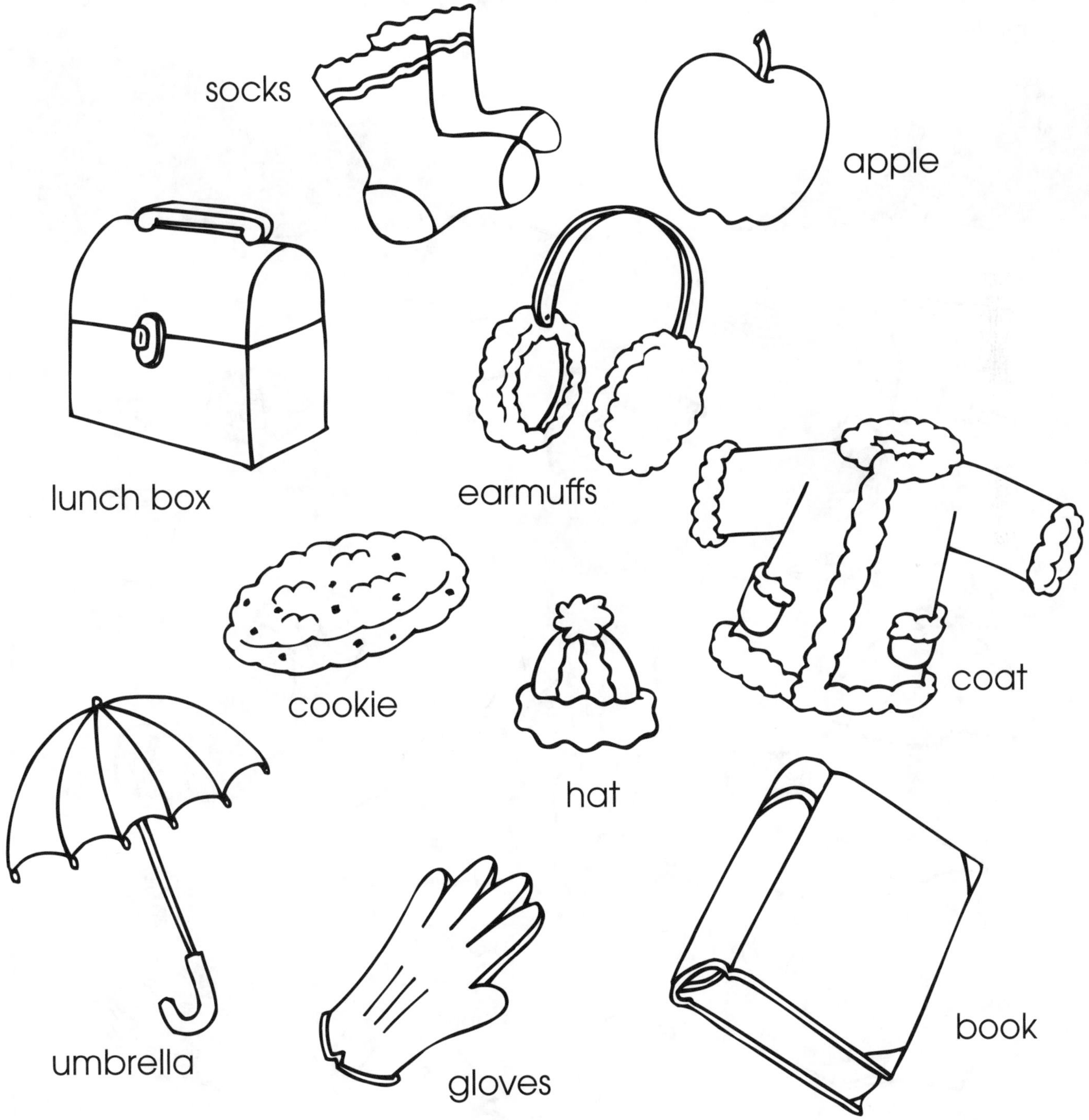

Name ____________________

Classifying: Objects

Help Dan clean up the park.

Directions: Circle the litter. Underline the coins. Draw a box around the balls.

Name ______________________________

Classifying: Things to Drink

Directions: Circle the pictures of things you can drink. Write the names of those things in the blanks.

milk

ice

soup and crackers

juice

soda

ice-cream bar

Name ______________________________

Vocabulary

Directions: Read the words. Trace and write them on the lines. Look at each picture. Write **hot** or **cold** on the lines to show if it is hot or cold.

hot hot

cold cold

 ______	 ______
 ______	 ______

Name ______________________

Vocabulary

Directions: Read the words. Trace and write them on the lines. Look at each picture and write **day** or **night** on the lines to show if they happen during the day or night.

day day

night night

Name ______________________________

Classifying: Night and Day

Directions: Write the words from the box under the pictures they describe.

stars	sun	moon	rays	dark	light	night	day

Name ________________________________

Classifying: Clowns and Balloons

Some words describe clowns. Some words describe balloons.

Directions: Read the words. Write the words that match in the correct columns.

float	laughs	hat	string
air	feet	pop	nose

clown

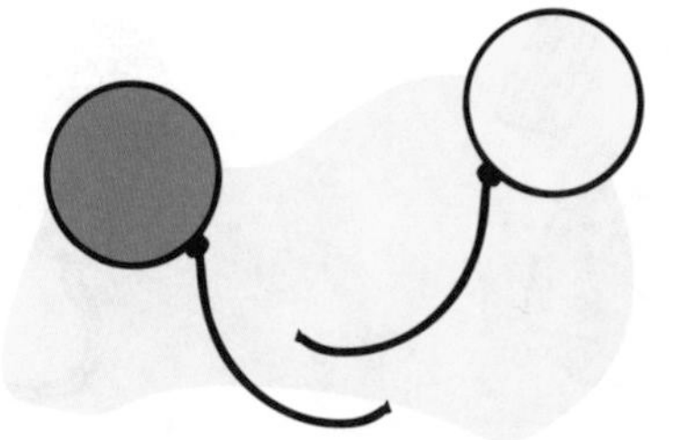

balloons

________________________________ ________________________________

________________________________ ________________________________

________________________________ ________________________________

________________________________ ________________________________

Name ____________________

Similarities: Objects

Directions: Circle the picture in each row that is most like the first picture.

Example:

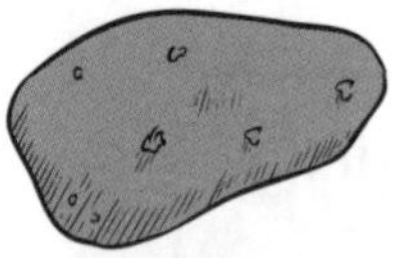

potato   rose   tomato   tree

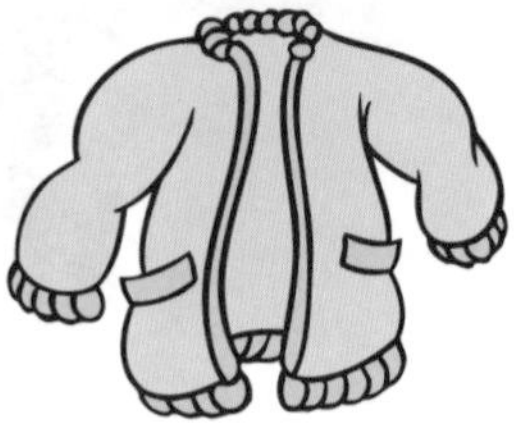

shirt   mittens   boots   jacket

whale   cat   dolphin   monkey

tiger   giraffe   lion   zebra

Name ______________________________

Similarities: Objects

Directions: Circle the picture in each row that is most like the first picture.

Example:

carrot

jacks

bread

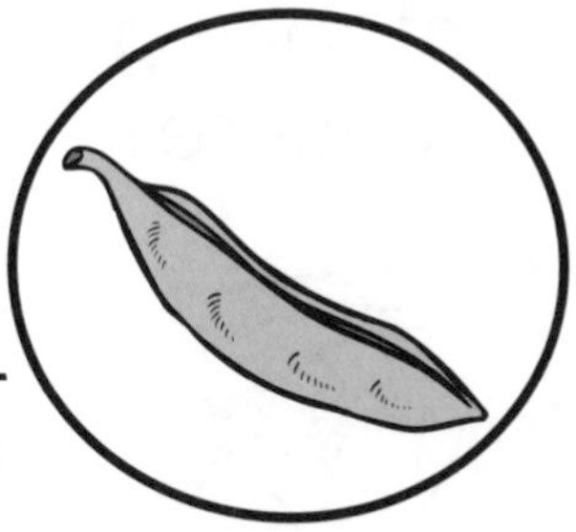

pea

baseball

sneakers

basketball

bat

store

school

home

bakery

kitten

dog

fox

cat

Name ____

Classifying: Food Groups

Directions: Color the meats and eggs blue. Color the fruits and vegetables green. Color the breads tan. Color the dairy foods (milk and cheese) yellow.

fish

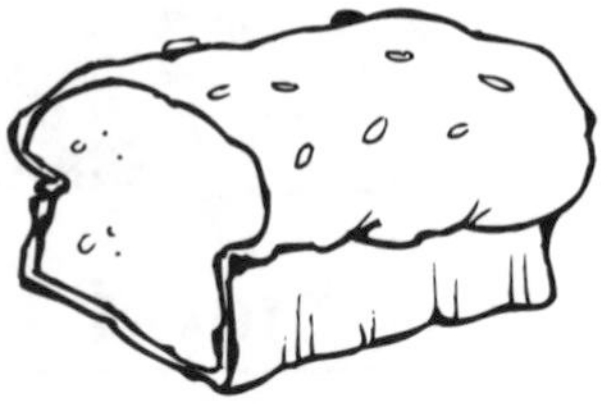
bread

apple

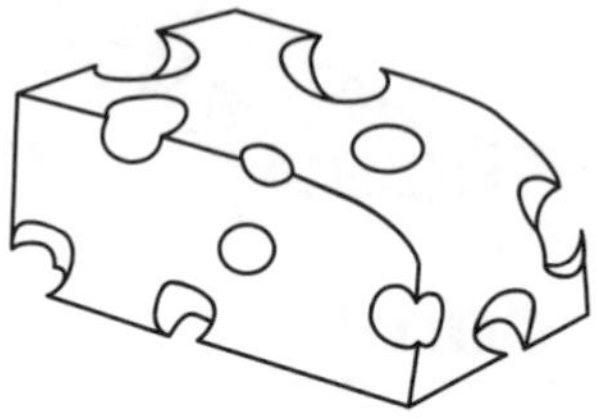
cheese

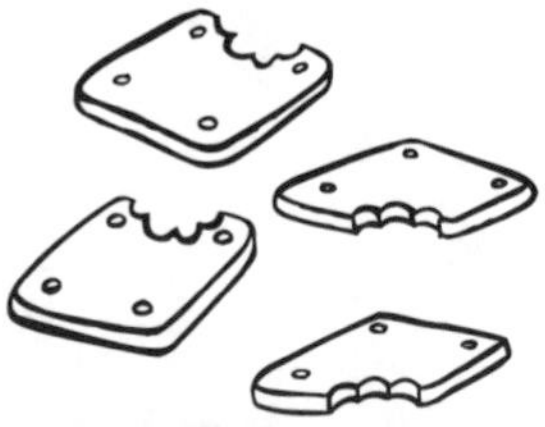
crackers

carrot

orange

eggs

steaks

pear

milk

yogurt

ice cream

chicken

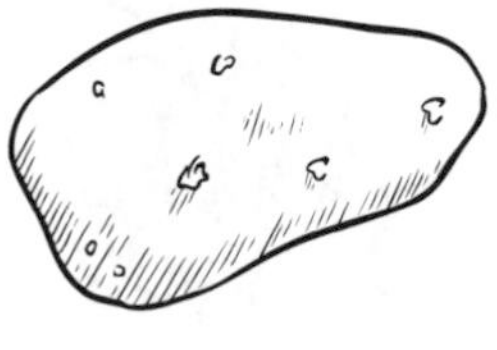
potato

pretzel

Name ______________________________

Classifying: What Does Not Belong?

Directions: Draw an **X** on the picture that does not belong in each group.

fruit

apple

peach

corn

watermelon

---

wild animals

bear

kitten

gorilla

lion

---

pets

cat

fish

elephant

dog

---

flowers

grass

rose

daisy

tulip

Name ____________________

Classifying: What Does Not Belong?

Directions: Draw an **X** on the word in each row that does not belong.

1.	flashlight	candle	radio	fire
2.	shirt	pants	coat	bat
3.	cow	car	bus	train
4.	beans	hot dog	ball	bread
5.	gloves	hat	book	boots
6.	fork	butter	cup	plate
7.	book	ball	bat	milk
8.	dogs	bees	flies	ants

Name ____________________

Classifying: Objects

Directions: Write each word in the correct row at the bottom of the page.

airplane

drum

radio

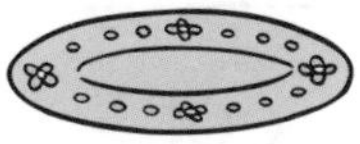
plate

car

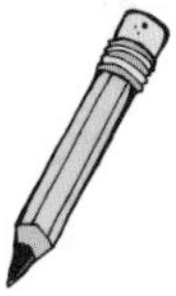
pencil

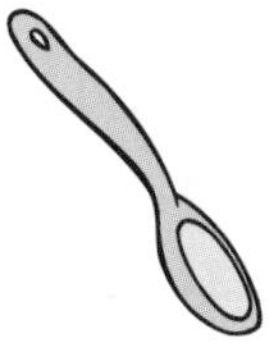
spoon

crayon

chalk

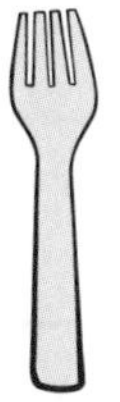
fork

television

boat

Things we ride in:

Things we eat with:

Things we draw with:

Things we listen to:

Name ______________________

Classifying: Names, Numbers, Animals, Colors

Directions: Write the words from the box next to the words they describe.

Joe	cat	blue	Tim
two	dog	red	ten
Sue	green	pig	six

Name Words ______________________

Number Words ______________________

Animal Words ______________________

Color Words ______________________

Name ____________________

Classifying: Things That Belong Together

Directions: Circle the pictures in each row that belong together.

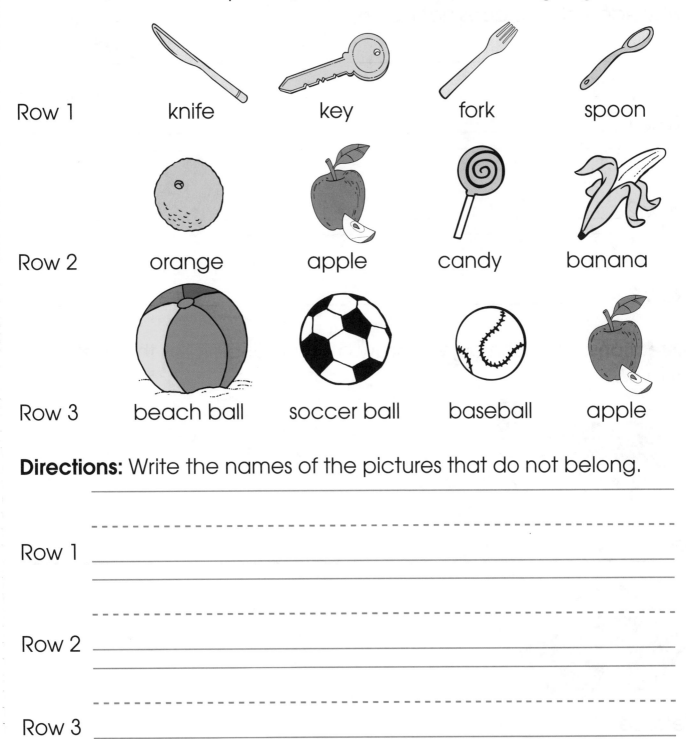

Row 1 knife key fork spoon

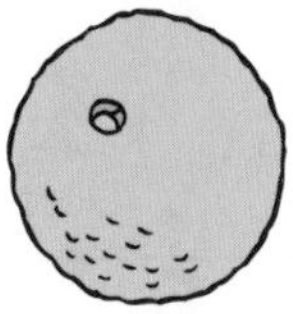

Row 2 orange apple candy banana

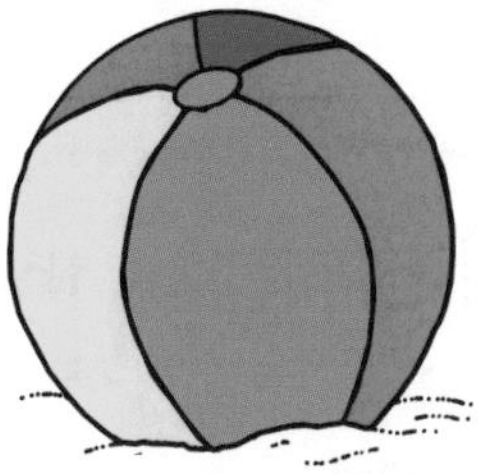

Row 3 beach ball soccer ball baseball apple

Directions: Write the names of the pictures that do not belong.

Row 1 ____________________

Row 2 ____________________

Row 3 ____________________

Name ______________________________

Classifying: Why They Are Different

Directions: Look at your answers on page 83. Write why each object does not belong.

Row 1 ______________________________

Row 2 ______________________________

Row 3 ______________________________

Directions: For each object, draw a group of pictures that belong with it.

candy bar

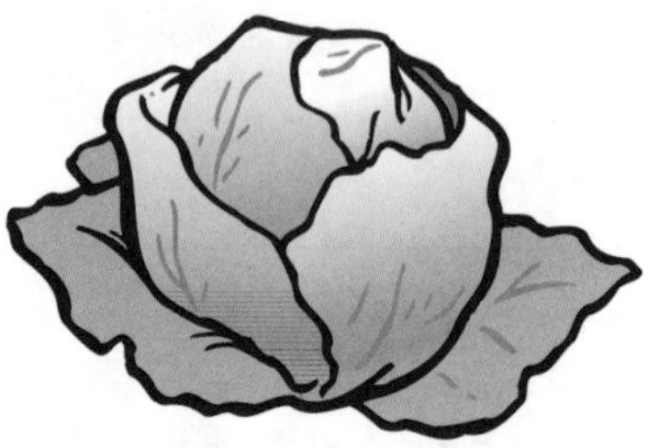

lettuce

Name ______________________________

Sequencing: Fill the Glasses

Directions: Follow the instructions to fill each glass. Use crayons to draw your favorite drink in the ones that are full and half-full.

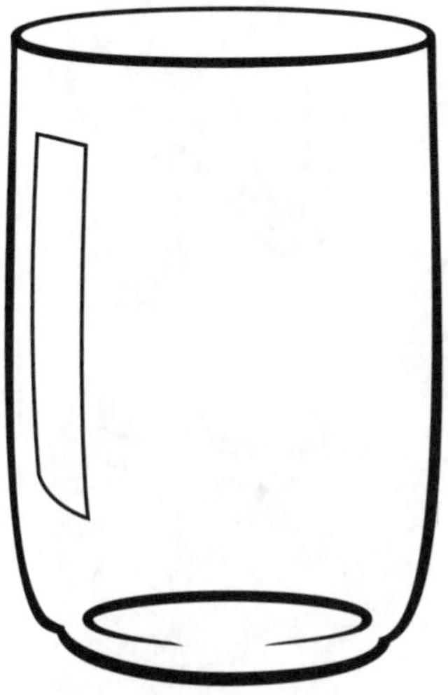

full

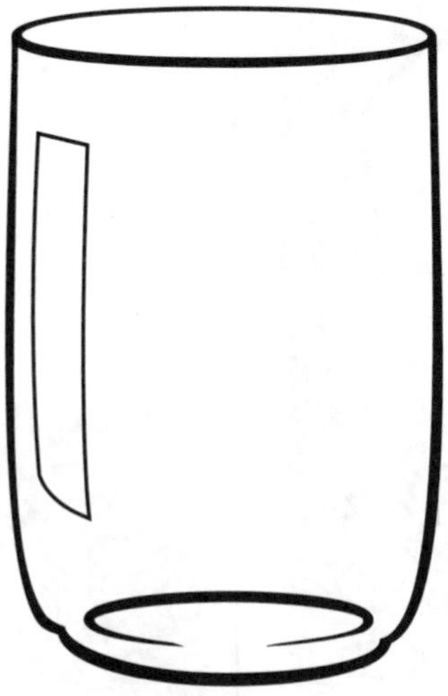

half-full

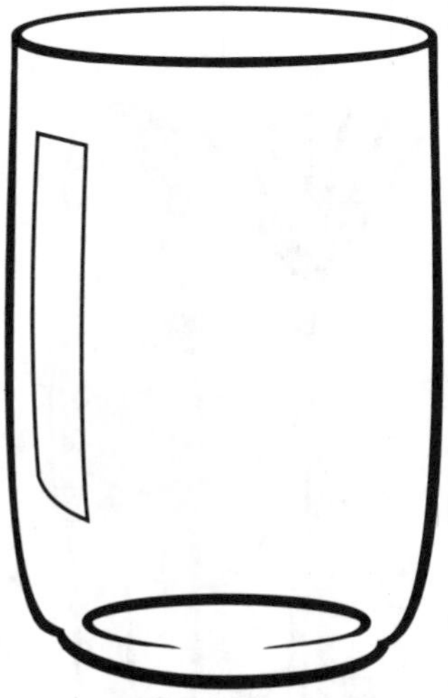

empty

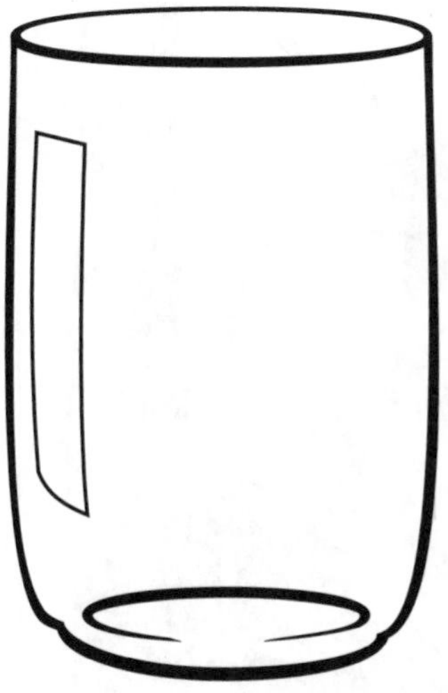

empty

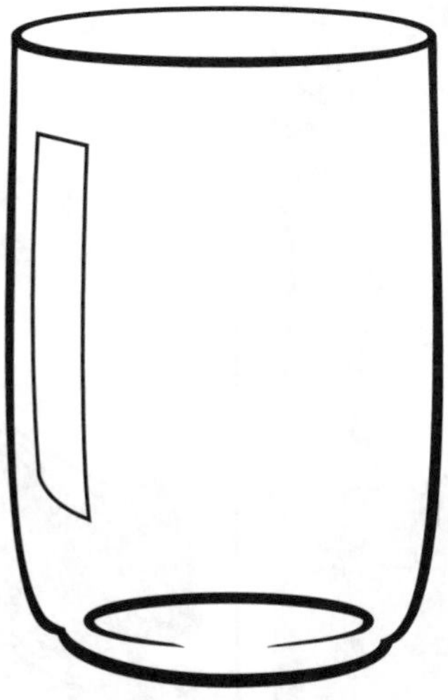

half-full

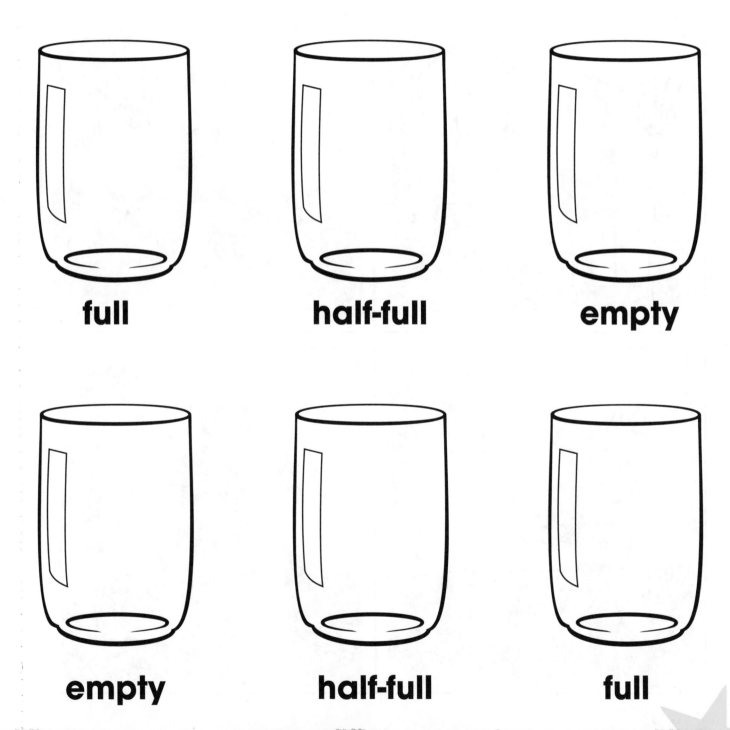

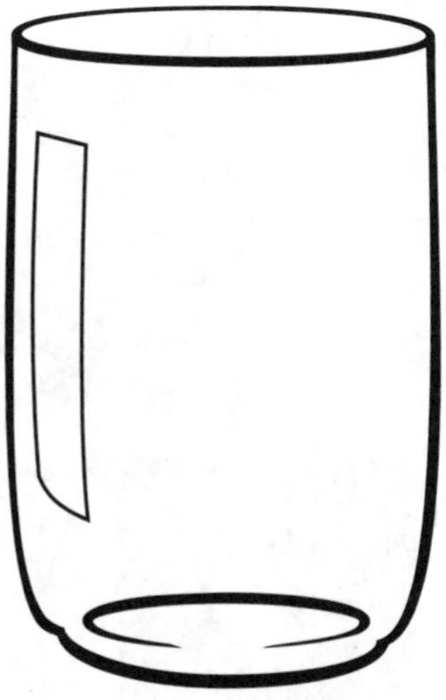

full

Name ________________________________

Sequencing: Raking Leaves

Directions: Write a number in each box to show the order of the story.

Name ______________________________

Sequencing: Make a Snowman!

Directions: Write the number of the sentence that goes with each picture in the box.

1. Roll a large snowball for the snowman's bottom.
2. Make another snowball and put it on top of the first.
3. Put the last snowball on top.
4. Dress the snowman.

Name ______________________________

Sequencing: A Recipe

Directions: Look at the recipe below. Put each step in order. Write **1, 2, 3** or **4** in the box.

HOW TO MAKE BREAD BUDDIES

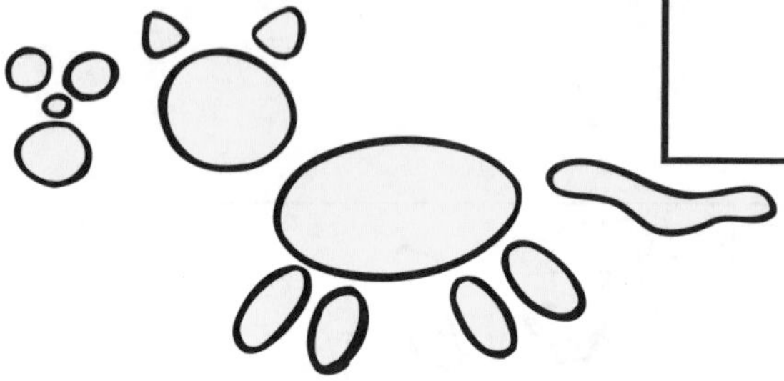

Roll dough into balls and shapes. Connect pieces with a drop of water.

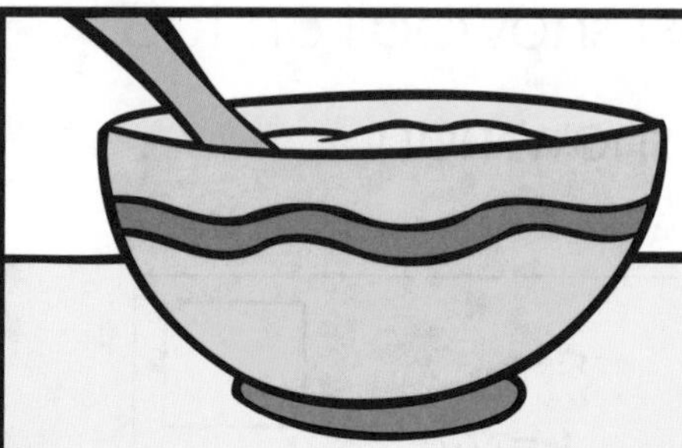

Mix 1 cup of water, 1 cup of salt and 3 cups of flour.

Knead the dough.

Have an adult bake your bread buddy for 2-3 hours at 300°. Let it cool. Then paint it!

What kind of bread buddy did you make?

____

Name ______________________

Sequencing: How Flowers Grow

Directions: Read the story. Then write the steps to grow a flower.

First find a sunny spot. Then plant the seed. Water it. The flower will start to grow. Pull the weeds around it. Remember to keep giving the flower water. Enjoy your flower.

1. ______________________.

2. ______________________.

3. ______________________.

4. ______________________.

5. ______________________.

Name ______________________________

Comprehension: Apples

Directions: Read about apples. Then write the answers.

I like  . Do you?

Some  are red.

Some  are green.

Some  are yellow.

1. How many kinds of apples does the story tell about?

____

2. Name the kinds of apples.

__________ __________ __________

3. What kind of apple do you like best?

____

Name ____________________

Comprehension: Crayons

Directions: Read about crayons. Then write your answers.

Crayons come in many colors.
Some crayons are dark colors.
Some crayons are light colors.
All crayons have wax in them.

1. How many colors of crayons are there? many few

____

2. Crayons come in ____________________ colors

and ____________________ colors.

3. What do all crayons have in them?

____

Name ______________________________

Comprehension: Clocks

Directions: Read about clocks. Then answer the questions.

Ticking Clocks

Many clocks make two sounds. The sounds are tick and tock. Big clocks often make loud tick-tocks. Little clocks often make quiet tick-tocks. Sometimes people put little clocks in a box with a new puppy. The puppy likes the sound. The tick-tock makes the puppy feel safe.

1. What two sounds do many clocks make?

______________________ and ______________________

2. What kind of tick-tocks do big clocks make?

____

3. What kind of clock makes a new puppy feel safe?

____

Name ______________________

Comprehension: Soup

Directions: Read about soup. Then write the answers.

I Like Soup

Soup is good! It is good for you, too. We eat most kinds of soup hot. Some people eat cold soup in the summer. Carrots and beans are in some soups. Do you like crackers with soup?

1. Name two ways people eat soup.

2. Name two things that are in some soups.

3. Name the kind of soup you like best.

Name ______________________________

Comprehension: The Teddy Bear Song

Do you know the Teddy Bear Song? It is very old!

Directions: Read the Teddy Bear Song. Then answer the questions.

Teddy bear, teddy bear, turn around.
Teddy bear, teddy bear, touch the ground.
Teddy bear, teddy bear, climb upstairs.
Teddy bear, teddy bear, say your prayers.
Teddy bear, teddy bear, turn out the light.
Teddy bear, teddy bear, say, "Good night!"

1. What is the first thing the teddy bear does?

____

2. What is the last thing the teddy bear does?

____

3. What would you name a teddy bear?

____

Name ________________________________

Comprehension: A New Teddy Bear Song

Directions: Write words to make a new teddy bear song. Act out your new song with your teddy bear as you read it.

Teddy bear, teddy bear, turn ____________________.

Teddy bear, teddy bear, touch the ____________________.

Teddy bear, teddy bear, climb ____________________.

Teddy bear, teddy bear, turn out ____________________.

Teddy bear, teddy bear, say, ____________________.

Name ______________________________

Sequencing: Put Teddy Bear to Bed

Directions: Read the song about the teddy bear again. Write a number in each box to show the order of the story.

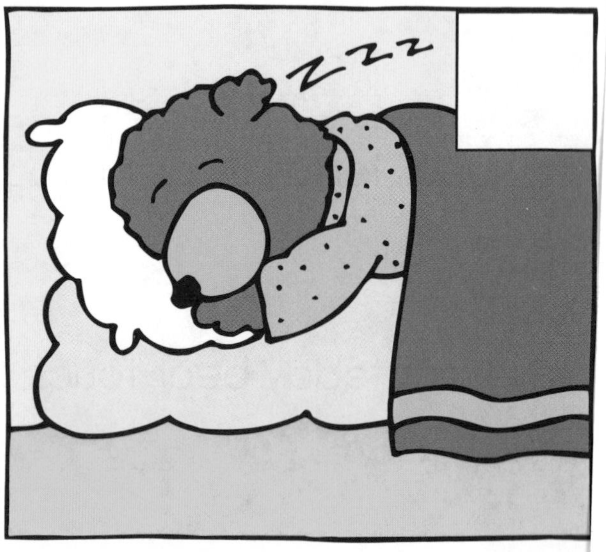

Name ______________________

Sequencing: Petting a Cat

Directions: Read the story. Then write the answers.

Do you like cats? I do. To pet a cat, move slowly. Hold out your hand. The cat will come to you. Then pet its head. Do not grab a cat! It will run away.

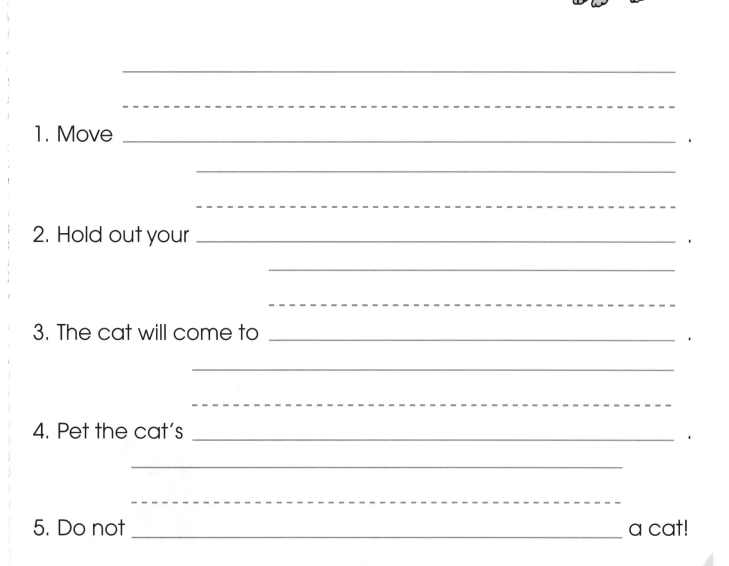

To pet a cat . . .

1. Move ______________________ .

2. Hold out your ______________________ .

3. The cat will come to ______________________ .

4. Pet the cat's ______________________ .

5. Do not ______________________ a cat!

Comprehension: Cats

Directions: Read the story about cats again. Then write the answers.

1. What is a good title for the story?

2. The story tells you how to ____________________.

3. What part of your body should you pet a cat with?

4. Why should you move slowly to pet a cat?

5. Why do you think a cat will run away if you grab it?

Name ___________________________

Comprehension: Cats

Directions: Look at the pictures and read about four cats. Then write the correct name beside each cat.

Fluffy, Blackie and Tiger are playing. Tom is sleeping. Blackie has spots. Tiger has stripes.

Name ______________________________

Same and Different: Cats

Directions: Compare the picture of the cats on page 99 to this picture. Write a word from the box to tell what is different about each cat.

purple ball	green bow	blue brush	red collar

1. Tom is wearing a ______________________.

2. Blackie has a ______________________.

3. Fluffy is wearing a ______________________.

4. Tiger has a ______________________.

Name ______________________________

Comprehension: Tigers

Directions: Read about tigers. Then write the answers.

Tigers sleep during the day. They hunt at night. Tigers eat meat. They hunt deer. They like to eat wild pigs. If they cannot find meat, tigers will eat fish.

1. When do tigers sleep?

2. Name two things tigers eat.

3. When do tigers hunt?

Name ______________________________

Following Directions: Tiger Puzzle

Directions: Read the story about tigers again. Then complete the puzzle.

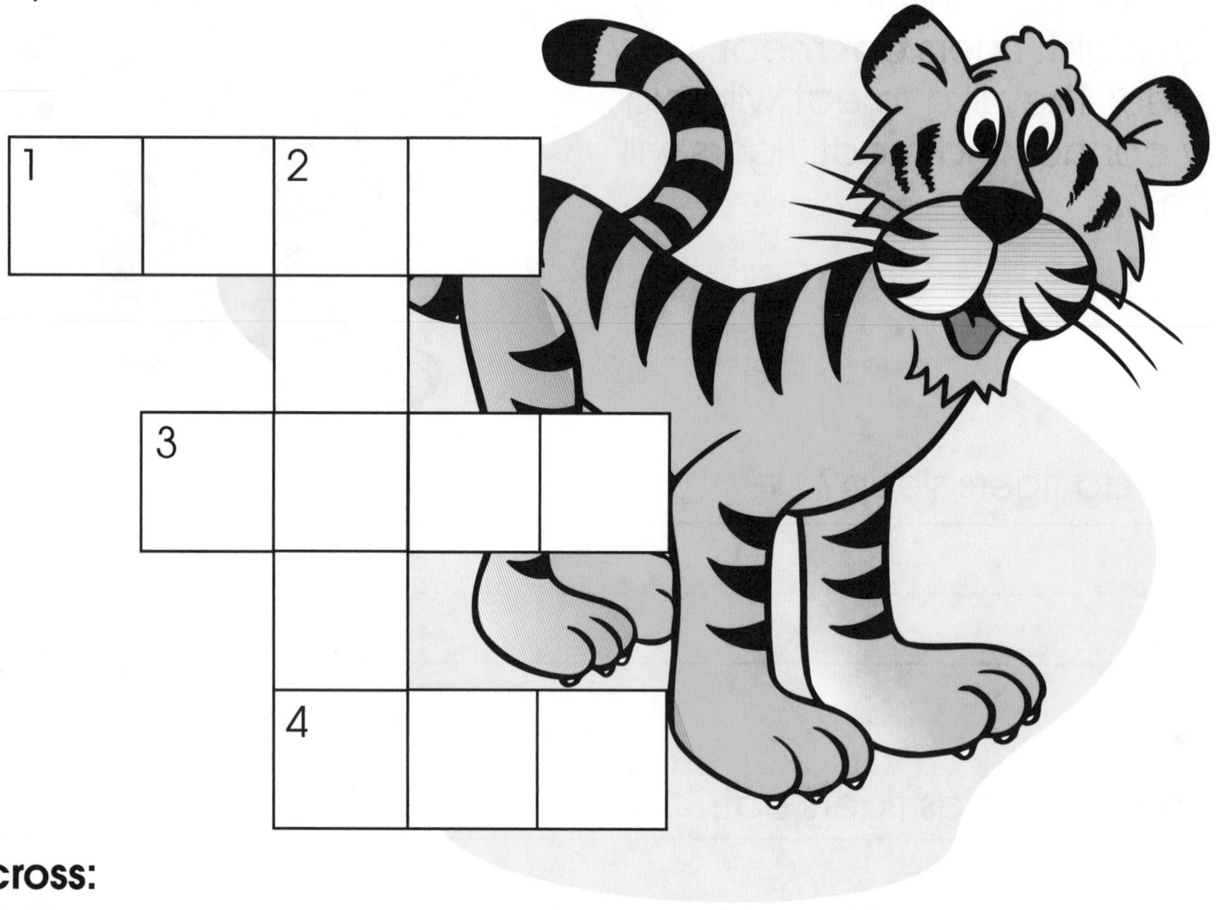

Across:

1. When tigers cannot get meat, they eat ______________ .

3. The food tigers like best is ______________ .

4. Tigers like to eat this meat: wild ______________ .

Down:

2. Tigers do this during the day.

Name ______________________________

Following Directions: Draw a Tiger

Directions: Follow directions to complete the picture of the tiger.

1. Draw black stripes on the tiger's body and tail.
2. Color the tiger's tongue red.
3. Draw claws on the feet.
4. Draw a black nose and two black eyes on the tiger's face.
5. Color the rest of the tiger orange.
6. Draw tall, green grass for the tiger to sleep in.

Name ________________________________

Comprehension: Write a Party Invitation

Directions: Read about the party. Then complete the invitation.

The party will be at Dog's house. The party will start at 1:00 P.M. It will last 2 hours. Write your birthday for the date of the party.

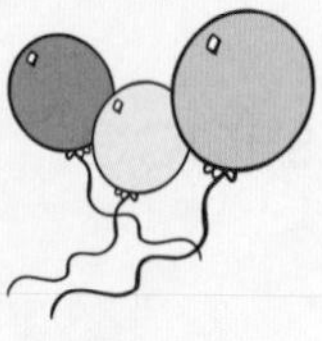

Party Invitation

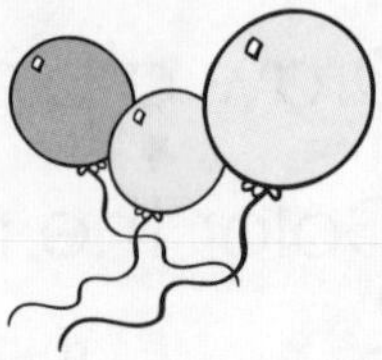

Where: ________________________________

Date: ________________________________

Time It Begins: ________________________________

Time It Ends: ________________________________

____

Directions: On the last line, write something else about the party.

Name ________________________________

Sequencing: Pig Gets Ready

Directions: Number the pictures of Pig getting ready for the party to show the order of the story.

What kind of party do you think Pig is going to? ________________________________

Name ______________________

Comprehension: An Animal Party

Directions: Use the picture for clues. Write words from the box to answer the questions.

bear	cat
dog	elephant
giraffe	hippo
pig	tiger

1. Which animals have bow ties?

2. Which animal has a hat?

3. Which animal has a striped shirt?

Name ______________________________

Classifying: Party Items

Directions: Draw a □ around objects that are food for the party. Draw a △ around the party guests. Draw a ○ around the objects used for fun at the party.

ice cream

candy

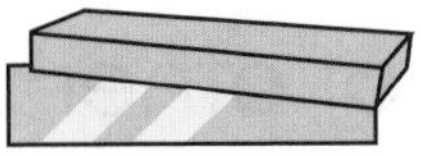
games

tiger

noise makers

cake

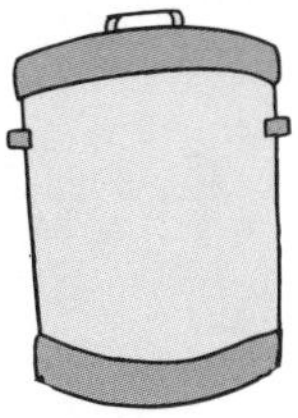
garbage can

cat

hat

glasses

candle

bear

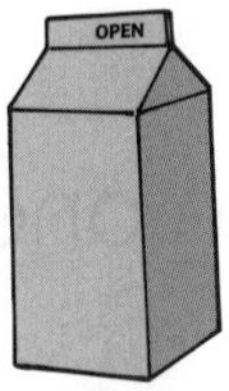

juice

balloons

giraffe

pig

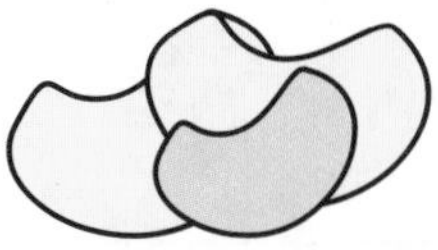
potato chips

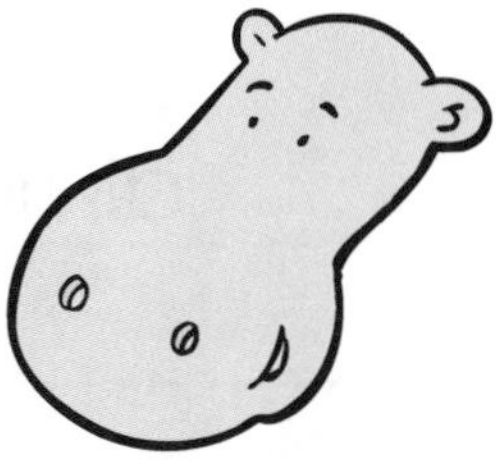
hippo

Name ________________________________

Comprehension: Rhymes

Directions: Read about words that rhyme. Then circle the answers.

Words that rhyme have the same end sounds. "Wing" and "sing" rhyme. "Boy" and "toy" rhyme. "Dime" and "time" rhyme. Can you think of other words that rhyme?

1. Words that rhyme have the same   end sounds.
   end letters.

2. Time rhymes with   "tree."
   "dime."

Directions: Write one rhyme for each word.

wing ________________

boy ________________

dime ________________

pink ________________

Name ______________________________

Rhyming Words

Many poems have rhyming words. The rhyming words are usually at the end of the line.

Directions: Complete the poem with words from the box.

My Glue

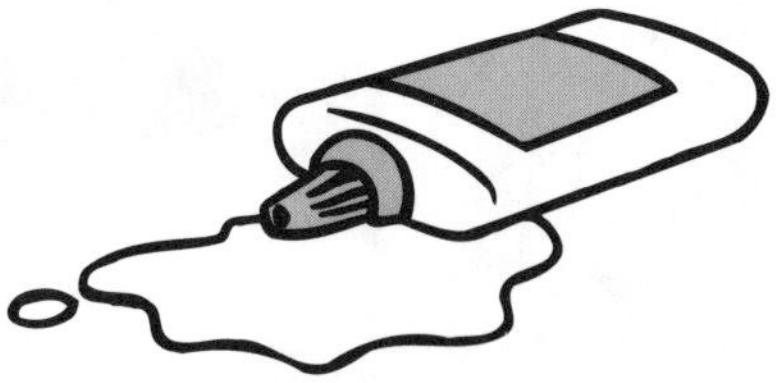

I spilled my ____________________.

I felt ____________________.

What could I ____________________?

Hey! I have a ____________________!

I'll make it ____________________.

The cleanest you've ____________________.

No one will ____________________.

Wouldn't that be ____________________?

blue	clue	scream	seen
glue	do	clean	mean

Name ______________________________

Classifying: Rhymes

Directions: Circle the pictures in each row that rhyme.

Row 1

Row 2

Row 3

Directions: Write the names of the pictures that do not rhyme.

These words do not rhyme:

Row 1	Row 2	Row 3
______________	______________	______________

Name ______________________________

Predicting: Words and Pictures

Directions: Complete each story by choosing the correct picture. Draw a line from the story to the picture.

1. Shawnda got her books. She went to the bus stop. Shawnda got on the bus.

2. Marco planted a seed. He watered it. He pulled the weeds around it.

3. Abraham's dog was barking. Abraham got out the dog food. He put it in the dog bowl.

Predicting: Story Ending

Directions: Read the story. Draw a picture in the last box to complete the story.

Name ______________________________

Predicting: Story Ending

Directions: Read the story. Draw a picture in the last box to complete the story.

Marco likes to paint.

He likes to help his dad.

4

He is tired when he's finished.

Name ___________________________

Predicting: Story Ending

Directions: Read each story. Circle the sentence that tells how the story will end.

Ann was riding her bike. She saw a dog in the park. She stopped to pet it. Ann left to go home.

The dog went swimming.

The dog followed Ann.

The dog went home with a cat.

Antonio went to a baseball game. A baseball player hit a ball toward him. He reached out his hands.

The player caught the ball.

The ball bounced on a car.

Antonio caught the ball.

Name ______________________________

Making Inferences: Baseball

Traci likes baseball. She likes to win. Traci's team does not win.

Directions: Circle the correct answers.

1. Traci likes

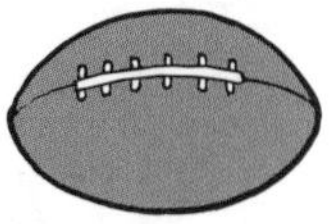
football.

soccer.

baseball.

2. Traci likes to

3. Traci uses a bat.

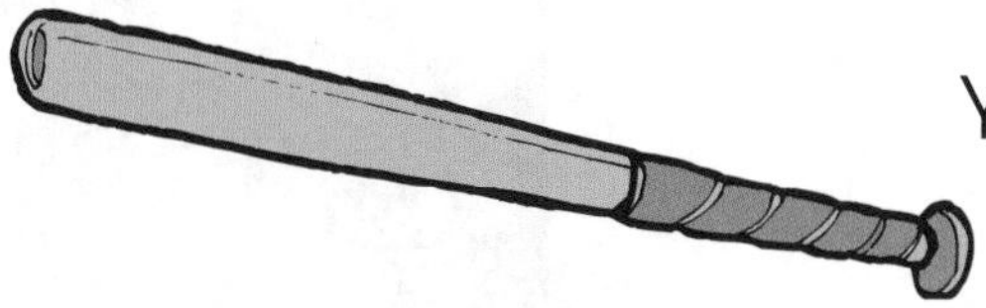

Yes No

4. Traci is

happy.

sad.

Name ______________________________

Making Inferences: The Stars

Lynn looks at the stars. She sings a song about them. She makes a wish on them. The stars help Lynn sleep.

Directions: Circle the correct answers.

1. Lynn likes the

moon.

sun.

stars.

2. What song do you think she sings?

Row, Row, Row Your Boat

Twinkle, Twinkle Little Star

Happy Birthday to You

3. What does Lynn "make" on the stars?

a wish | a spaceship | lunch

Name ______________________________

Making Inferences: Feelings

Directions: Read each story. Choose a word from the box to show how each person feels.

happy	excited	sad	mad

1. Andy and Sam were best friends. Sam and his family moved far away. How does Sam feel?

____

2. Deana could not sleep. It was the night before her birthday party. How does Deana feel?

____

3. Jacob let his baby brother play with his teddy bear. His brother lost the bear. How does Jacob feel?

____

4. Kia picked flowers for her mom. Her mom smiled when she got them. How does Kia feel?

____

Name ________________________________

Books

Directions: What do you know about books? Use the words in the box below to help fill in the lines.

title	book	author
illustrator	pages	left to right
fun	library	glossary

The name of the book is the ________________.

________________ is the direction we read.

The person who wrote the words is the ________________.

Reading is ________________!

There are many books in the ________________.

The person who draws the pictures is the ________________.

The ________________ is a kind of dictionary in the book to help you find the meanings of words.

ENGLISH

Name ______________________________

Nouns

A noun is a word that names a person, place or thing. When you read a sentence, the noun is what the sentence is about.

Directions: Complete each sentence with a noun.

The ______________________ is fat.

My ______________________ is blue.

The ______________________ has apples.

The ______________________ is hot.

Name ______________________________

Nouns

Directions: Write these naming words in the correct box.

store	zoo	child	baby	teacher	table
cat	park	gym	woman	sock	horse

Person

Place

Thing

Name ____

Things That Go Together

Some nouns name things that go together.

Directions: Draw a line to match the nouns on the left with the things they go with on the right.

toothpaste

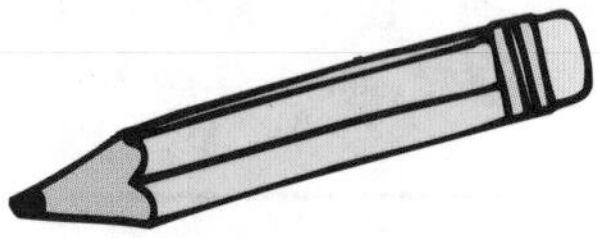

pencil

salt

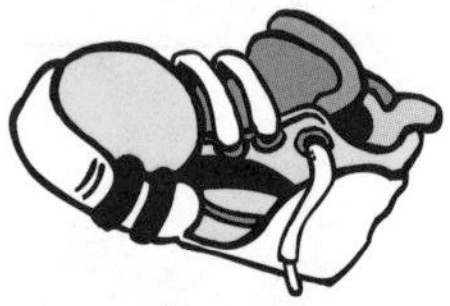

shoe

soap

pillow

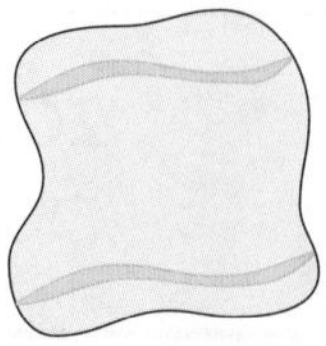

washcloth

sock

toothbrush

pepper

paper

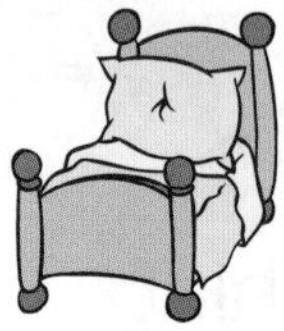

bed

Name ______________________________

Things That Go Together

Directions: Draw a line to connect the objects that go together.

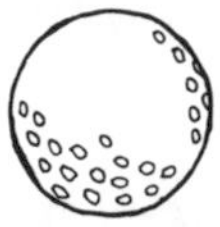
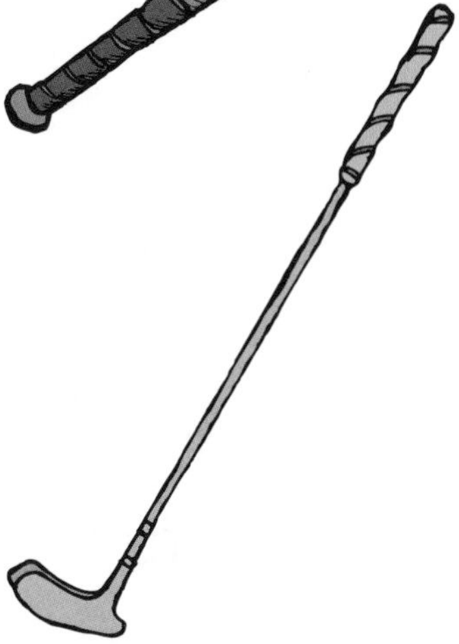

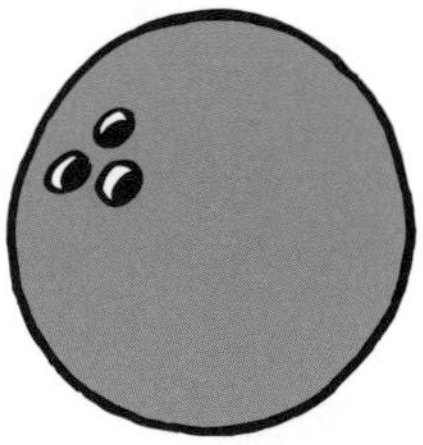

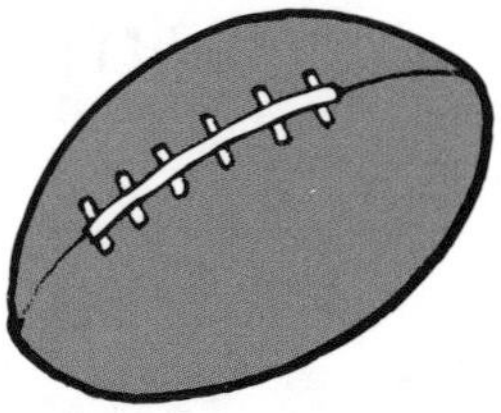

Name ______________________________

Verbs

Verbs are words that tell what a person or a thing can do.

Example: The girl pats the dog.
The word **pats** is the verb. It shows action.

Directions: Draw a line between the verbs and the pictures that show the action.

eat

run

sleep

swim

sing

hop

Name ____________________

Verbs

Directions:
Look at the picture and read the words. Write an action word in each sentence below.

1. The two boys like to ______________ together.

2. The children ______________ the soccer ball.

3. Some children like to ______________ on the swing.

4. The girl can ______________ very fast.

5. The teacher ______________ the bell.

Name ______________________

Adjectives

Describing words tell us more about a person, place or thing.

Directions: Read the words in the box. Choose the word that describes the picture. Write it next to the picture.

happy	round	sick	cold	long

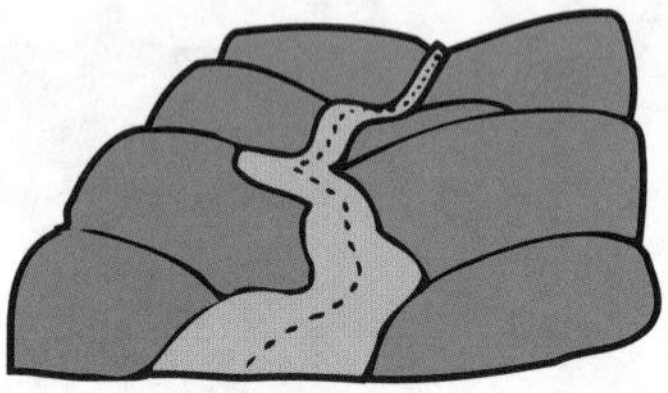

ame ______________________________

Adjectives

irections: Circle the describing word in each sentence. Draw a
ne from the sentence to the picture.

. The hungry dog is eating.

. The tiny bird is flying.

. Horses have long legs.

. She is a fast runner.

. The little boy was lost.

Name ____________________

Adjectives

Directions: Read the words in the box. Choose the word that desc
the picture. Write it next to the picture.

wet	round	funny	soft	sad	tc

____

____

____

____

____

____

Name ______________________

Adjectives: Colors and Numbers

Colors and numbers can describe nouns.

Directions: Underline the describing word in each sentence. Draw a picture to go with each sentence.

A yellow moon was in the sky.

Two worms are on the road.

The tree had red apples.

The girl wore a blue dress.

Name ____________________

Comparative Adjectives

Directions: Look at each group of pictures. Write 1, 2 or 3 under the picture to show where it should be.

Example:

tallest ___3___ **tall** ___1___ **taller** ___2___

small ______ **smallest** ______ **smaller** ______

biggest ______ **big** ______ **bigger** ______

wider ______ **wide** ______ **widest** ______

Name ________________________________

Comparative Adjectives

Directions: Look at the pictures in each row. Write 1, 2 or 3 under the picture to show where it should be.

shortest ______ **shorter** ______ **short** ______

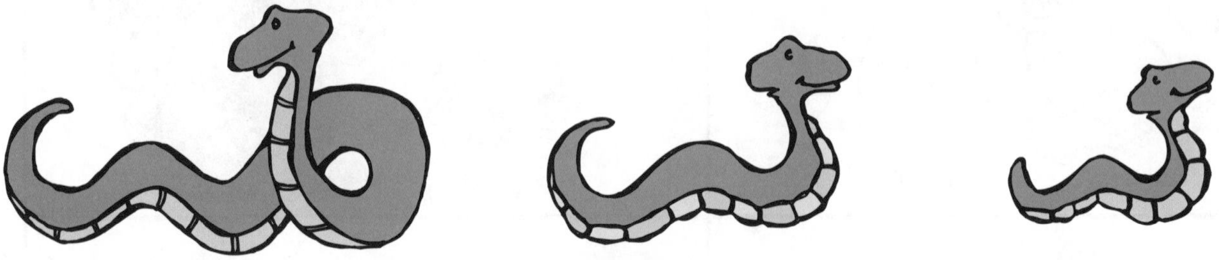

longest ______ **longer** ______ **long** ______

happy ______ **happier** ______ **happiest** ______

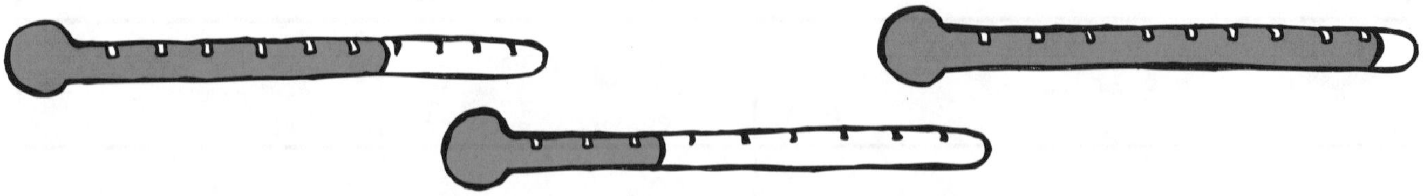

hotter ______ **hot** ______ **hottest** ______

Name ______________________________

Synonyms

Synonyms are words that mean almost the same thing. **Start** and **begin** are synonyms.

Directions: Find the synonyms that describe each picture. Write the words in the boxes below the picture.

small funny large sad silly little big unhappy

Name ____________________

Synonyms

Directions: Circle the word in each row that is most like the first word in the row.

Example:

grin		**smile** (circled)	**frown**	**mad**
bag	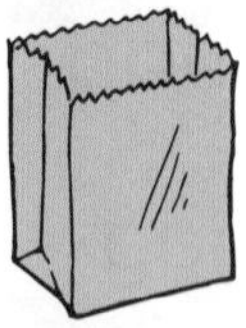	**jar**	**sack**	**box**
cat		**fruit**	**animal**	**flower**
apple		**rot**	**cookie**	**fruit**
around		**circle**	**square**	**dot**
bird		**dog**	**cat**	**duck**
bee		**fish**	**ant**	**snake**

Name ______________________________

Synonyms

Directions: Read each sentence and look at the underlined word. Circle the word that means the same thing. Write the new words.

1. The boy was <u>mad</u>.	happy	angry	pup
2. The <u>dog</u> is brown.	pup	cat	rat
3. I like to <u>scream</u>.	soar	mad	shout
4. The bird can <u>fly</u>.	soar	jog	warm
5. The girl can <u>run</u>.	sleep	jog	shout
6. I am <u>hot</u>.	warm	cold	soar

Name ________________________________

Synonyms

Directions: Read the story. Write a word on the line that means almost the same as the word under the line.

Dan went to the ______________________.
store

He wanted to buy ______________________.
food

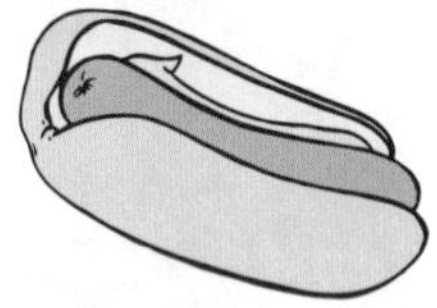

He walked very ______________________.
quickly

The store had what he wanted.

He bought it using ______________________.
dimes

Instead of walking home, Dan ______________________.
jogged

Name ____________________

Antonyms

Antonyms are words that are opposites. **Hot** and **cold** are antonyms.

Directions: Draw a line between the antonyms.

closed

below

full

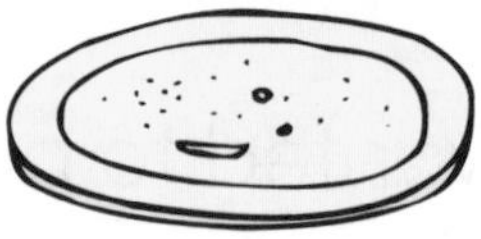

empty

above

old

new

open

Name ______________________

Antonyms

Directions: Draw lines to connect the words that are opposites.

up	**wet**
over	**down**
dry	**dirty**
clean	**under**

Name ______________________________

Antonyms

Opposites are things that are different in every way.

Directions: Draw a line between the opposites.

day

happy

big

open

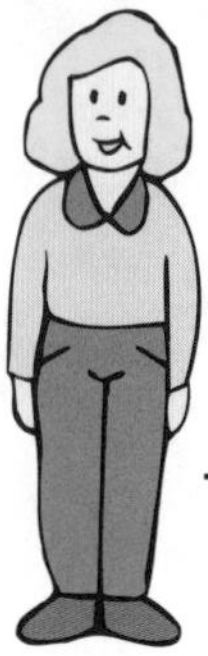
front

little

closed

night

back

sad

Name ______________________________

Antonyms

Directions: Circle the picture in each row that is the opposite of the first picture.

up

down

over

across

cold

frozen

hot

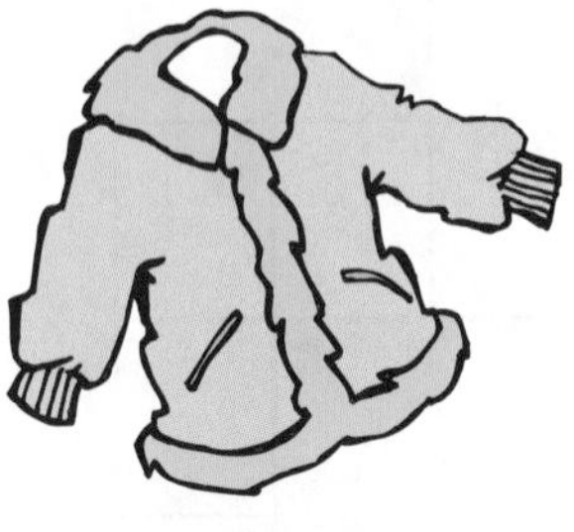
warm

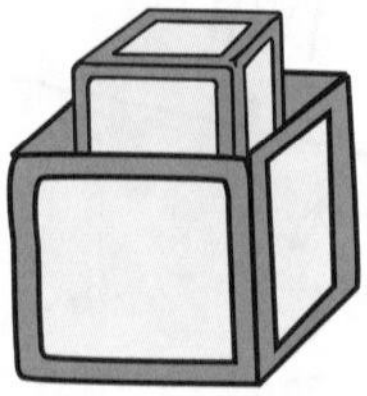
in

beside

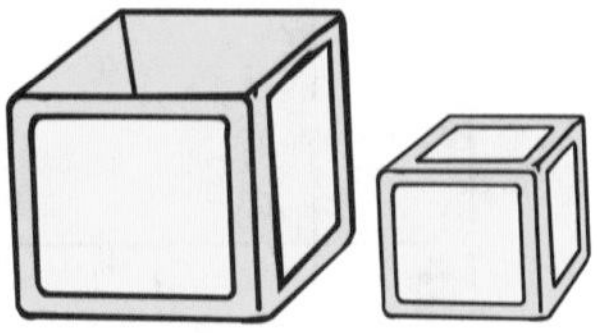
out

over

cloud

rain

storm

sun

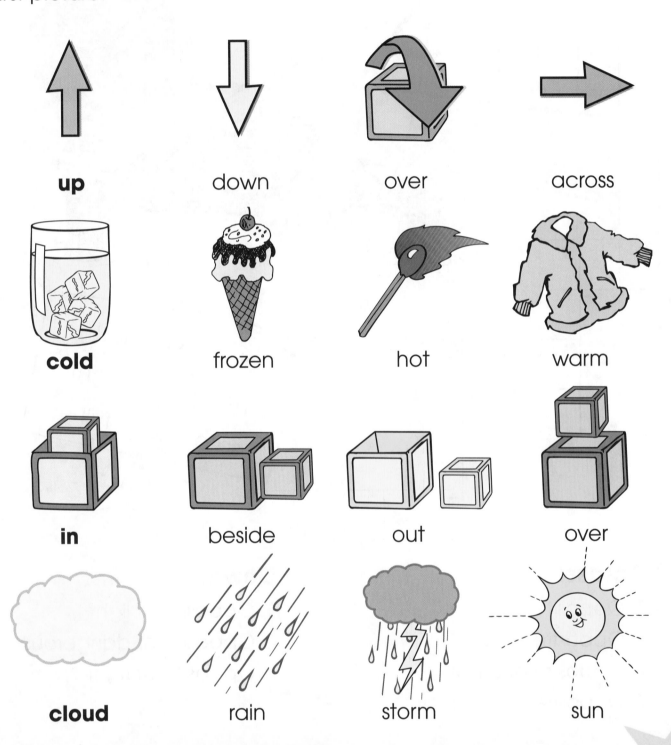

Antonyms

Directions: Read each clue. Write the answers in the puzzle.

Across:

1. Opposite of low
2. Opposite of no
4. Opposite of empty
6. Opposite of loose

Down:

1. Opposite of light
3. Opposite of dangerous
5. Opposite of right

Name ______________________

Homophones

Homophones are words that **sound** the same but are spelled differently and mean something different. **Blew** and **blue** are homophones.

Directions: Look at the word pairs. Choose the word that describes the picture. Write the word on the line next to the picture.

1. sew so ______________________

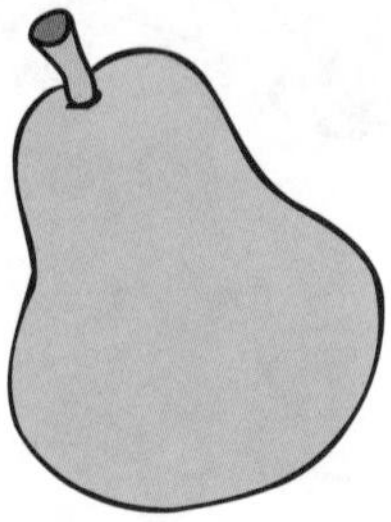

2. pair pear ______________________

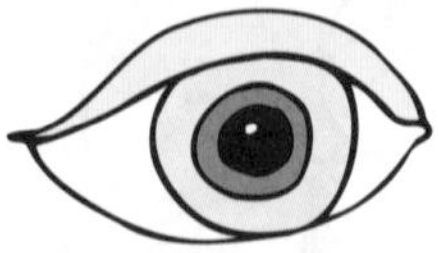

3. eye I ______________________

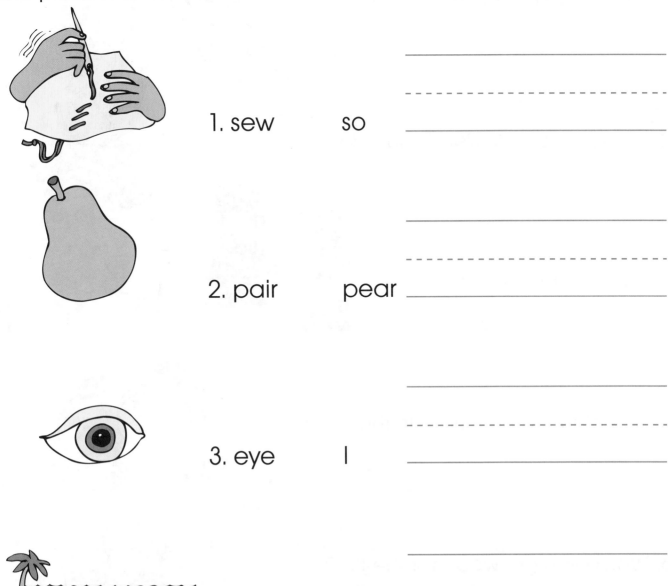

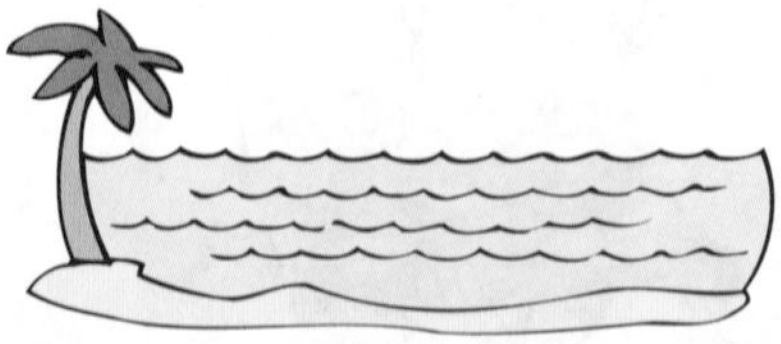

4. see sea ______________________

Name ___________________________________

Homophones

Directions: Read each sentence. Underline the two words that sound the same but are spelled differently and mean something different.

1. Tom ate eight grapes.

2. Becky read *Little Red Riding Hood*.

3. I went to buy two dolls.

4. Five blue feathers blew in the wind.

5. Would you get wood for the fire?

Name ______________________________

Sentences

Sentences begin with capital letters.

Directions: Read the sentences and write them below. Begin each sentence with a capital letter.

Example: the cat is fat.

The cat is fat.

my dog is big.

the boy is sad.

bikes are fun!

dad can bake.

Name ______________________________

Word Order

If you change the order of the words in a sentence, you can change the meaning of the sentence.

Directions: Read the sentences. Draw a circle around the sentence that describes the picture.

Example:

The fox jumped over the dogs.

The dogs jumped over the fox.

1. The cat watched the bird.
   The bird watched the cat.

2. The girl looked at the boy.
   The boy looked at the girl.

3. The turtle ran past the rabbit.
   The rabbit ran past the turtle.

Name ___________________________

Word Order

Directions: Look at the picture. Put the words in order. Write the sentences on the lines below.

1. We made lemonade. some
2. good. It was
3. We the sold lemonade.
4. cost It five cents.
5. fun. We had

1. ___________________________

2. ___________________________

3. ___________________________

4. ___________________________

5. ___________________________

Name ______________________________

Telling Sentences

Directions: Read the sentences and write them below. Begin each sentence with a capital letter. End each sentence with a period.

1. most children like pets
2. some children like dogs
3. some children like cats
4. some children like snakes
5. some children like all animals

1. ______________________________

2. ______________________________

3. ______________________________

4. ______________________________

5. ______________________________

Name ______________________________

Telling Sentences

Directions: Read the sentences and write them below.
Begin each sentence with a capital letter.
End each sentence with a period.

1. i like to go to the store with Mom
2. we go on Friday
3. i get to push the cart
4. i get to buy the cookies
5. i like to help Mom

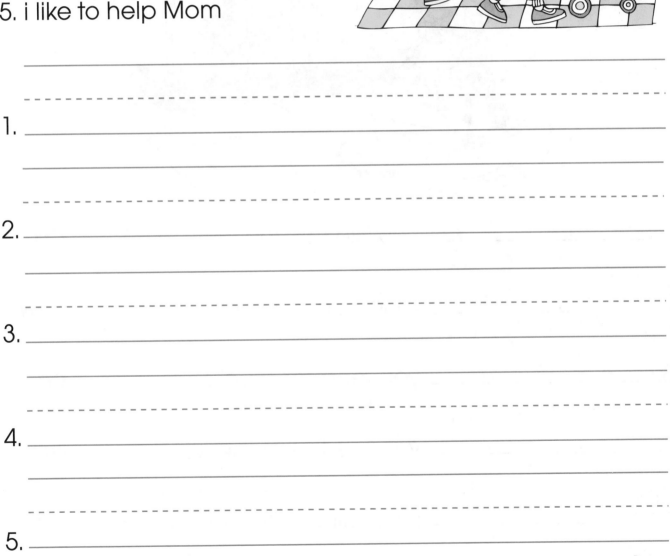

1. ______________________________

2. ______________________________

3. ______________________________

4. ______________________________

5. ______________________________

Name ______________________________

Asking Sentences

Directions: Write the first word of each asking sentence. Be sure to begin each question with a capital letter. End each question with a question mark.

1. ______________________ you like the zoo **do**

2. ______________________ much does it cost **how**

3. ______________________ you feed the ducks **can**

4. ______________________ you see the monkeys **will**

5. ______________________ time will you eat lunch **what**

Name ______________________________

Asking Sentences

Directions: Read the asking sentences. Write the sentences below. Begin each sentence with a capital letter. End each sentence with a question mark.

1. what game will we play
2. do you like to read
3. how old are you
4. who is your best friend
5. can you tie your shoes

1. ______________________________

2. ______________________________

3. ______________________________

4. ______________________________

5. ______________________________

Name ______________________________

Periods and Question Marks

Directions: Put a period or a question mark at the end of each sentence below.

1. Do you like parades

2. The clowns lead the parade

3. Can you hear the band

4. The balloons are big

5. Can you see the horses

Name ______________________________

Is and Are

We use **is** in sentences about one person or one thing. We use **are** in sentences about more than one person or thing.

Example: The dog **is** barking.
The dogs **are** barking.

Directions: Write **is** or **are** in the sentences below.

1. Jim ________________ playing baseball.

2. Fred and Sam ________________ good friends.

3. Cupcakes ________________ my favorite treat.

4. Lisa ________________ a good soccer player.

Name ____________________

Is and Are

Directions: Write **is** or **are** in the sentences below.

Example: Lisa <u>is</u> sleeping.

1. Cats and dogs ____________ good pets.

2. Bill ____________ my best friend.

3. Apples ____________ good to eat.

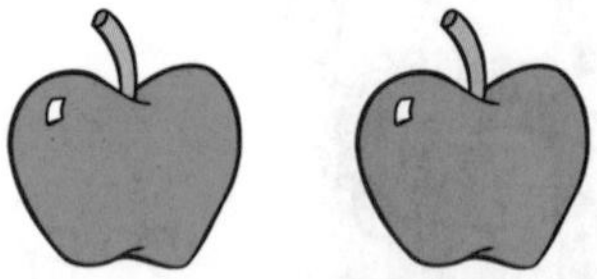

4. We ____________ going to the zoo.

5. Pedro ____________ coming to my house.

6. When ____________ you all going to the zoo?

SPELLING

Name ______________________________

Color Names

Directions: Trace the letters to write the name of each color. Then write the name again by yourself.

Example:

orange   orange

blue

green

yellow

red

brown

Name ______________________________

Color Names: Sentences

Directions: Use the color words to complete these sentences. Then put a period at the end.

Example: My new 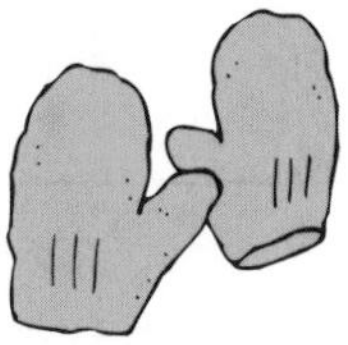 are orange.

green tree

blue bike

yellow chick

red ball

1. The baby  is ______________________ ☐

2. This  is ______________________ ☐

3. My 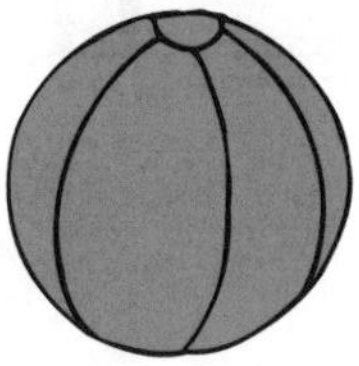 is big and ______________________ ☐

4. My sister's  is ______________________ ☐

Name ______________________________

Animal Names

Directions: Fill in the missing letters for each word.

Example:

frog frog

fi__ f_sh

d_g _og

b__d _ir_

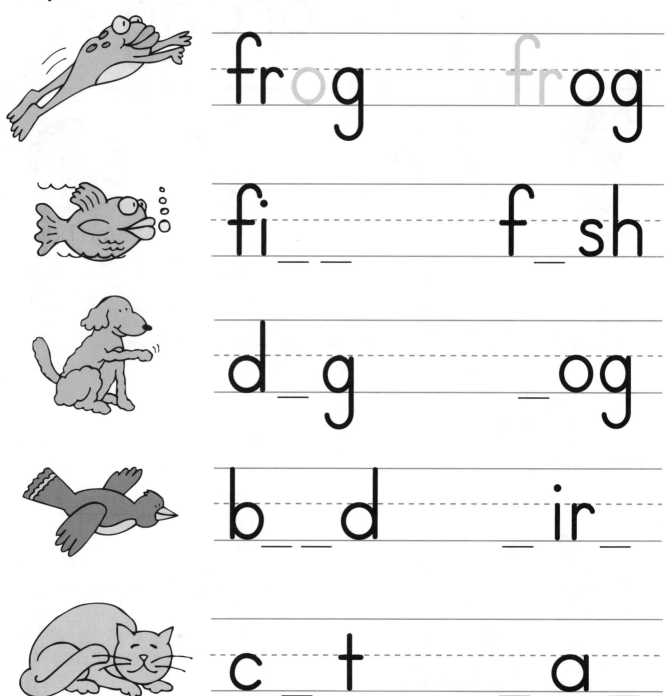

c_t _a_

Name ______________________

Animal Names: Sentences

A **sentence** tells about something.

Directions: These sentences tell about animals. Write the word that completes each sentence.

Example:

My frog  jumps high.

1. I take my ______  for a walk.

2. My ______  lives in water.

3. My ______  can sing.

4. My ______  has a long tail.

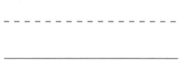

Name ______________________________

Things That Go

Directions: Trace the letters to write the name of each thing. Write each name again by yourself. Then color the pictures.

Example:

car car

truck

train

bike

plane

Name ______________________________

Things That Go: Sentences

Directions: These sentences tell about things that go. Write the word that completes each sentence.

Example:

The ___car___ is in the garage.

1. The ______________ was at the farm.

2. My ______________ had a flat tire.

3. The ______________ flew high.

4. The ______________ went fast.

Name ______________________________

Clothing Words

Directions: Trace the letters to write the name of each clothing word. Then write each name again by yourself.

Example:

shirt shirt

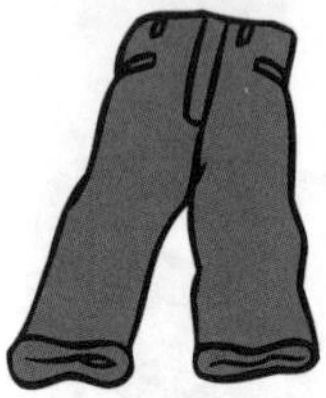

pants

jacket

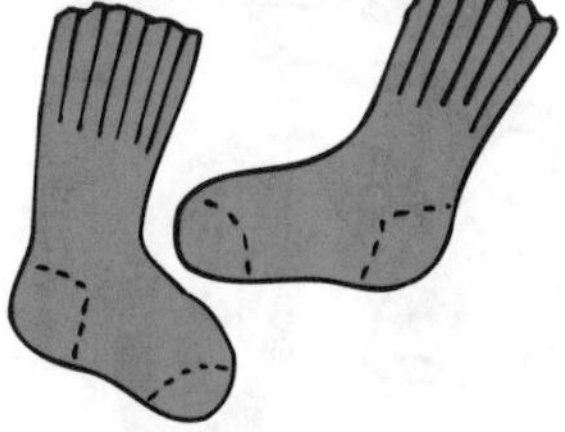

socks

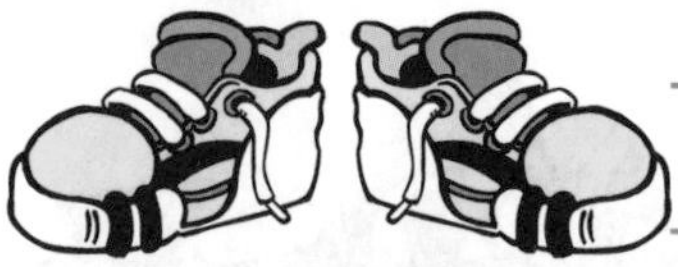

shoes

dress

hat

Name ____

Clothing Words: Sentences

Directions: Some of these sentences tell a whole idea. Others have something missing. If something is missing, draw a line to the word that completes the sentence. Put a period at the end of each sentence.

Example:

She is wearing a polka-dot

holes

1. The baseball player wore a

2. His pants were torn.

dress .

3. The socks had

4. The jacket had blue buttons.

hat

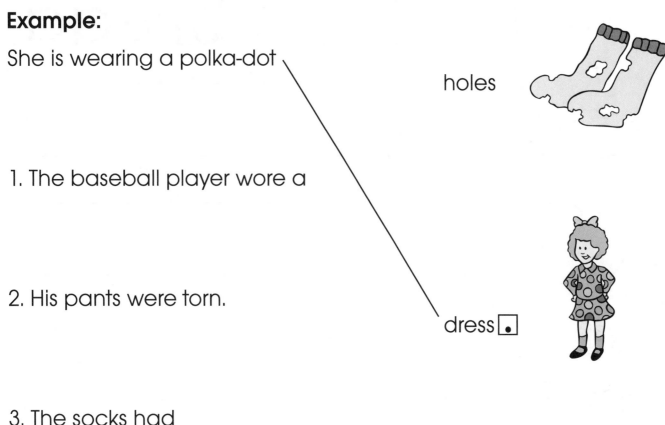

5. The shoes were brown.

Name ______________________________

Food Names

Directions: Trace the letters to write the name of each food word. Write each name again by yourself. Then color the pictures.

Example:  bread **bread**

 cookie

 apple

 cake

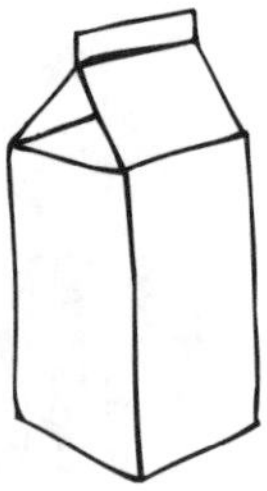 milk

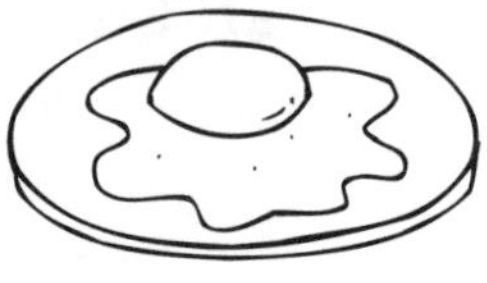 egg

Name ____________________

Food Names: Asking Sentences

An **asking sentence** asks a question. Asking sentences end with a question mark.

Directions: Write each sentence on the line. Begin each sentence with a capital letter. Put a period at the end of the telling sentences and a question mark at the end of the asking sentences.

Example: do you like cake 

Do you like cake?

1. the cow has spots 

2. is that cookie good 

3. she ate the apple 

Name ___________________________________

Number Words

Directions: Trace the letters to write the name of each number. Write the numbers again by yourself. Then color the number pictures.

Example: 1 one one

2 two

3 three

4 four

5 five

6 six

7 seven

8 eight

9 nine

10 ten

Name ______________________________

Number Words: Asking Sentences

Directions: Use a number word to answer each question.

one	five	seven	three	eight

1. How many trees are there? ______________________

2. How many flowers are there? ______________________

3. How many presents are there? ______________________

4. How many clocks are there? ______________________

5. How many forks are there? ______________________

Name ____________________

Action Words

Action words tell things we can do.

Directions: Trace the letters to write each action word. Then write the action word again by yourself.

Example:

sleep sleep

run

make

ride

play

stop

Name ____________________

Action Words: More Than One

To show more than one of something, add **s** to the end of the word.

Example: one cat  two cats 

Directions: In each sentence, add **s** to show more than one. Then write the action word that completes each sentence.

sit	jump	stop	ride

Example:

The frog **s** **sleep** in the sun.

1. The boy ____ ____________ on the fence.

2. The car ____ ____________ at the sign.

3. The girl ____ ____________ in the water.

4. The dog ____ ____________ in the wagon.

Name ______________________________

Action Words: Asking Sentences

Directions: Write an asking sentence about each picture. Begin each sentence with **can**. Add an action word. Begin each asking sentence with a capital letter and end it with a question mark.

Example:

I with you can 

Can I sit with you?

she can 

____

with you can I 

____

can she fast 

____

Name ______________________________

Sense Words

Directions: Circle the word that is spelled correctly. Then write the correct spelling in the blank.

Example:

tast
taste
tste

taste

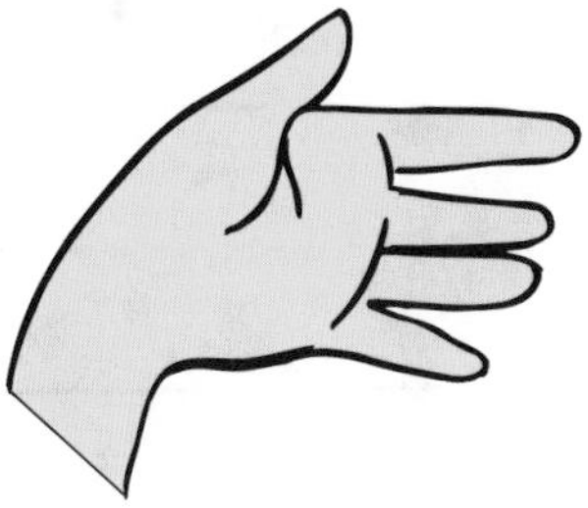

touch
tuch
touh

____

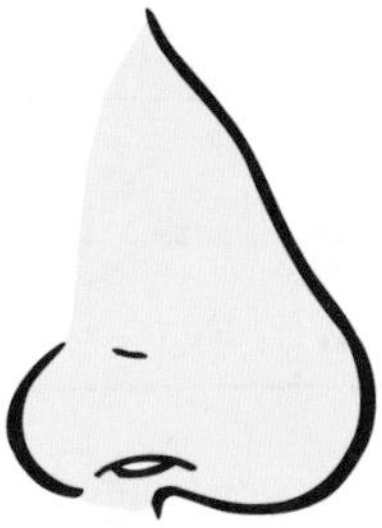

smel
smll
smell

____

her
hear
har

____

see
se
sea

____

Name ______________________________

Sense Words: Sentences

Directions: Read each sentence and write the correct words in the blanks.

Example:

taste
mouth I can taste things with my mouth.

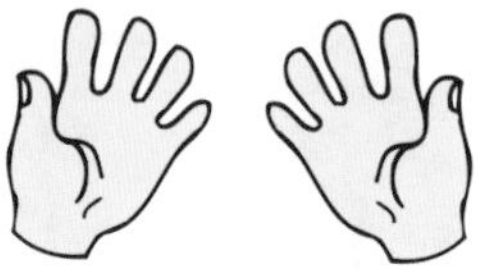

touch
hands 1. I can ____________ things with my ____________.

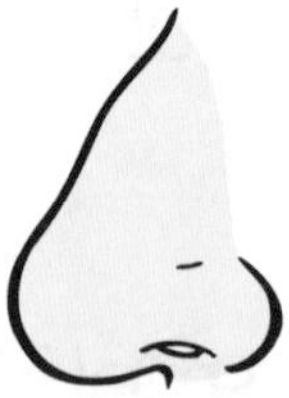

nose
smell 2. I can ____________ things with my ____________.

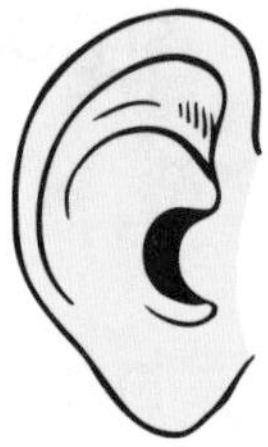

hear
ears 3. I can ____________ with my ____________.

see
eyes 4. I can ____________ things with my ____________.

Name ____________________

My World

Directions: Fill in the missing letters for each word.

tree  tree

gr_ ss 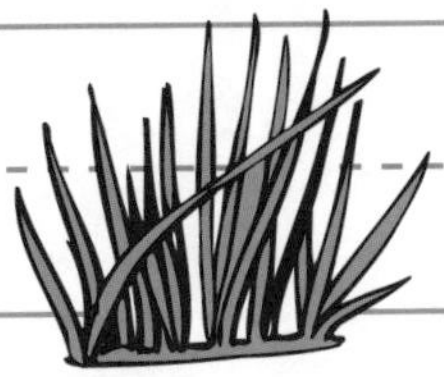 _ _ a _ _

fl_ _ er  _ _ ow _ _

p_ nd  _ o _ _

s_ nd 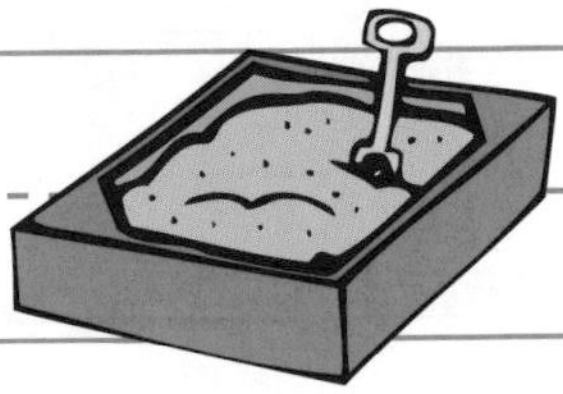 _ a _ _

sk_  _ _ y

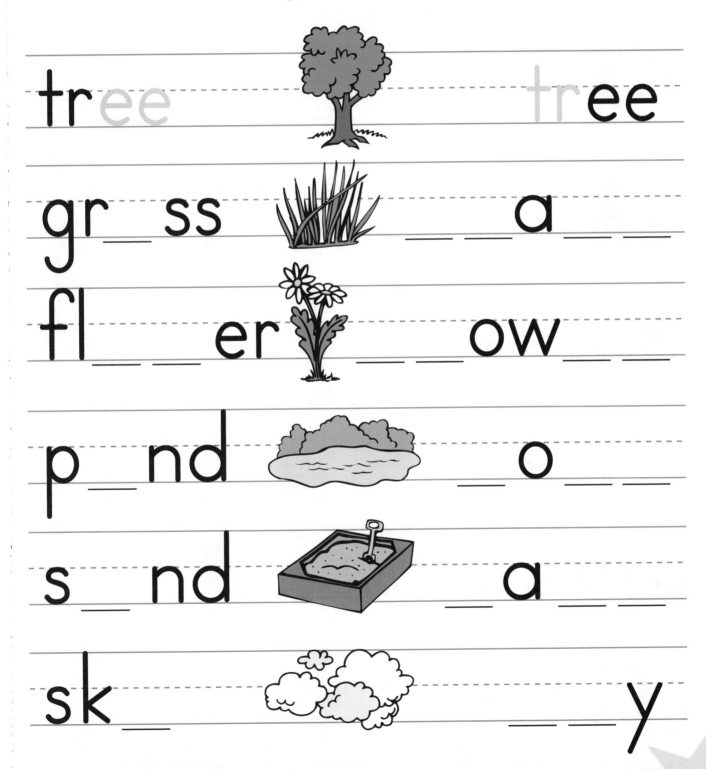

Name ______________________

My World

Directions: The letters in the words below are mixed up. Unscramble the letters and write each word correctly.

etre ______________________

srags ______________________

loefwr ______________________

dnop ______________________

dnsa ______________________

yks ______________________

Name ______________________

My World: Sentences

Directions: Write the word that completes each sentence. Put a period at the end of the telling sentences and a question mark at the end of the asking sentences.

Example: Does the sun shine on the flowers?

tree	grass	pond	sand	sky

1. The ______________ was full of dark clouds☐

2. Can you climb the ______________☐

3. Did you see the duck in the ______________☐

4. Is the child playing in the ______________☐

5. The ______________ in the yard was tall☐

Name ______________________________

The Parts of My Body: Sentences

Directions: Write the word that completes each sentence. Put a period at the end of the telling sentences and a question mark at the end of the asking sentences.

Example:  I wear my hat on my head.

arms	legs	feet	hands

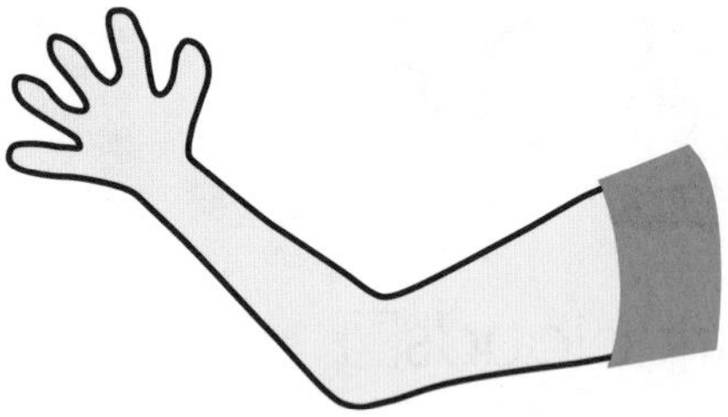

1. How strong are your ______________ ☐

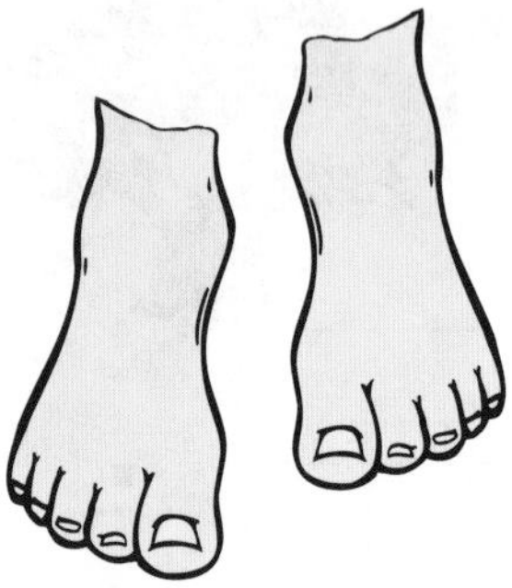

2. You wear shoes on your ______________ ☐

3. If you're happy and you know it, clap your ______________ ☐

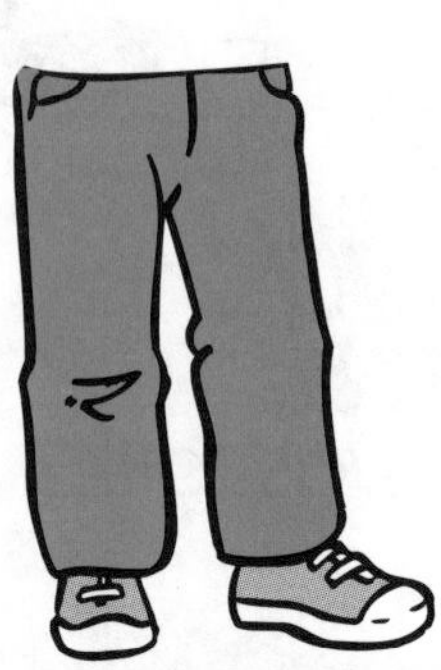

4. My pants covered my ______________ ☐

Name ______________________________

The Parts of My Body: Sentences

Directions: Read the sentence parts below. Draw a line from the first part of the sentence to the second part that completes it.

1. I give big hugs

with my arms.

with my car.

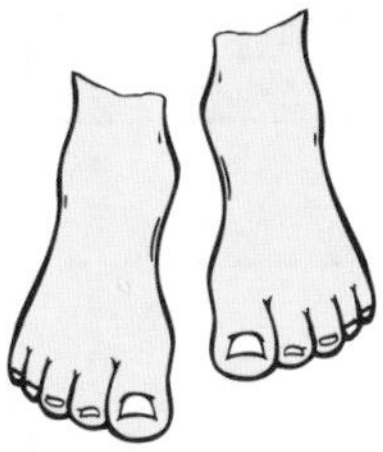

2. My feet

drive the car.

got wet in the rain.

3. I have a bump

on my head.

on my coat.

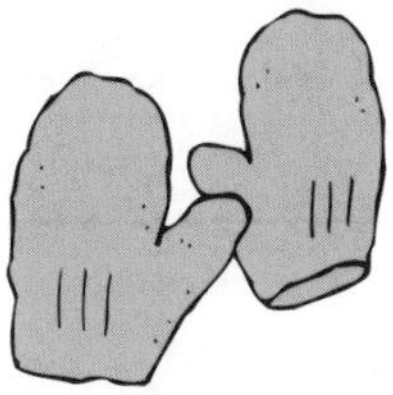

4. My mittens

keep my arms warm.

keep my hands warm.

5. I can jump high

using my legs.

using a spoon.

Name ______________________________

The Parts of My Body: Sentences

Directions: Read the two sentences on each line and draw a line between them. Then write each sentence again on the lines below. Begin each sentence with a capital letter, and end each one with a period or a question mark.

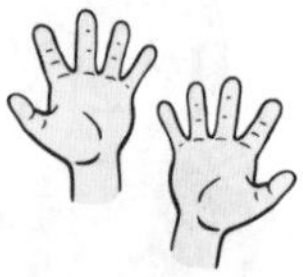

Example: wash your hands|they are dirty

Wash your hands.

They are dirty.

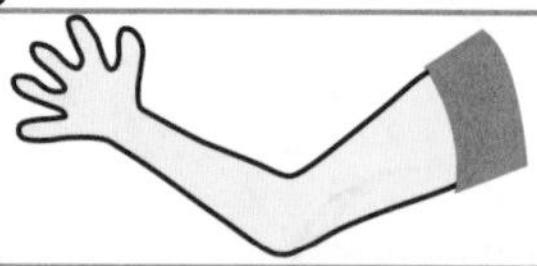

1. you have big arms are you very strong

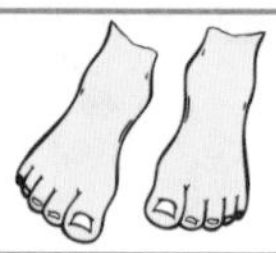

2. I have two feet I can run fast

MATH

Name ________________________________

Number Recognition

Directions: Write the numbers 1-10. Color the bear.

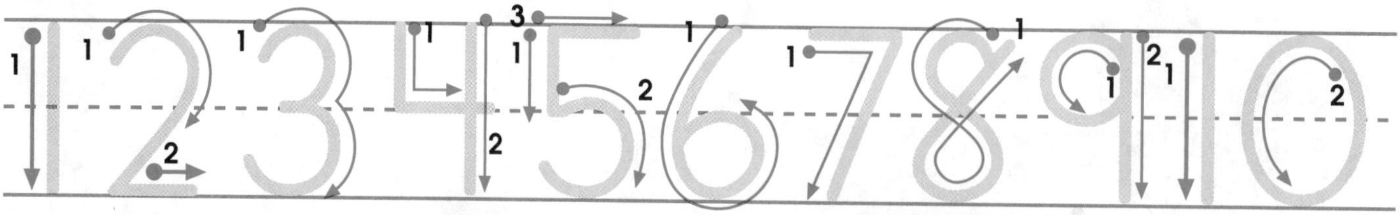

Name ________________________________

Number Recognition

Directions: Count the number of objects in each group. Draw a line to the correct number.

1

2

3

4

5

6

7

8

9

10

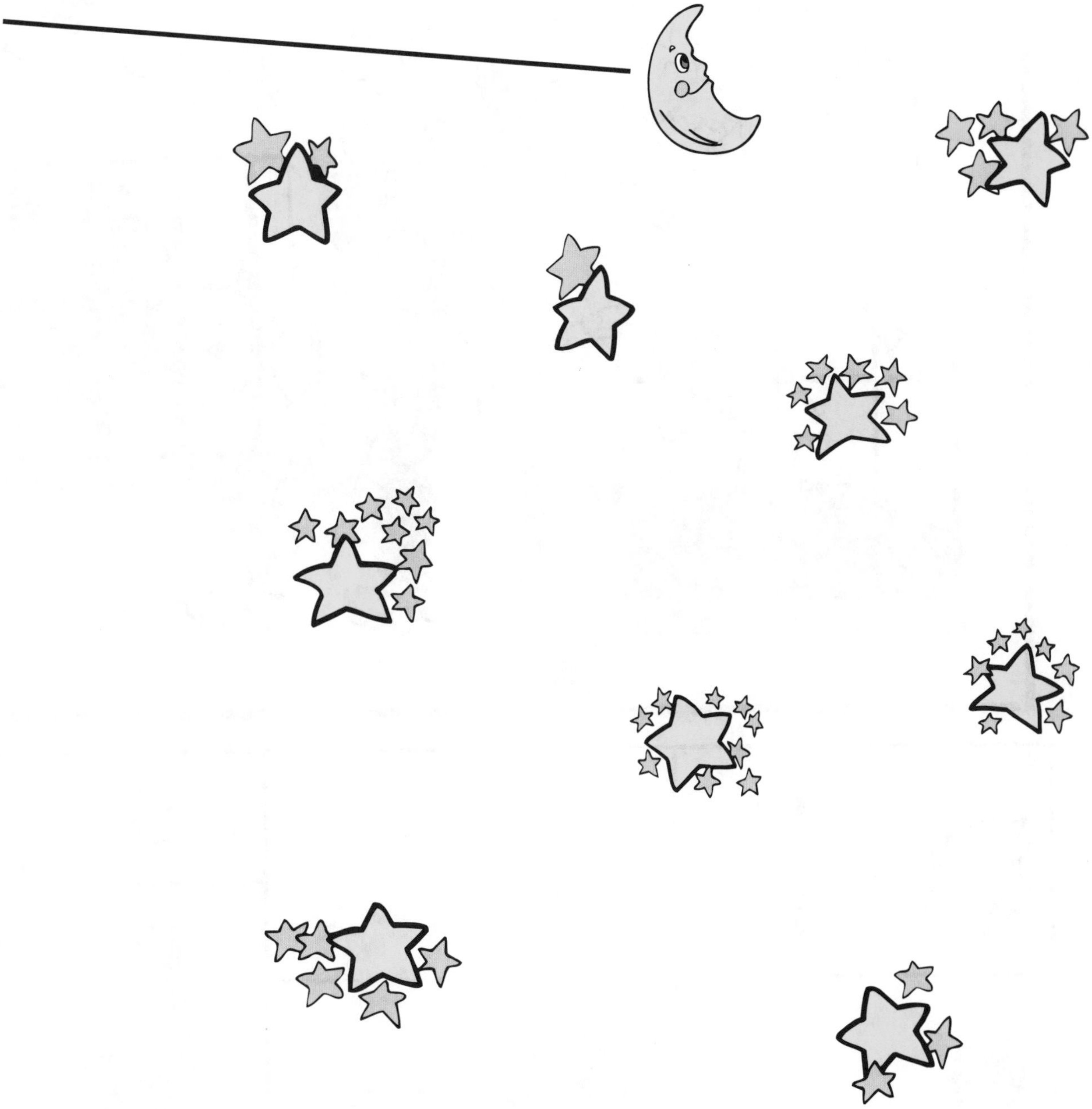

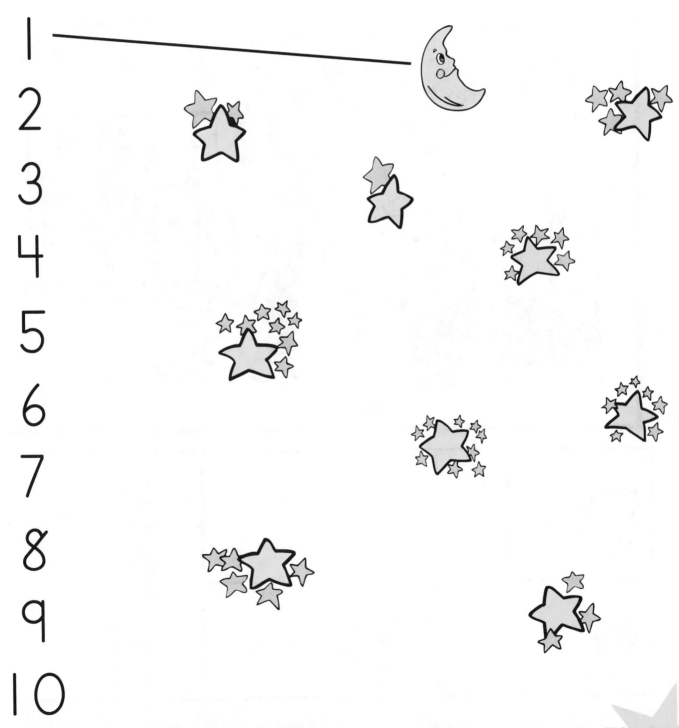

Name ______________________________

Counting

Directions: How many are there of each shape? Write the answers in the boxes. The first one is done for you.

 1		

Name ________________________________

Counting

Directions: How many are there of each picture? Write the answers in the boxes. The first one is done for you.

Name ____________________________________

Number Word Find

Directions: Find the number words 0 through 12 hidden in the box.

t	e	a	z	w	z	x	a	b	i	g	t	e	n
o	l	z	r	b	e	r	e	v	e	d	l	a	j
t	w	e	l	v	e	a	b	o	n	e	c	d	z
i	a	r	p	q	d	p	s	u	j	x	e	i	w
c	f	o	p	l	s	c	k	i	q	u	i	i	o
m	s	t	f	v	i	o	e	t	t	f	g	h	d
t	n	u	w	u	x	g	z	w	h	g	h	r	o
n	i	n	e	k	f	d	f	o	u	r	t	j	f
a	s	g	l	q	c	w	k	o	s	n	v	m	i
n	y	c	e	b	o	n	h	h	p	o	m	p	v
b	e	x	v	s	s	e	v	e	n	w	e	n	e
t	h	r	e	e	r	t	a	l	j	k	x	q	z
m	o	a	n	e	n	i	m	u	t	w	a	y	x

Words to find:

zero	four	eight	eleven
one	five	nine	twelve
two	six	ten	
three	seven		

Name ______________________________

Number Words

Directions: Number the buildings from one to six.

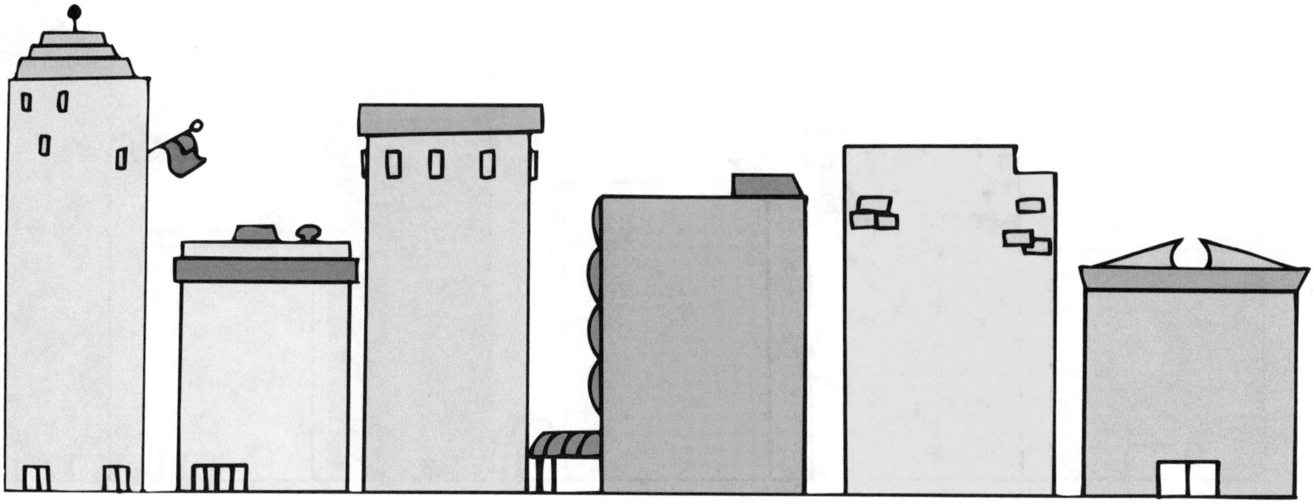

Directions: Draw a line from the word to the number.

two	1
five	3
six	5
four	6
one	2
three	4

Name ___________________________

Number Words

Directions: Number the buildings from five to ten.

Directions: Draw a line from the word to the number.

nine	8
seven	10
five	7
eight	5
six	9
ten	6

Name ____________________

Number Recognition Review

Directions: Match the correct number of objects with the number. Then match the number with the word.

1	four
2	ten
3	two
4	six
5	one
6	nine
7	three
8	eight
9	five
10	seven

Name ______________________________

Sequencing Numbers

Sequencing is putting numbers in the correct order.

1, 2, 3, 4, 5, 6, 7, 8, 9, 10

Directions: Write the missing numbers.

Example: 4, ___5___ ,6

3, ________ ,5	7, ________ ,9	8, ________ ,10
6, ________ ,8	________ ,3,4	________ ,5,6
5, 6, ________	________ ,6,7	________ ,3,4
________ ,4,5	________ ,7,8	5, ________ ,7
2, 3, ________	1, 2, ________	7, 8, ________
2, ________ ,4	________ ,2,3	4, ________ ,6
6, 7, ________	3, 4, ________	1, ________ ,3
7, 8, ________	________ ,3,4	________ ,9,10

Name ______________________________

Number Match

Directions: Cut out the pictures and number words below. Mix them up and match them again.

one		two	eight
		five	
	three		nine
four	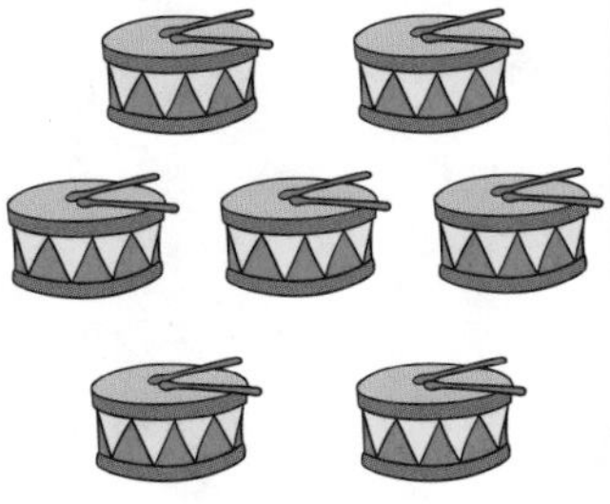	seven	
	six		ten

Name ______________________________

Page is blank for cutting exercise on previous page.

Name ____________________

Number Crossword Puzzle

Directions: Write the correct number word in the boxes provided.

Across
2. 4
3. 8
5. 2
7. 7
9. 10

Down
1. 0
2. 5
4. 3
6. 1
7. 6
8. 9

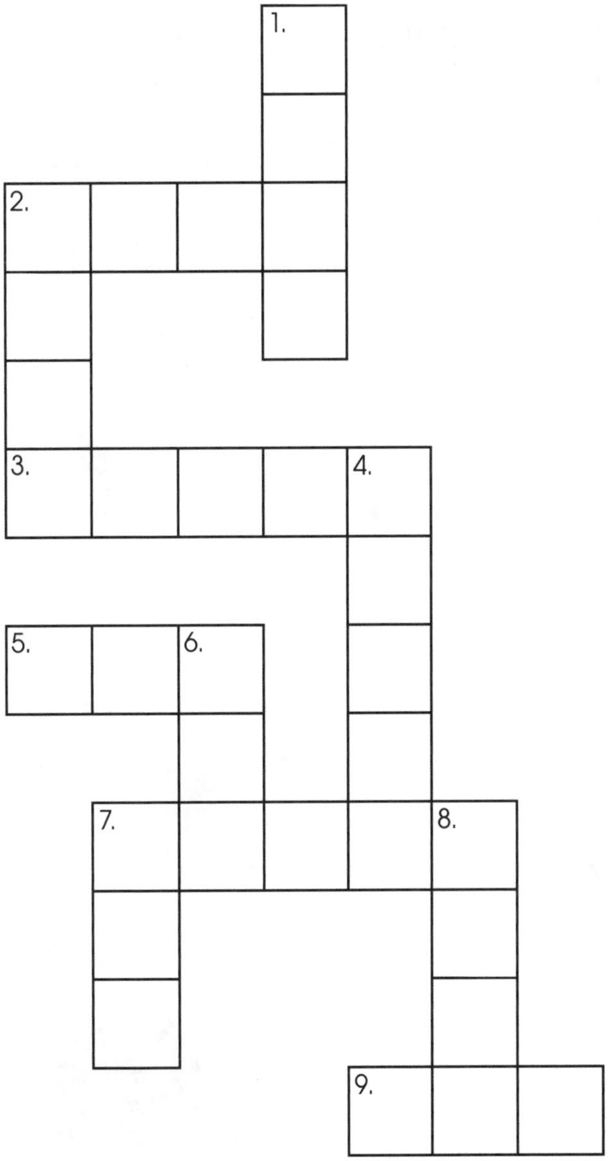

one ●	two ●●	three ●●●	four ●●●●	five ●●●●●	
six ●●●●●●	seven ●●●●●●●	eight ●●●●●●●●	nine ●●●●●●●●●	ten ●●●●●●●●●●	zero

Name ______________________________

Ordinal Numbers

Ordinal numbers are used to indicate order in a series, such as **first**, **second** or **third**.

Directions: Draw a line to the picture that corresponds to the ordinal number in the left column.

eighth

third

sixth

ninth

seventh

second

fourth

first

fifth

tenth

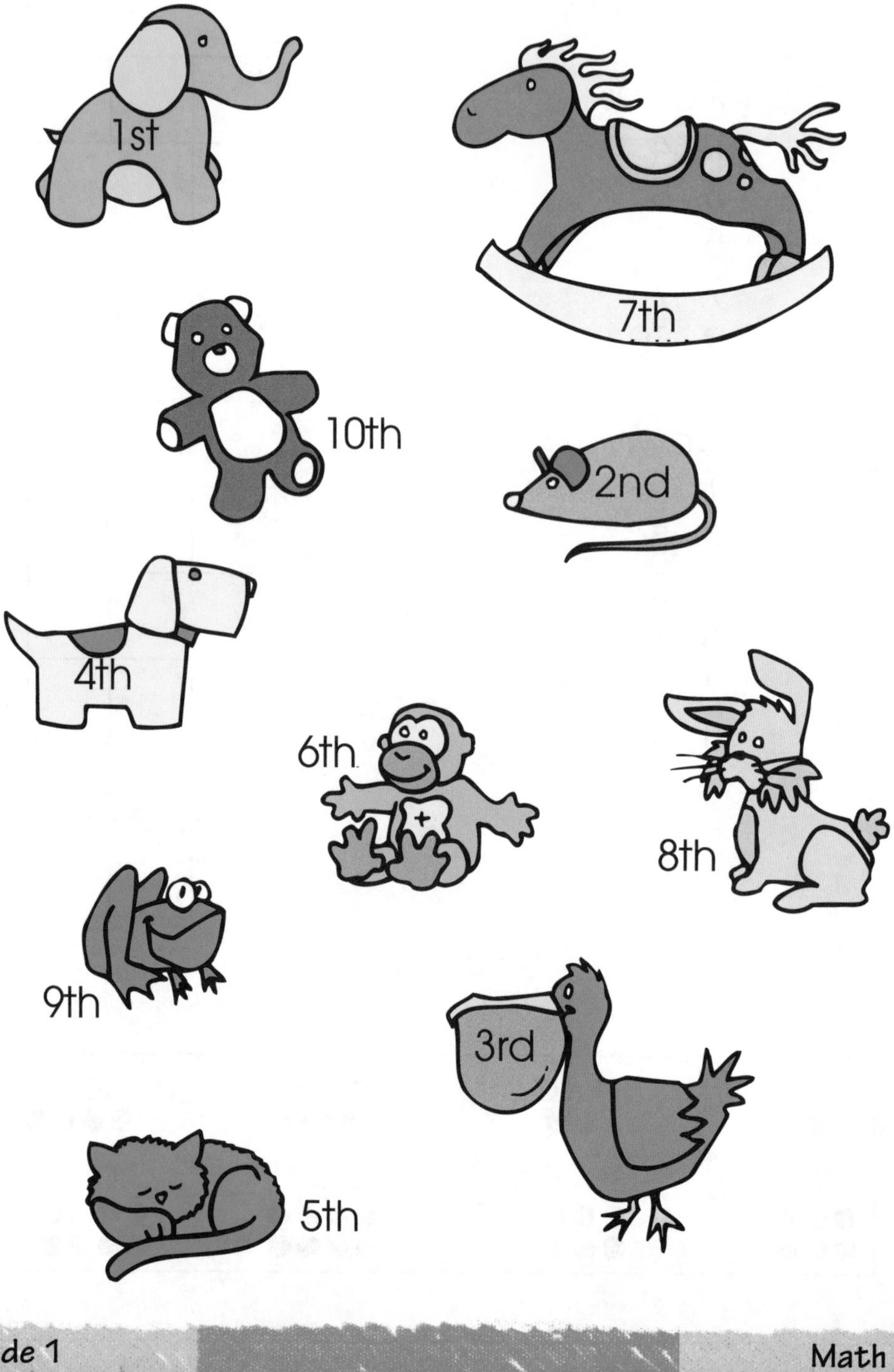

Name ______________________________

Ordinal Numbers

Directions: Draw an **X** on the first vegetable, draw a circle around the second vegetable, and draw a square around the third vegetable.

Directions: Write the ordinal number below the picture.

✂ **Cut** the children apart. Mix them up. Then put them back in the correct order.

first | second | third | fourth | fifth | sixth | seventh | eighth | ninth | tenth

Name ____________________

Page is blank for cutting exercise on previous page.

Name ______________________

Sequencing: Standing in Line

Directions: These children are waiting to see a movie. Look at them and follow the instructions.

1. Color the person who is first in line yellow.
2. Color the person who is last in line brown.
3. Color the person who is second in line pink.
4. Circle the person who is at the end of the line.

Name ______________________________

Addition 1, 2

Addition means "putting together" or adding two or more numbers to find the sum. "+" is a plus sign. It means to add the 2 numbers. "=" is an equals sign. It tells how much they are together.

Directions: Count the cats and tell how many.

 +  =  ______

 +  =  ______

 +  =  ______

Name ______________________________

Addition

Directions: Count the shapes and write the numbers below to tell how many in all.

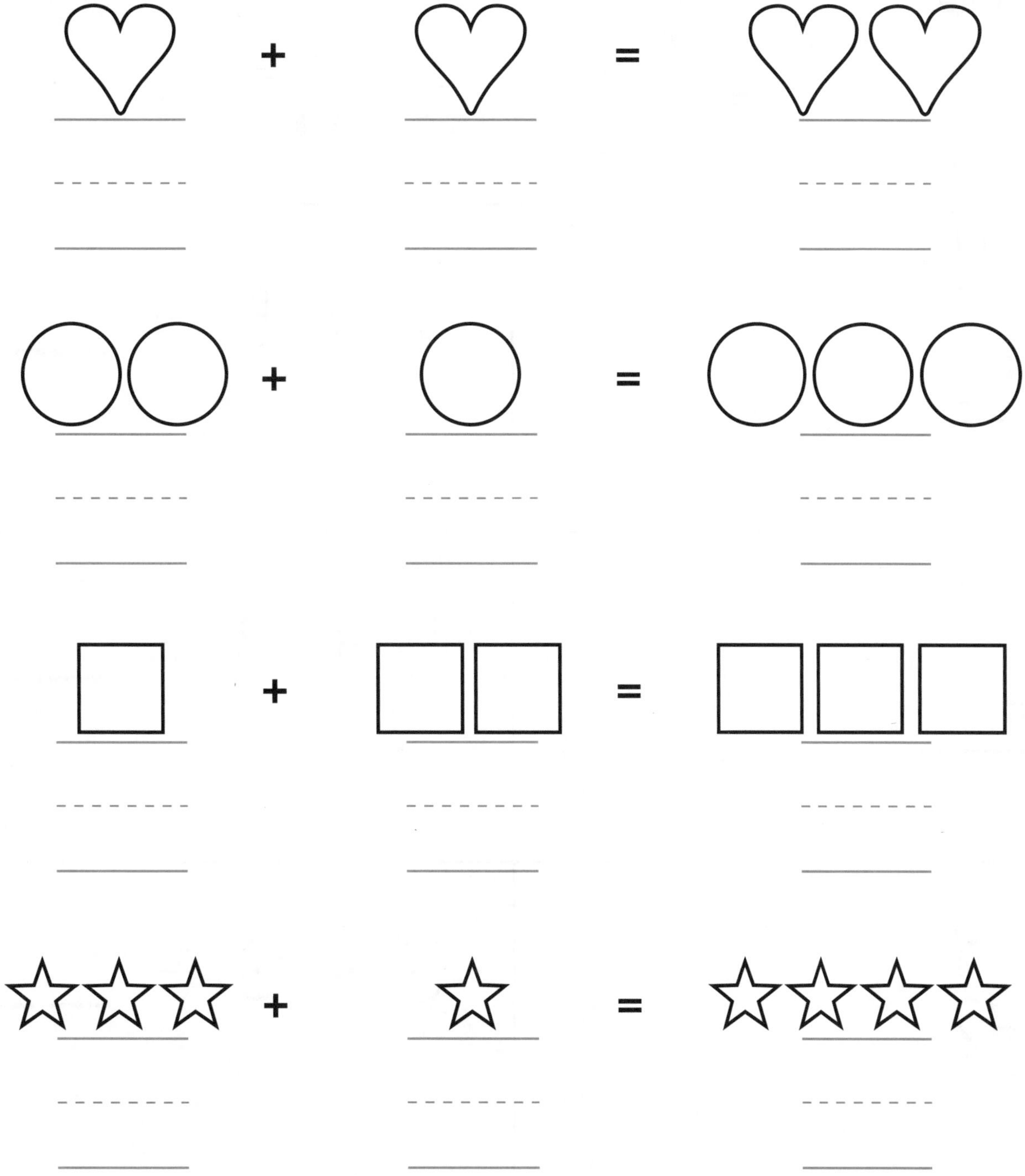

Name ________________________________

Addition

Directions: Draw the correct number of dots next to the numbers in each problem. Add up the number of dots to find your answer.

Example:

3 ●●● +2 ●● 5	2 + 2 = 4 ●● ●●

4 +2	1 + 5 = ___
3 +1	4 + 3 = ___
6 +2	5 + 3 = ___

Name ______________________________

Addition 3, 4, 5, 6

Directions: Practice writing the numbers and then add. Draw dots to help, if needed.

3 ______________________

4 ______________________

5 ______________________

6 ______________________

$$\begin{array}{r} 2 \\ +4 \\ \hline \end{array} \qquad \begin{array}{r} 1 \\ +4 \\ \hline \end{array}$$

$$\begin{array}{r} 3 \\ +2 \\ \hline \end{array} \qquad \begin{array}{r} 1 \\ +2 \\ \hline \end{array}$$

Name ________________________________

Addition 4, 5, 6, 7

Directions: Practice writing the numbers and then add. Draw dots to help, if needed.

4 ____________

5 ____________

6 ____________

7 ____________

$$\begin{array}{r} 2 \\ +5 \\ \hline \end{array} \qquad \begin{array}{r} 3 \\ +1 \\ \hline \end{array}$$

$$\begin{array}{r} 4 \\ +1 \\ \hline \end{array} \qquad \begin{array}{r} 2 \\ +4 \\ \hline \end{array}$$

Name ______________________________

Addition 6, 7, 8

Directions: Practice writing the numbers and then add. Draw dots to help, if needed.

6 ______________________

7 ______________________

8 ______________________

$$\begin{array}{r} 3 \\ +4 \\ \hline \end{array} \qquad \begin{array}{r} 5 \\ +1 \\ \hline \end{array}$$

$$\begin{array}{r} 2 \\ +6 \\ \hline \end{array} \qquad \begin{array}{r} 4 \\ +4 \\ \hline \end{array}$$

Name

Addition 7, 8, 9

Directions: Practice writing the numbers and then add. Draw dots to help, if needed.

7 ____________________

8 ____________________

9 ____________________

8	3
+1	+5
___	___

2	6
+7	+1
___	___

Addition Table

Directions: Add across and down with a friend. Fill in the spaces.

+	0	1	2	3	4	5
0	0					
1	1	2				
2			4			
3	3			6		
4						
5						10

Do you notice any number patterns in the Addition Table?

Name ____________________

Subtraction 1, 2, 3

Subtraction means "taking away" or subtracting one number from another. "–" is a minus sign. It means to subtract the second number from the first.

Directions: Practice writing the numbers and then subtract. Draw dots and cross them out, if needed.

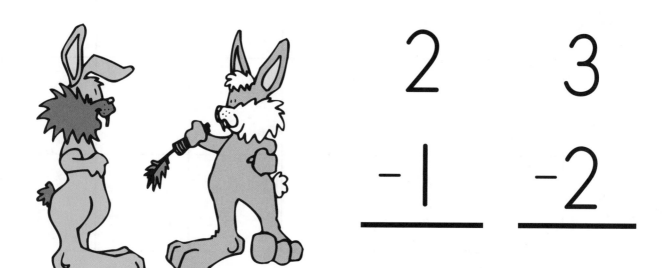

1 ____________________

2 ____________________

3 ____________________

3	4
−1	−3
2	

2	3
−1	−2

Name ____________________

Subtraction 3, 4, 5, 6

Directions: Practice writing the numbers and then subtract. Draw dots and cross them out, if needed.

3 ____________________

4 ____________________

5 ____________________

6 ____________________

$$\begin{array}{r} 5 \\ -2 \\ \hline \end{array} \qquad \begin{array}{r} 6 \\ -1 \\ \hline \end{array}$$

$$\begin{array}{r} 6 \\ -3 \\ \hline \end{array} \qquad \begin{array}{r} 5 \\ -1 \\ \hline \end{array}$$

Name ______________________________

Subtraction

Directions: Draw the correct number of dots next to the numbers in each problem. Cross out the ones subtracted to find your answer.

Example:

$$\begin{array}{r} 5 \\ -2 \\ \hline 3 \end{array} \quad \bullet\bullet\bullet \;\; \times\times \qquad\qquad 2 - 1 = 1 \quad \bullet \;\; \times$$

$4 - 2 =$ ____	$\begin{array}{r} 8 \\ -6 \\ \hline \end{array}$
$\begin{array}{r} 6 \\ -1 \\ \hline \end{array}$	$3 - 1 =$ ____
$9 - 6 =$ ____	$\begin{array}{r} 4 \\ -3 \\ \hline \end{array}$

Name ______________________________

Review

Directions: Trace the numbers. Work the problems.

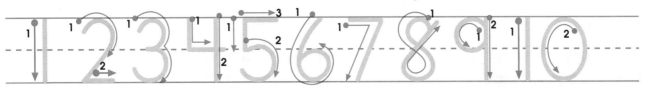

1 2 3 4 5 6 7 8 9 10

9 −3 ___	6 +2 ___	3 +4 ___	2 −1 ___

5 +4 ___	9 −5 ___	7 +2 ___	8 −6 ___

4 −2 ___	6 +3 ___	9 −7 ___	1 +7 ___

Name ______________________________

Zero

Directions: Write the number.

Example:

How many monkeys?

3

How many monkeys?

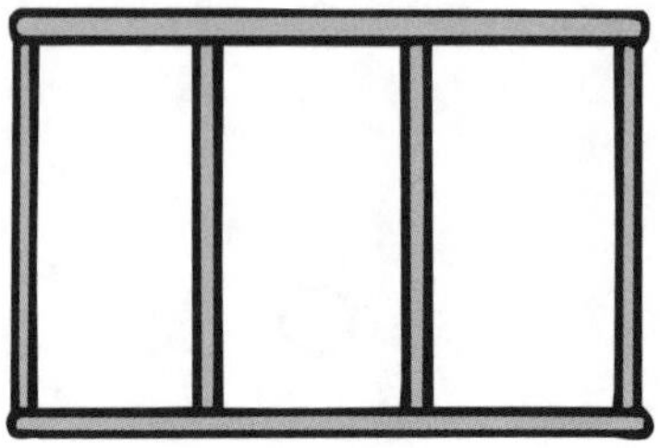

0

How many kites?

How many kites?

How many flowers?

How many flowers?

How many apples?

How many apples?

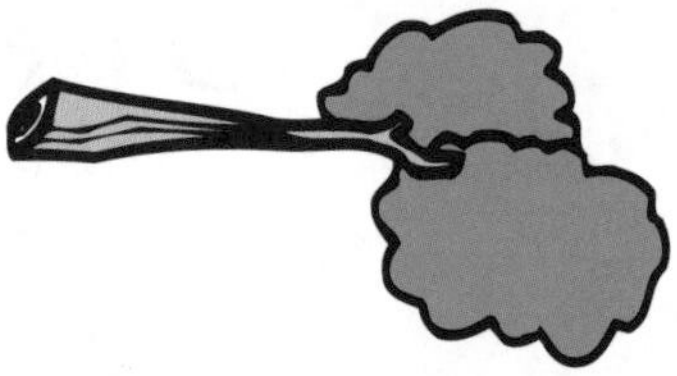

Name ______________________________

Zero

Directions: Write the number that tells how many.

How many sailboats?

How many sailboats?

How many eggs?

How many eggs?

How many marshmallows?

How many marshmallows?

How many candles?

How many candles?

Name ______________________________

Picture Problems: Addition

Directions: Solve the number problem under each picture.

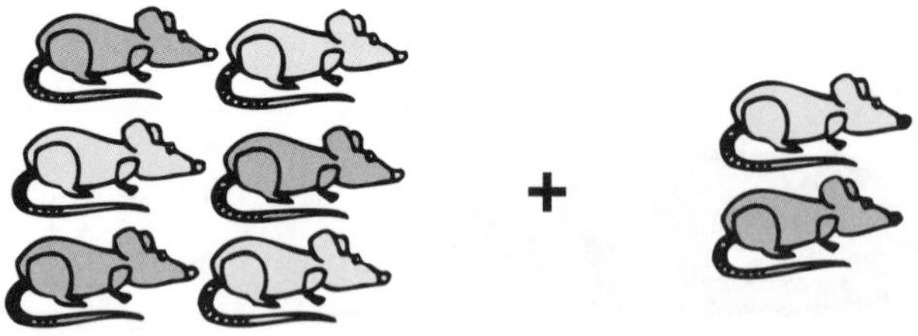 6 + 2 = ____	 3 + 1 = ____
 5 + 3 = ____	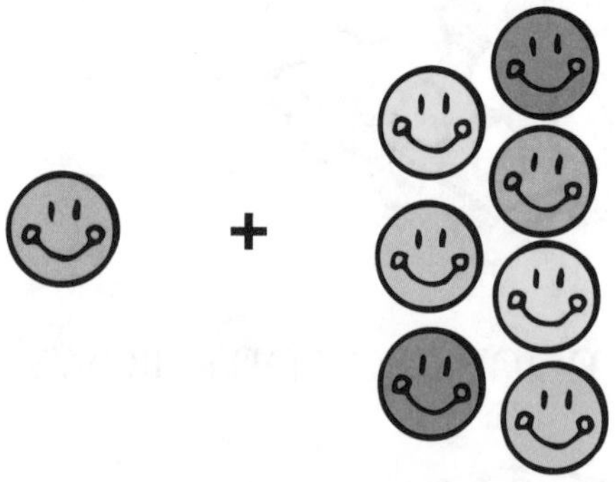 1 + 7 = ____
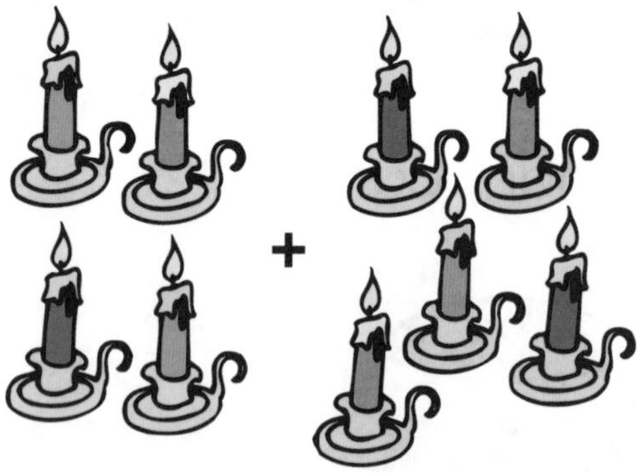 4 + 5 = ____	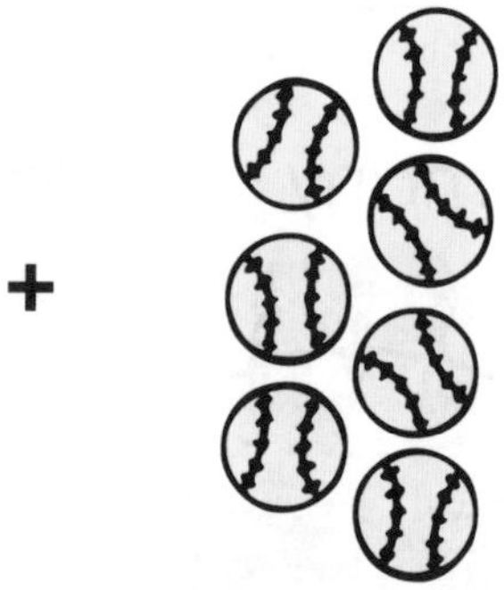 0 + 7 = ____

Name ______________________________

Picture Problems: Addition

Directions: Solve the number problem under each picture.

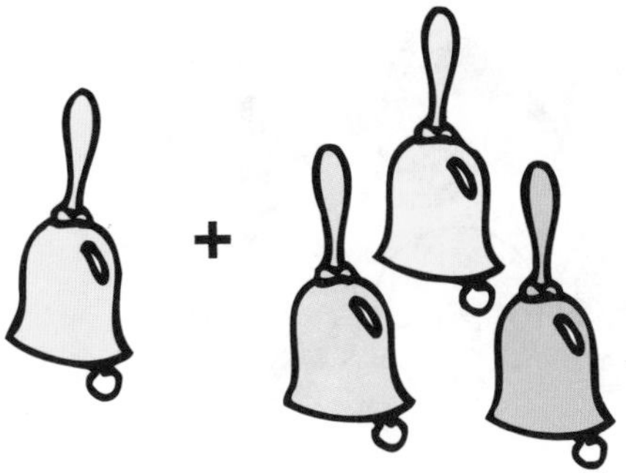

1 + 3 = ____

2 + 4 = ____

3 + 5 = ____

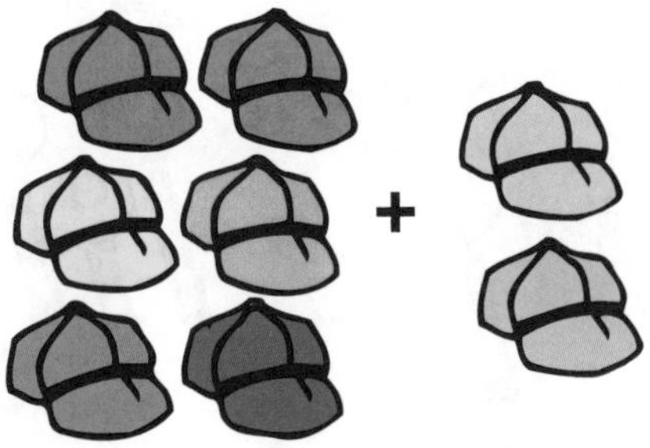

6 + 2 = ____

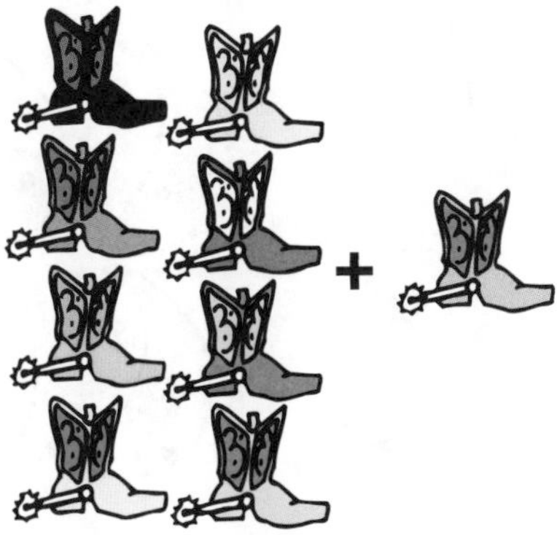

8 + 1 = ____

0 + 7 = ____

Name ______________________________

Picture Problems: Subtraction

Directions: Solve the number problem under each picture.

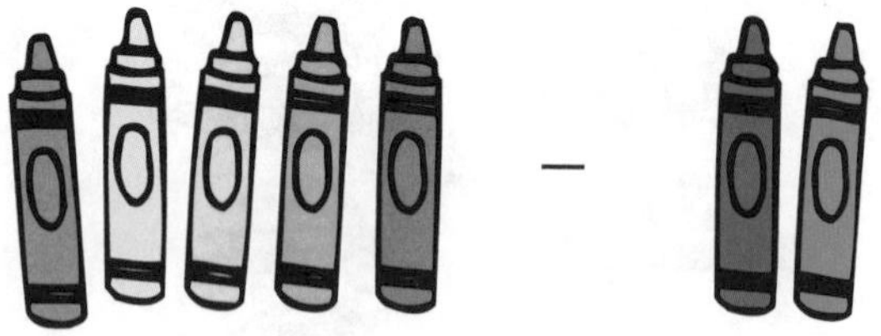

5 - 2 = ____

6 - 1 = ____

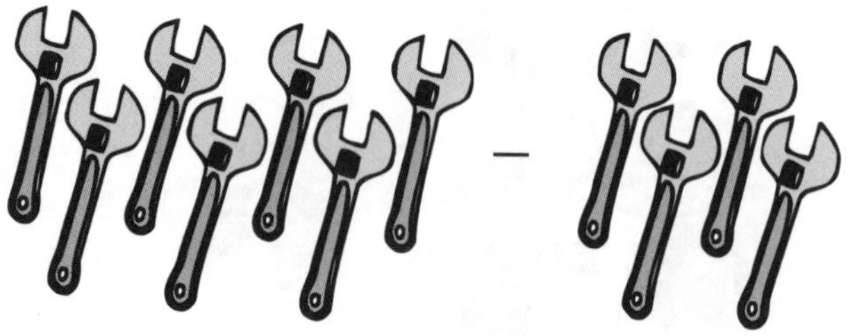

7 - 4 = ____

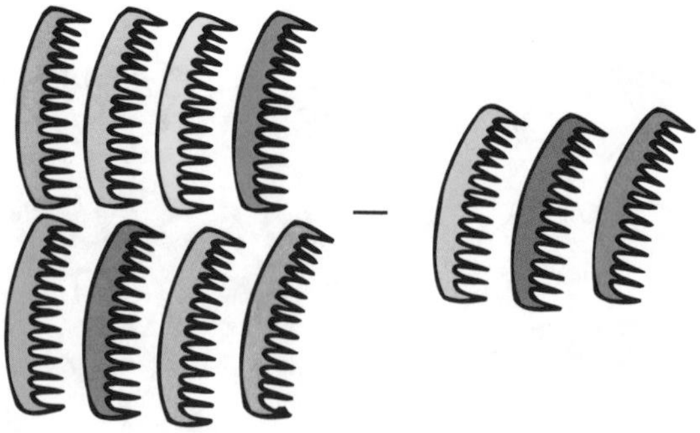

8 - 3 = ____

9 - 2 = ____

4 - 4 = ____

Name ____________________________

Picture Problems: Subtraction

Directions: Solve the number problem under each picture.

6 - 2 = ____

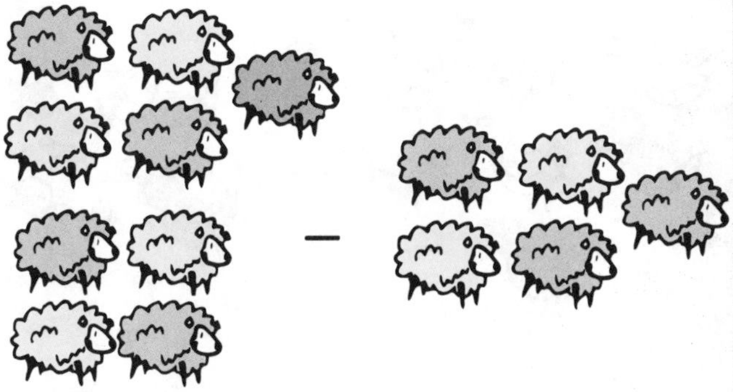

9 - 5 = ____

7 - 2 = ____

4 -1 = ____

8 - 1 = ____

4 - 0 = ____

Name ______________________

Picture Problems: Addition and Subtraction

Directions: Solve the number problem under each picture.

7 - 4 = ____

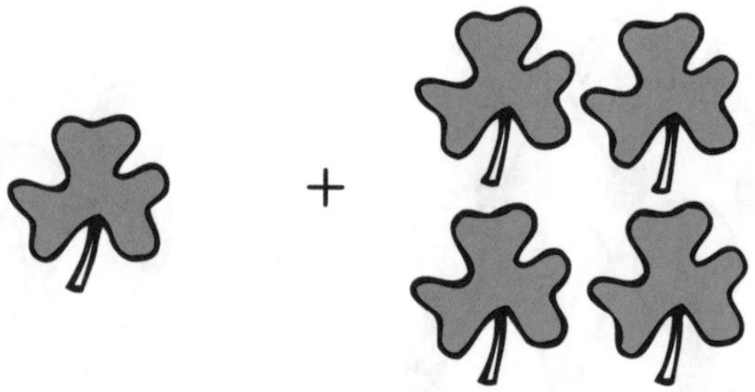

1 + 4 = ____

3 + 5 = ____

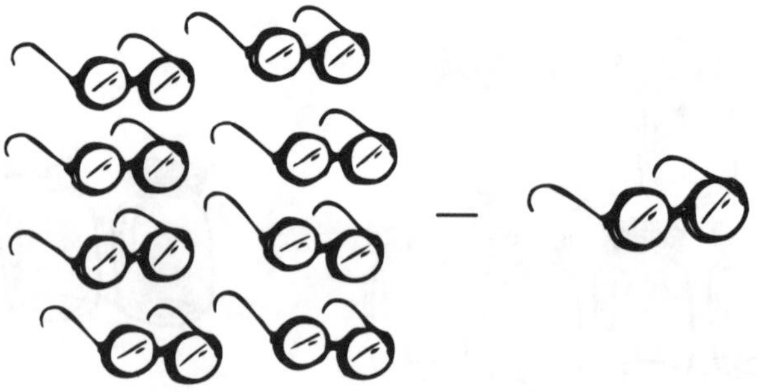

8 - 1 = ____

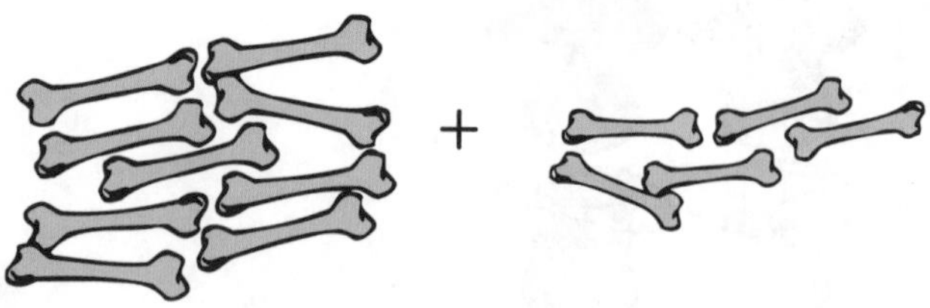

9 + 5 = ____

6 - 3 = ____

Name ______________________________

Picture Problems: Addition and Subtraction

Directions: Solve the number problem under each picture.
Write **+** or **–** to show if you should add or subtract.

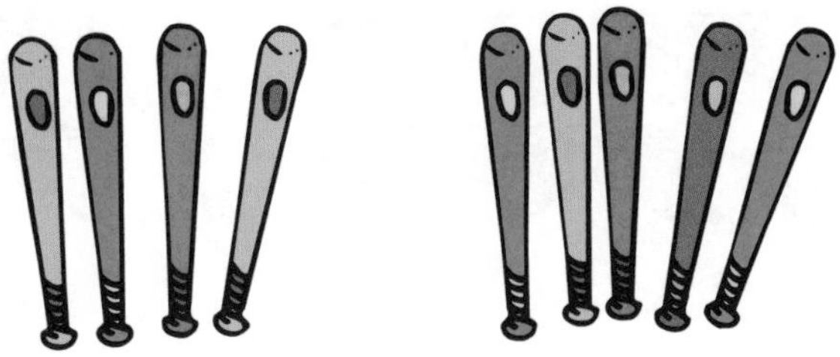

How many s in all?

4 + 5 = ______

How many s in all?

7 5 = ______

How many s are left?

12 3 = ______

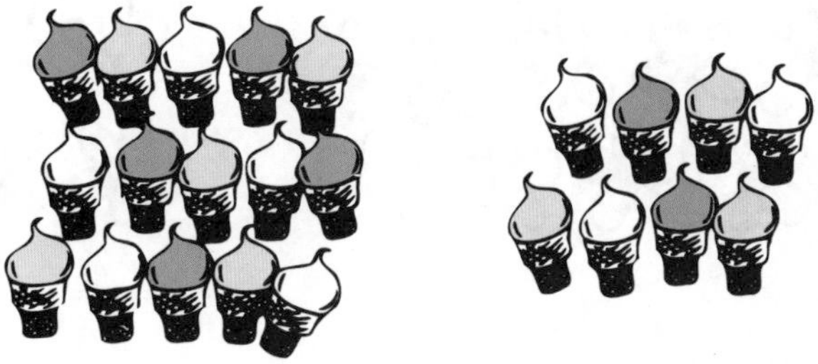

How many s are left?

15 8 = ______

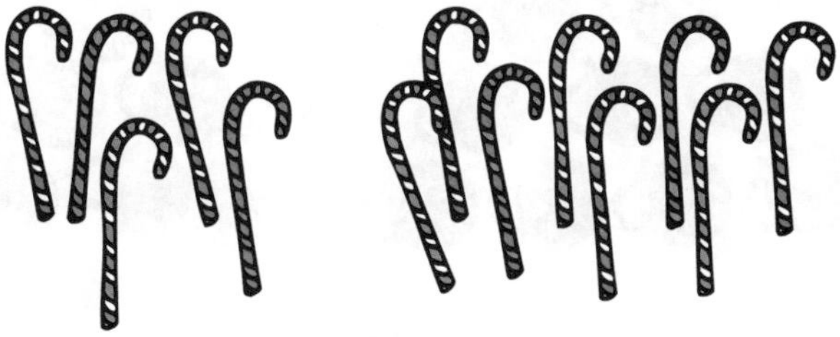

How many s in all?

5 8 = ______

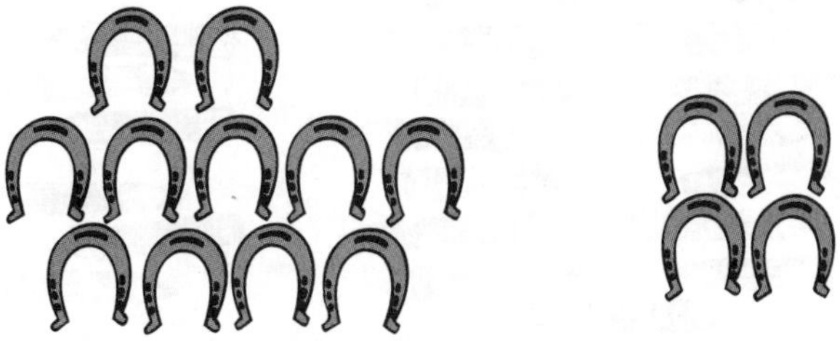

How many s are left?

11 4 = ______

Name ______________________________

Picture Problems: Addition and Subtraction

Directions: Solve the number problem under each picture.
Write **+** or **–** to show if you should add or subtract.

How many s in all?

7 + 5 = 12

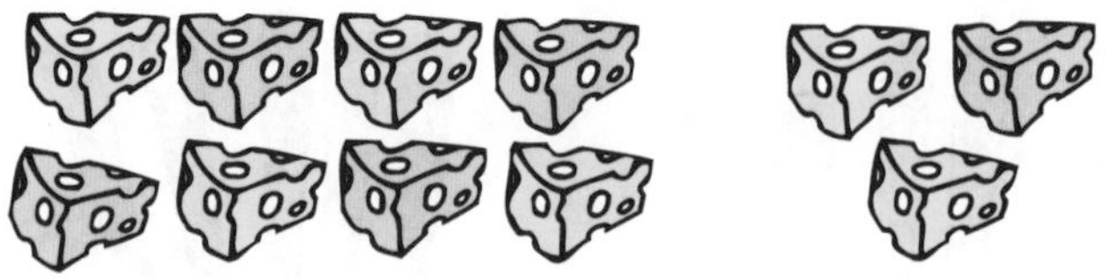

How many s are left?

8 3 = ______

How many s are left?

9 4 = ______

How many s in all?

14 1 = ______

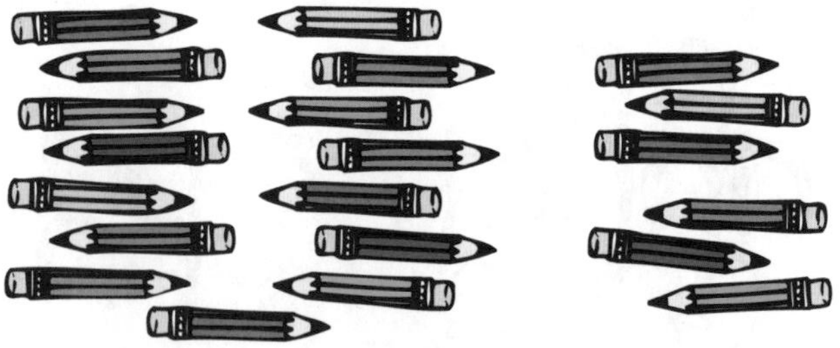

How many s are left?

15 6 = ______

How many s in all?

9 5 = ______

Name ____________________

Review: Addition and Subtraction

Directions: Solve the number problem under each picture. Write **+** or **–** to show if you should add or subtract.

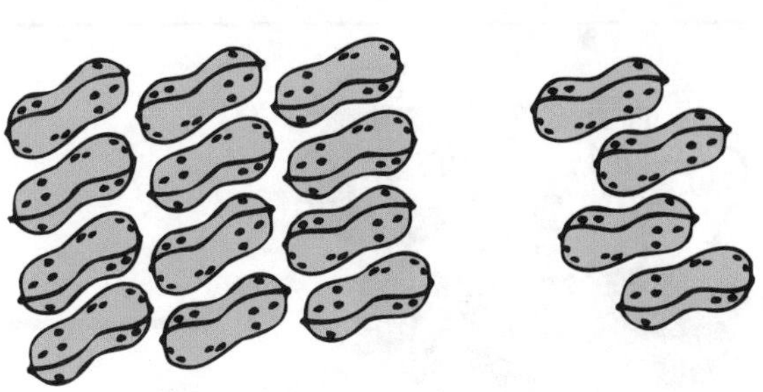

How many s are left?

12 4 = ____

How many s in all?

6 8 = ____

How many s are left?

4 4 = ____

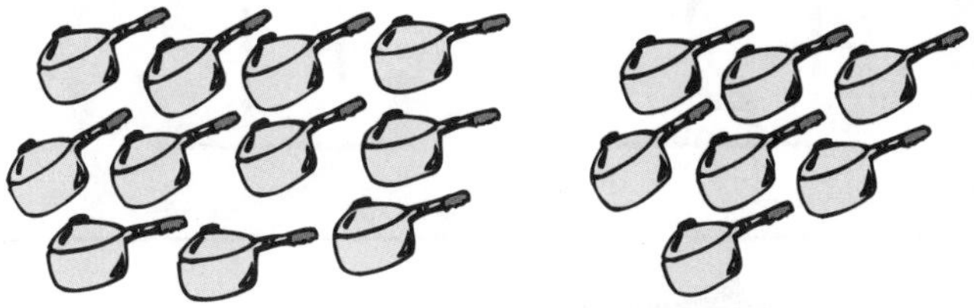

How many s are left?

11 7 = ____

How many s in all?

9 3 = ____

How many s in all?

10 0 = ____

Name ____________________

Addition 1-5

Directions: Count the tools in each tool box. Write your answers in the blanks. Circle the problem that matches your answer.

4
___

$$\begin{array}{r}2\\+2\\\hline\end{array}\qquad\begin{array}{r}2\\+1\\\hline\end{array}$$

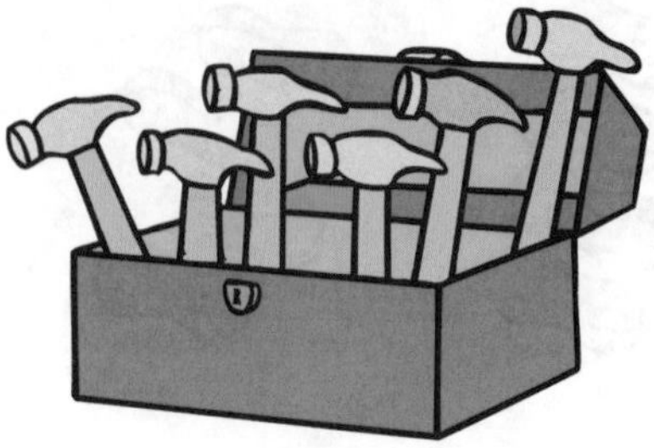

___

$$\begin{array}{r}5\\+0\\\hline\end{array}\qquad\begin{array}{r}4\\+2\\\hline\end{array}$$

___

$$\begin{array}{r}6\\+2\\\hline\end{array}\qquad\begin{array}{r}4\\+3\\\hline\end{array}$$

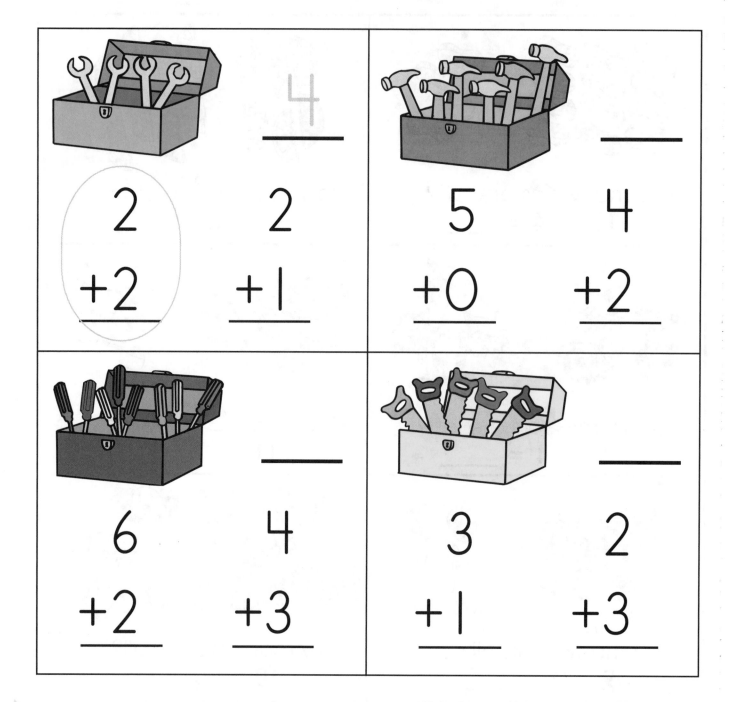

___

$$\begin{array}{r}3\\+1\\\hline\end{array}\qquad\begin{array}{r}2\\+3\\\hline\end{array}$$

Name ______________________

Addition 1-5

Directions: Look at the bold numbers and draw that many more flowers in the pot. Count them to get your total.

Example: 3 + **2** = 5

1 + **4** = ____

1
+ **1**
____

2
+ **2**
____

3 + **1** = ____

Name ___________________________________

Addition 1-5

Directions: Add the numbers. Put your answers in the nests.

Example: 2 + 3 =  5 

1 + 2 = 

1 + 3 = 

4 + 1 = 

1 + 1 = 

Name ______________________________

Addition 6-10

Directions: Add the numbers. Put your answers in the doghouses.

Example: 4 + 2 = 

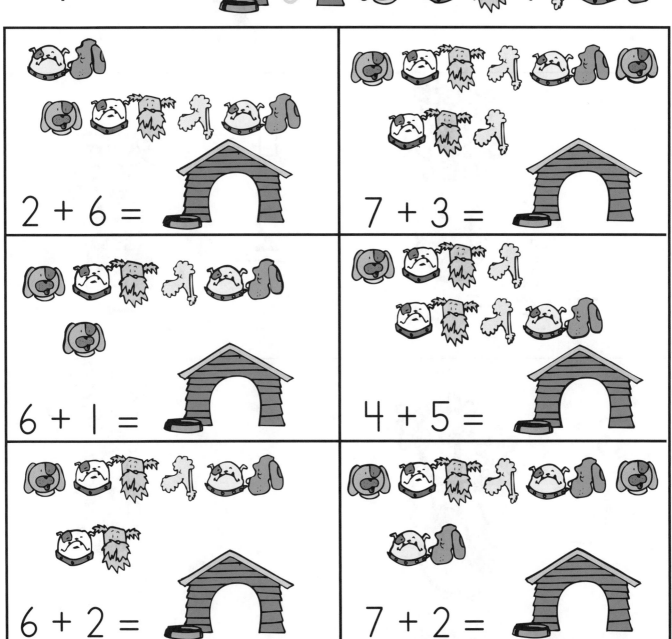

2 + 6 = 

7 + 3 = 

6 + 1 = 

4 + 5 = 

6 + 2 = 

7 + 2 = 

Name ______________________________

Subtraction 1-5

Directions: Subtract the bold numbers by crossing out that many flowers in the pot. Count the ones not crossed out to get the total.

Example: 2 - **1** = 1

5 - **2** = ____

4
-2
____

3
-1
____

4 - **3** = ____

Subtraction 1-5

Directions: Count the fruit in each bowl. Write your answers on the blanks. Circle the problem that matches your answer.

4

5	4
−1	−2

___

3	4
−0	−2

___

5	4
−1	−3

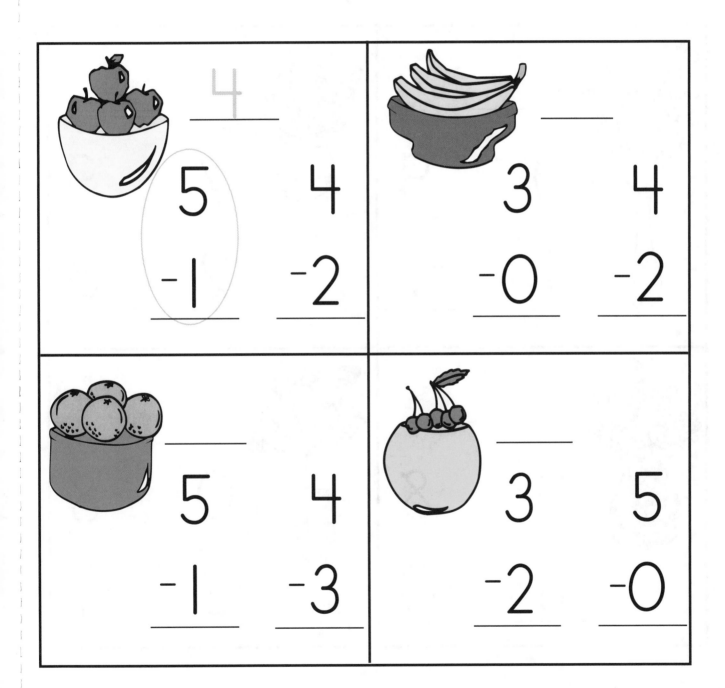

___

3	5
−2	−0

Name ________________________________

Subtraction 6-10

Directions: Count the flowers. Write your answer on the blank. Circle the problem that matches your answer.

______

10	9
−1	−1
____	____

______

7	9
−2	−3
____	____

______

9	8
−6	−0
____	____

______

10	8
−2	−1
____	____

Name ____

Addition and Subtraction

Directions: Solve the problems. Remember, addition means "putting together" or adding two or more numbers to find the sum. Subtraction means "taking away" or subtracting one number from another.

1 + 3 = ____ 4 - 3 = ____ 4 + 5 = ____

6 + 1 = ____ 7 - 2 = ____ 8 - 4 = ____

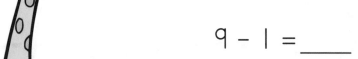

9 - 1 = ____ 10 - 3 = ____

5 - 2 = ____ 6 + 3 = ____

8 + 2 = ____ 5 + 5 = ____

Name ______________________________

Addition and Subtraction

Remember, addition means "putting together" or adding two or more numbers to find the sum. Subtraction means "taking away" or subtracting one number from another.

Directions: Solve the problems. From your answers, use the code to color the quilt.

Color:

6 = blue
7 = yellow
8 = green
9 = red
10 = orange

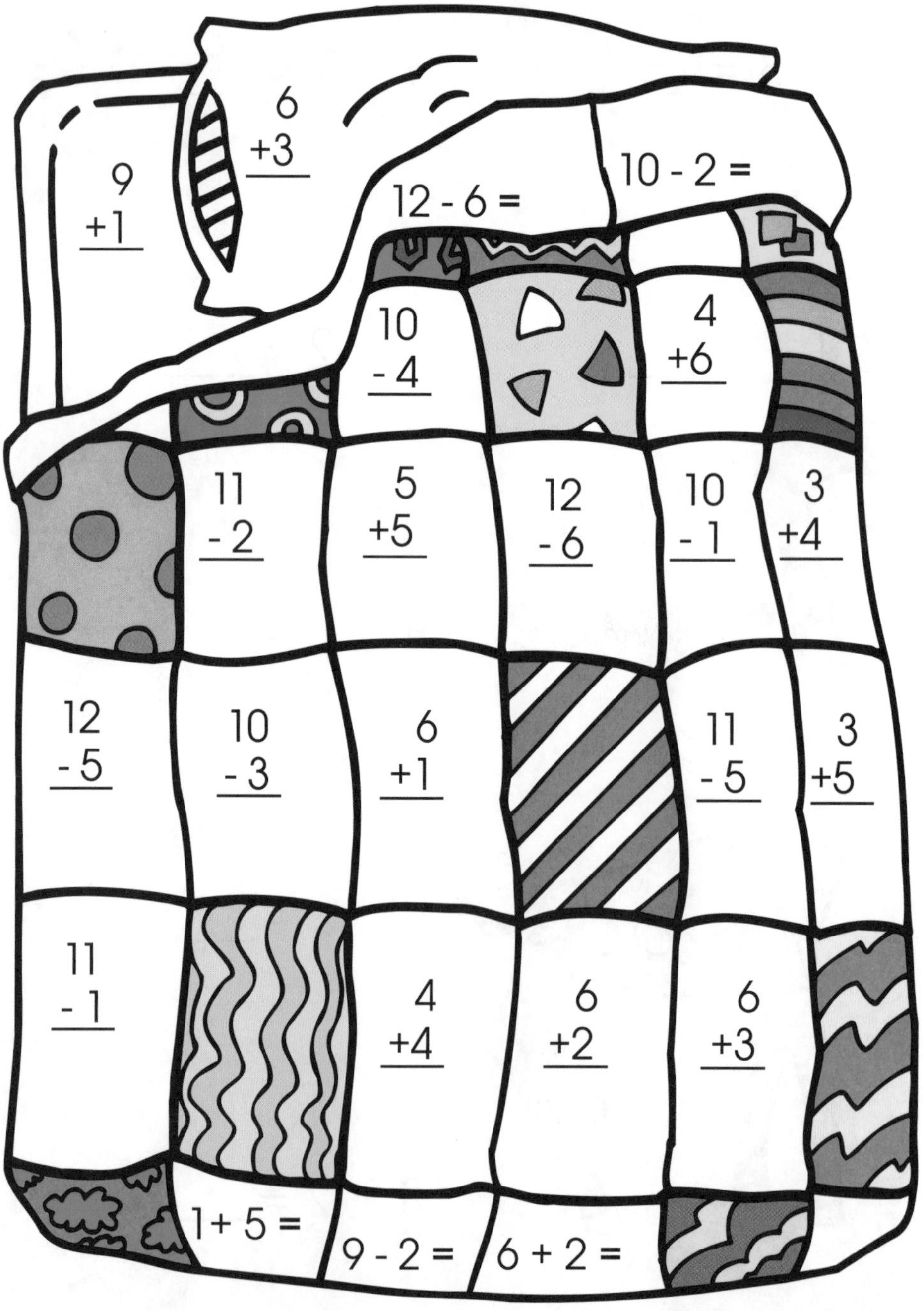

Name ______________________________

Place Value: Tens and Ones

The place value of a digit, or numeral, is shown by where it is in the number. For example, in the number **23**, **2** has the place value of **tens**, and **3** is ones.

Directions: Count the groups of ten crayons and write the number by the word **tens**. Count the other crayons and write the number by the word **ones**.

Example:  = 1 ten + 1 one

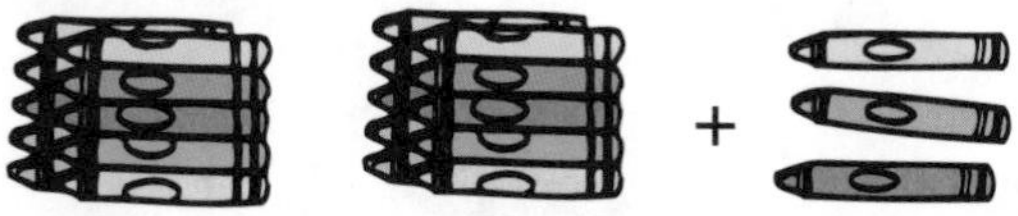 = ____ tens + ____ ones

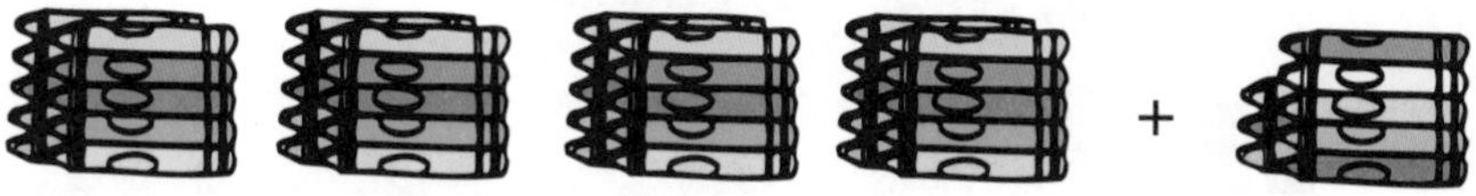 = ____ tens + ____ ones

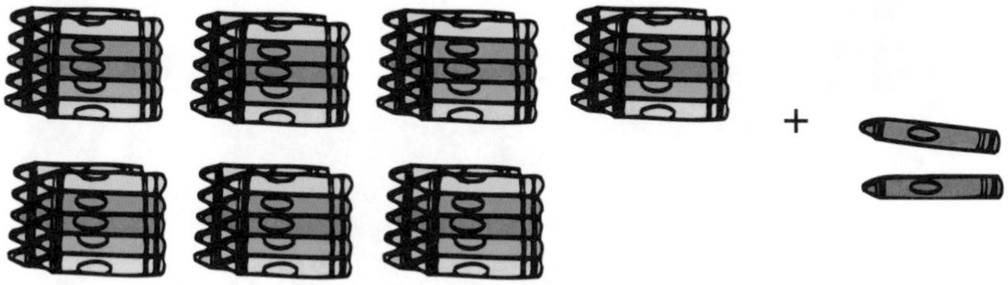 = ____ tens + ____ ones

---

6 tens + 3 ones = ____

5 tens + 1 one = ____

3 tens + 8 ones = ____

9 tens + 7 ones = ____

4 tens + 5 ones = ____

2 tens + 8 ones = ____

Place Value: Tens and Ones

Directions: Count the groups of ten blocks and write the number by the word tens. Count the other blocks and write the number by the word ones.

Example:

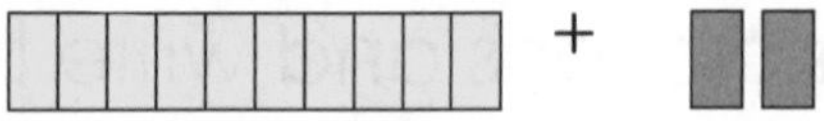

= __1__ ten + __2__ ones

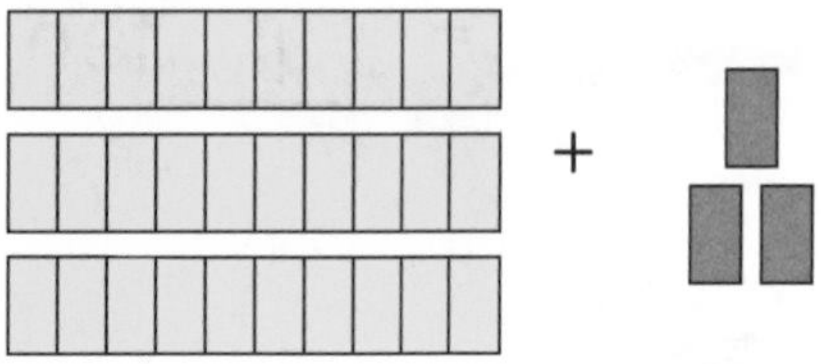

= ____ tens + ____ ones

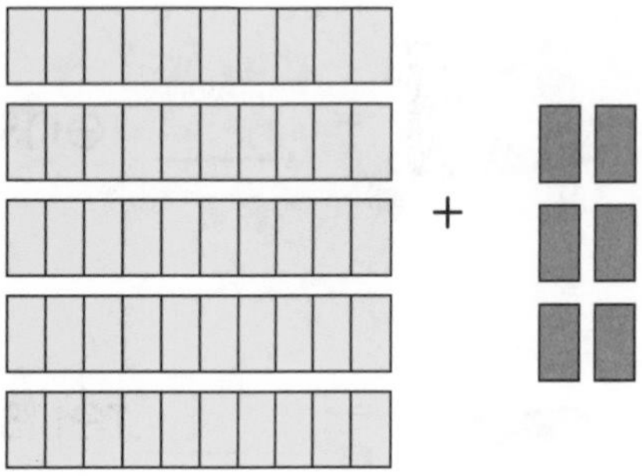

= ____ tens + ____ ones

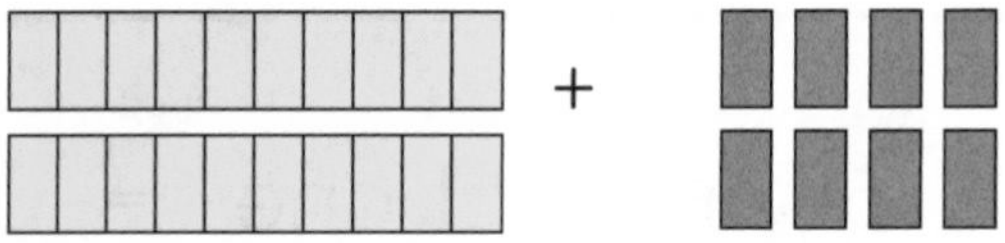

= ____ tens + ____ ones

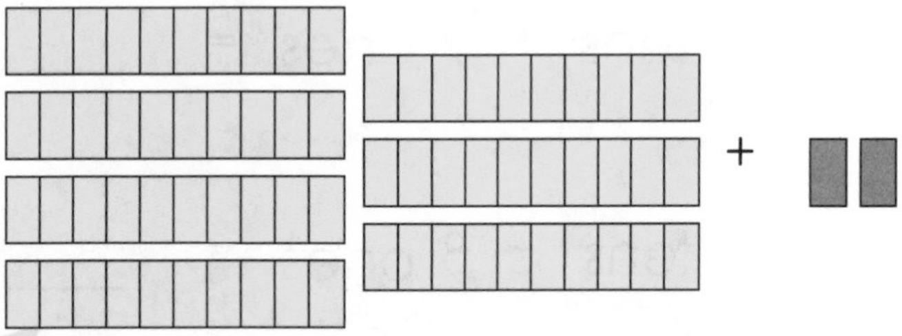

= ____ tens + ____ ones

Name ______________________________

Place Value: Tens and Ones

Directions: Write the answers in the correct spaces.

	tens	ones		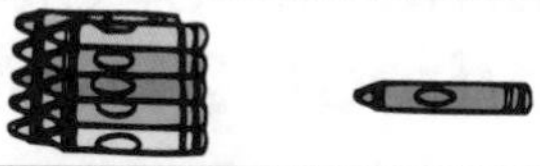
3 tens, 2 ones	3	2	=	32
3 tens, 7 ones	______	______	=	______
9 tens, 1 one	______	______	=	______
5 tens, 6 ones	______	______	=	______
6 tens, 5 ones	______	______	=	______
6 tens, 8 ones	______	______	=	______
2 tens, 8 ones	______	______	=	______
4 tens, 9 ones	______	______	=	______
1 ten, 4 ones	______	______	=	______
8 tens, 2 ones	______	______	=	______
4 tens, 2 ones	______	______	=	______

28	=	______	tens,	______	ones
64	=	______	tens,	______	ones
56	=	______	tens,	______	ones
72	=	______	tens,	______	ones
38	=	______	tens,	______	ones
17	=	______	ten,	______	ones
63	=	______	tens,	______	ones
12	=	______	ten,	______	ones

Name ______________________________

Review: Place Value

The place value of each digit, or numeral, is shown by where it is in the number. For example, in the number **123**, **1** has the place value of **hundreds**, **2** is **tens** and **3** is **ones**.

Directions: Count the groups of crayons and add.

Example:

						Hundreds	Tens	Ones
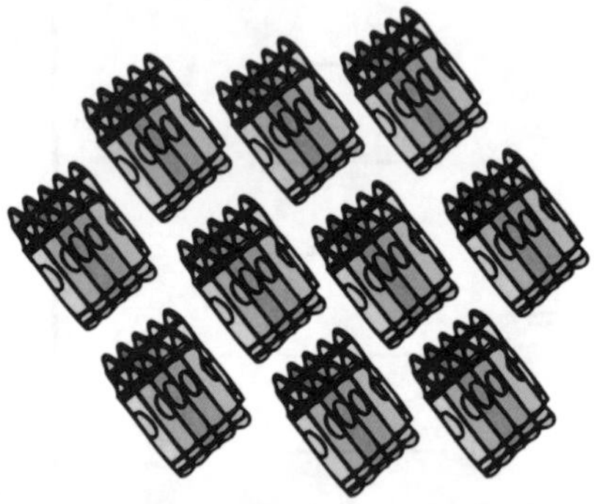	+		+		=	1	1	3
1 Hundred	+	1 Ten	+	3 Ones				
	+		+		=	____	____	____
	+	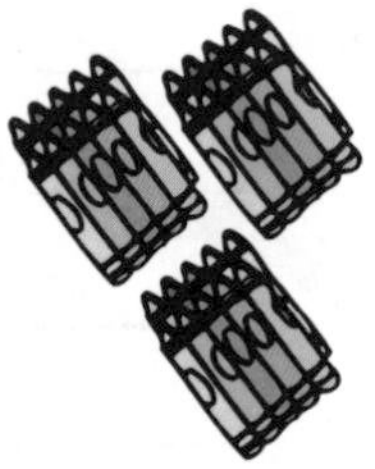	+		=	____	____	____

Name ______________________________

Counting by Fives

Directions: Count by fives to draw the path to the playground.

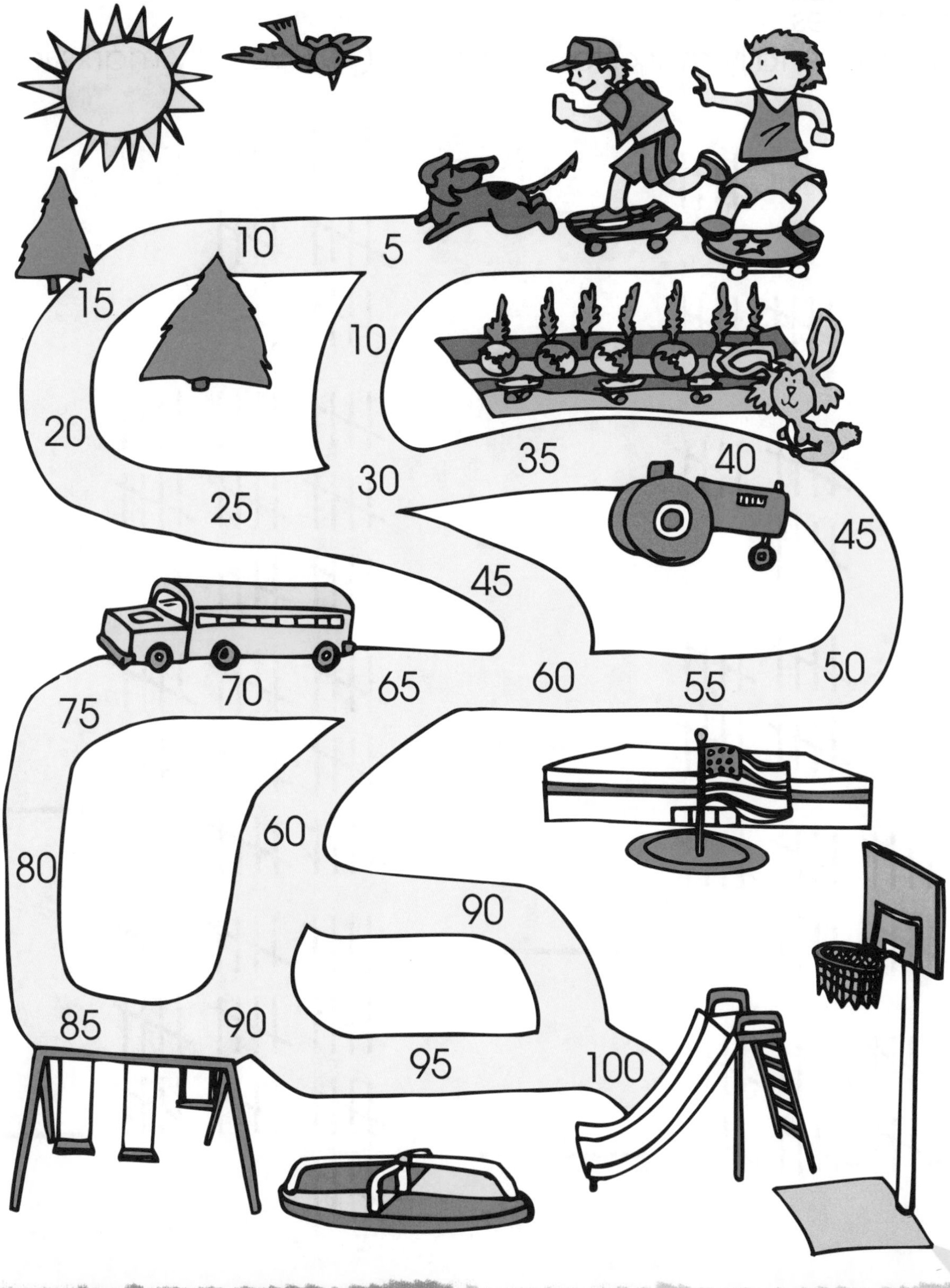

Counting by Fives

Directions: Use tally marks to count by fives. Write the number next to the tallies.

Example: A tally mark stands for one (1). Five tally marks look like this: 卌

卌 _____

卌 卌 _____

卌 卌
卌 _____

卌 卌
卌 卌 _____

卌 卌 卌
卌 卌 _____

卌 卌 卌
卌 卌 卌 _____

卌 卌 卌
卌 卌
卌 卌 _____

卌 卌 卌
卌 卌 卌
卌 卌 _____

卌 卌 卌
卌 卌 卌 _____

卌 卌 卌
卌 卌 卌
卌 卌 卌
卌 _____

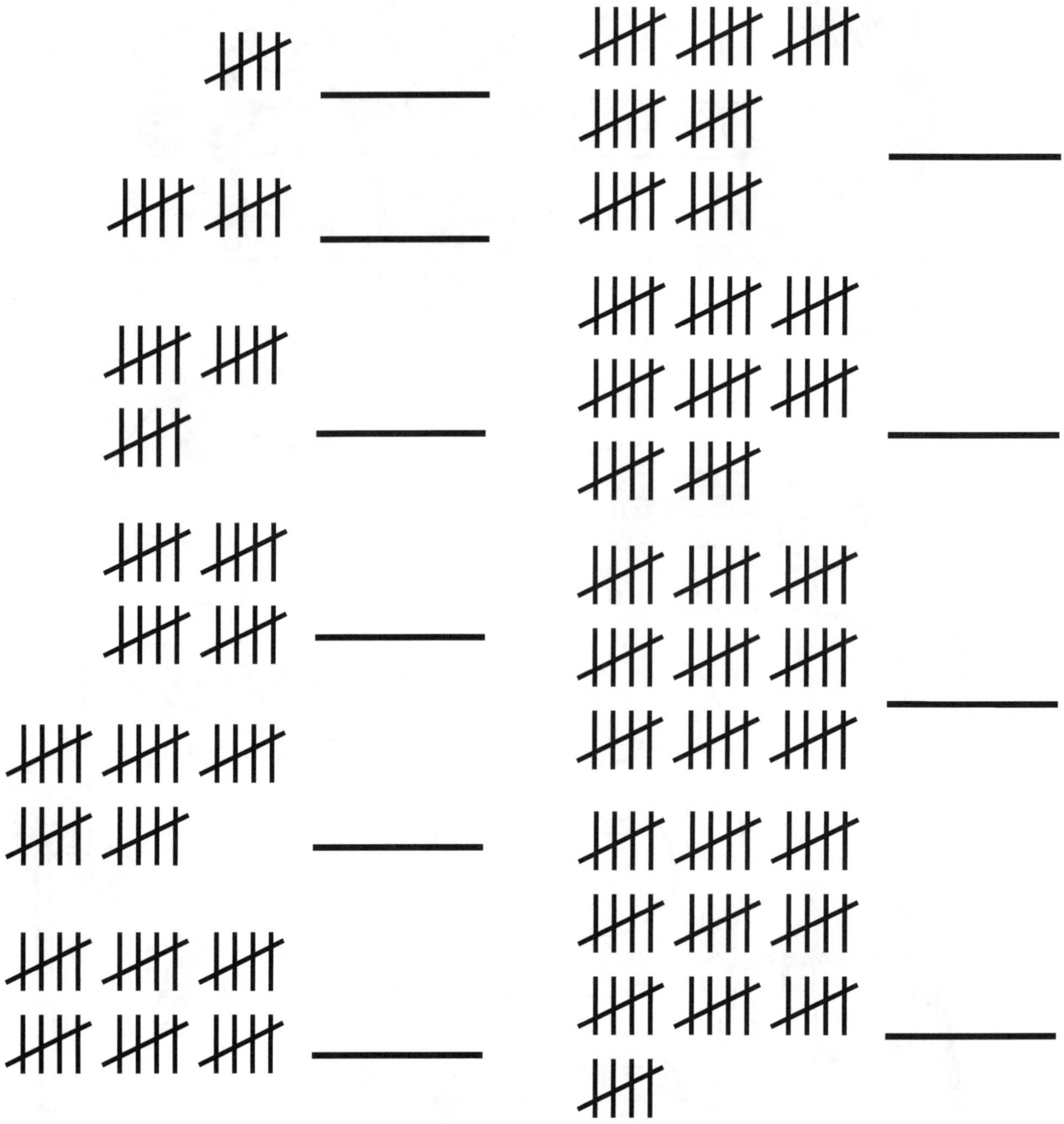

Name ____________________

Counting by Tens

Directions: Count in order by tens to draw the path the boy takes to the store.

Name ________________________________

Counting by Tens

Directions: Use the groups of 10's to count to 100.

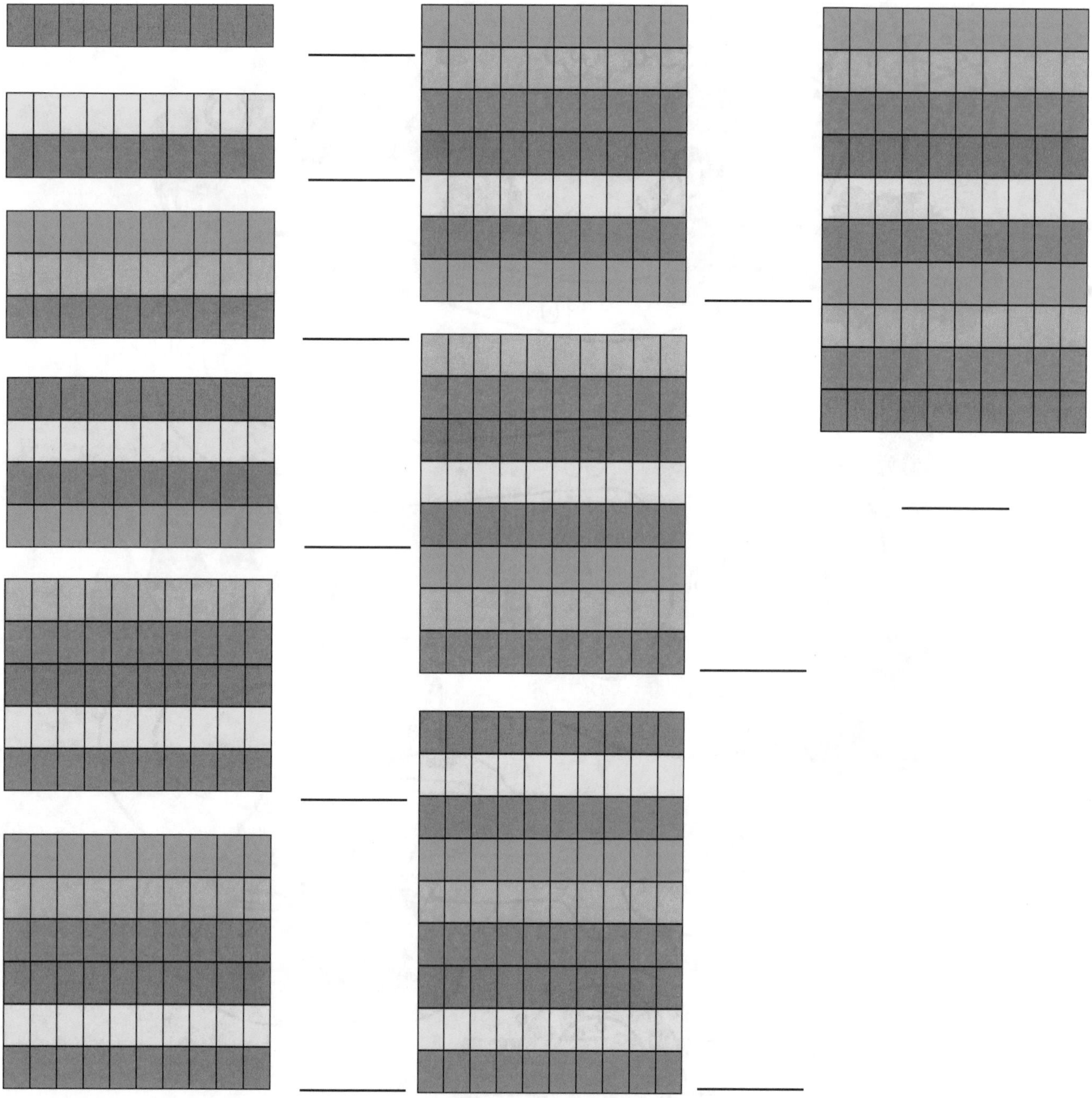

Name ______________________

Addition: 10-15

Directions: Circle groups of ten crayons. Add the remaining ones to make the correct number.

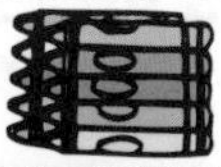				tens	ones
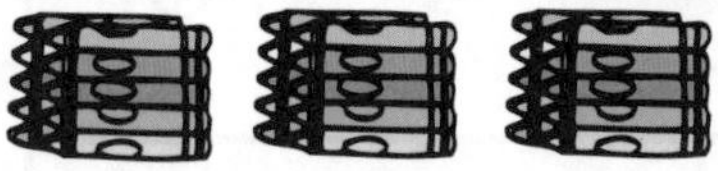	+	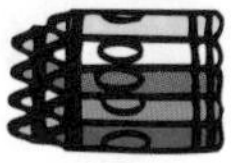	=	3	9
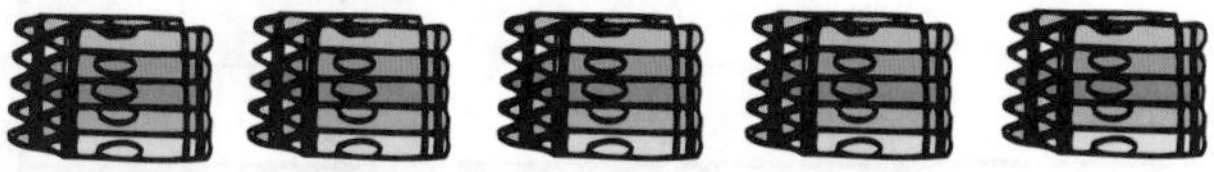	+	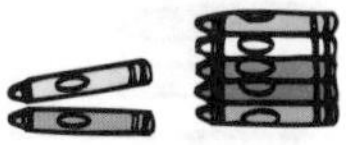	=	___	___
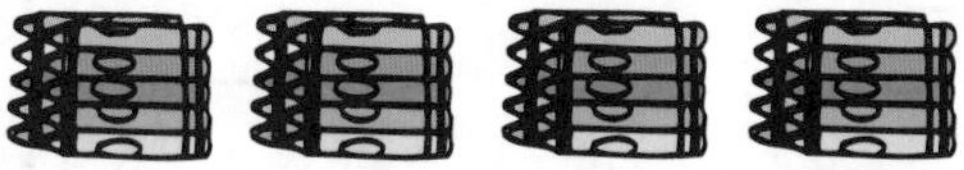	+		=	___	___
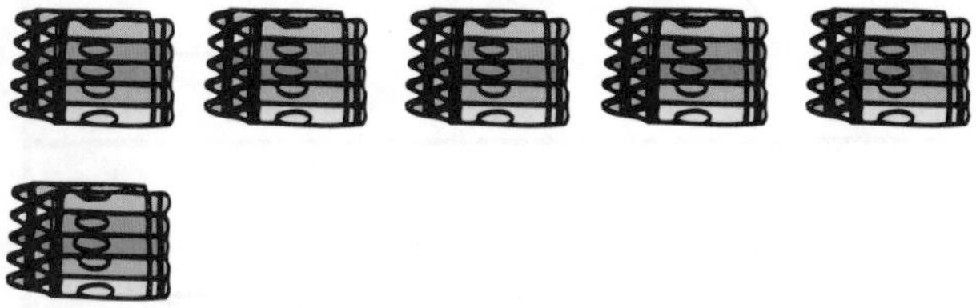	+		=	___	___
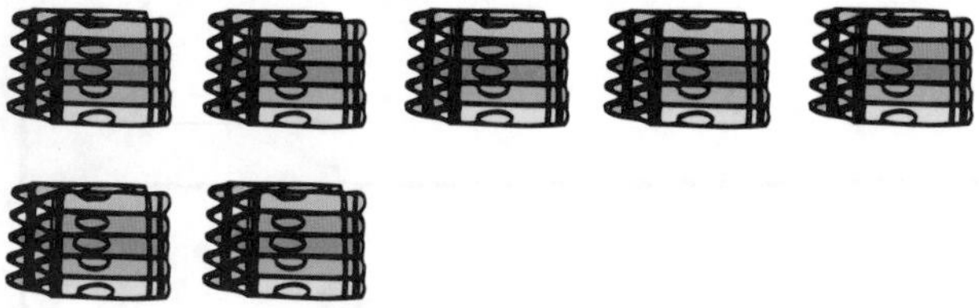	+	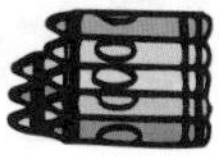	=	___	___
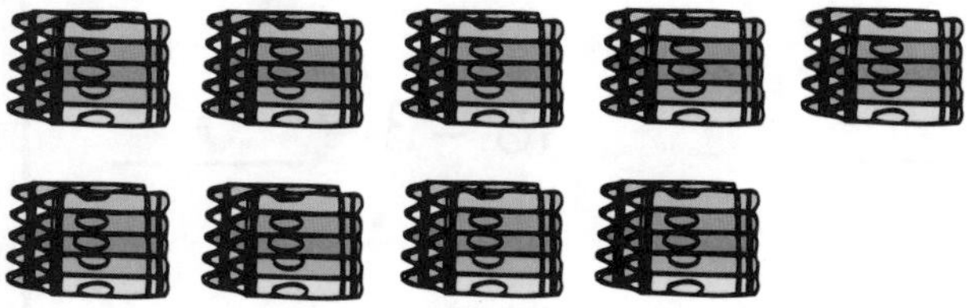	+	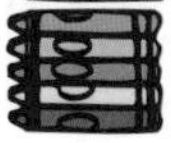	=	___	___

6 + 6 = ____ 8 + 4 = ____ 9 + 5 = ____

Name ____________________

Subtraction: 10-15

Directions: Count the crayons in each group. Put an **X** through the number of crayons being subtracted. How many are left?

	-	5	=	10
	-	4	=	____
	-	7	=	____
	-	6	=	____
	-	5	=	____
	-	8	=	____

13 - 8 = ____	11 - 5 = ____	12 - 9 = ____
14 - 7 = ____	10 - 7 = ____	13 - 3 = ____
15 - 9 = ____	11 - 8 = ____	12 - 10 = ____

Name ____________________

Shapes: Square

A square is a figure with four corners and four sides of the same length. This is a square □.

Directions: Find the squares and circle them.

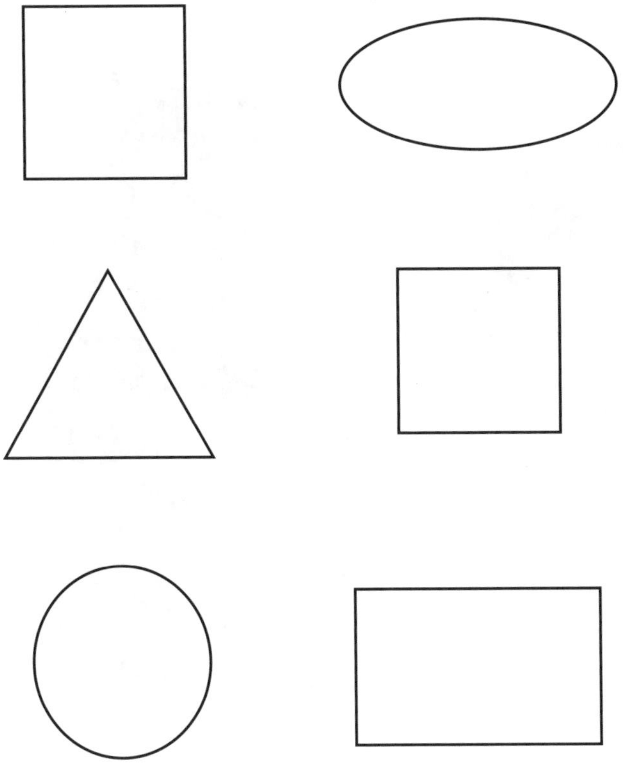

Directions: Trace the word. Write the word.

square

Name ______________________

Shapes: Circle

A circle is a figure that is round. This is a circle ○.

Directions: Find the circles and put a square around them.

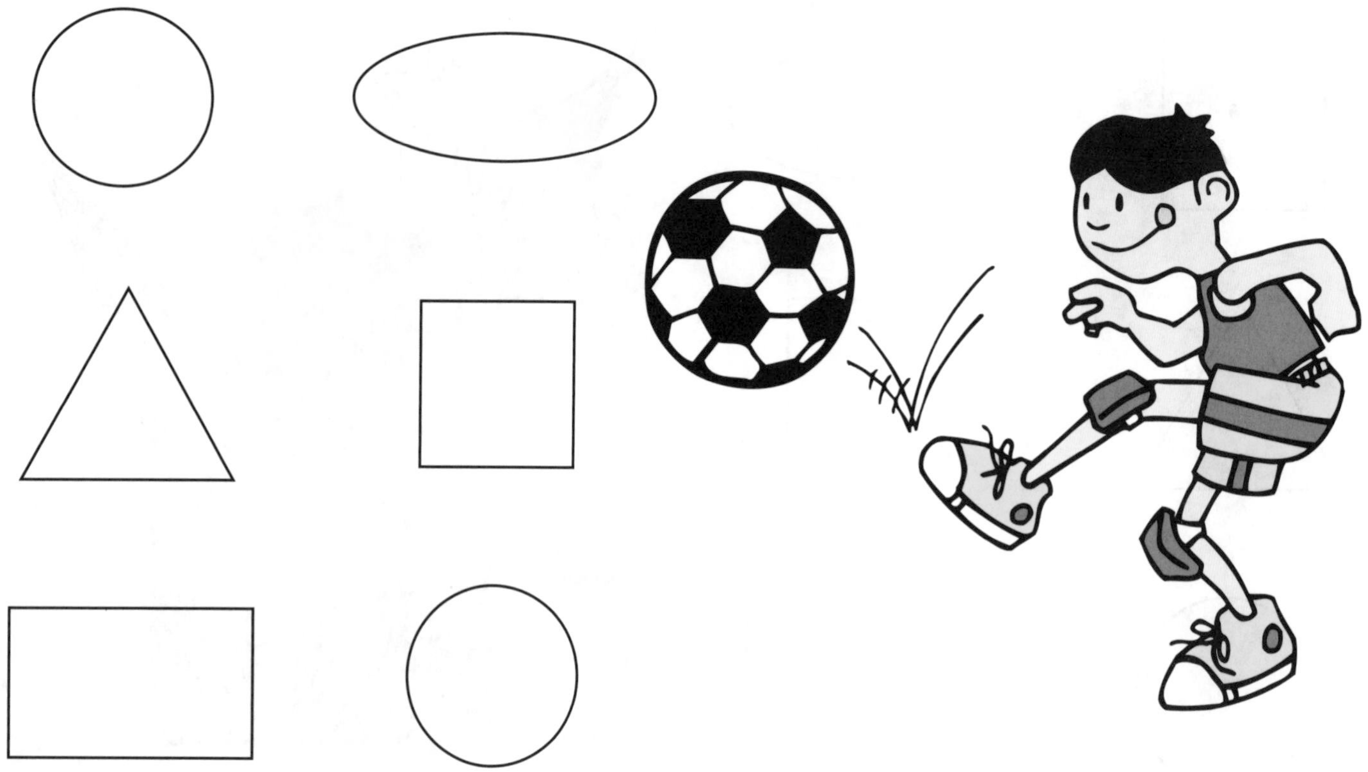

Directions: Trace the word. Write the word.

circle

Name ______________________________

Shapes: Square and Circle

Directions: Practice drawing squares. Trace the samples and make four of your own.

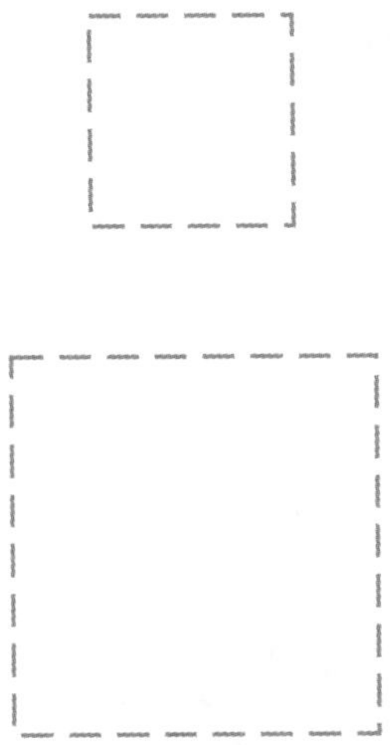

Directions: Practice drawing circles. Trace the samples and make four of your own.

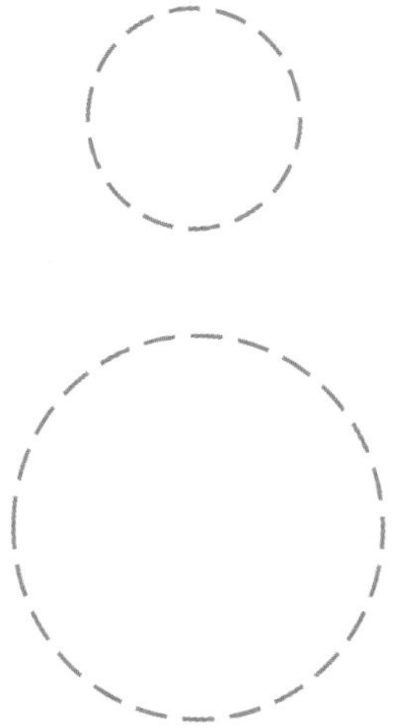

Name ______________________________

Shapes: Triangle

A triangle is a figure with three corners and three sides. This is a triangle △.

Directions: Find the triangles and put a circle around them.

Directions: Trace the word. Write the word.

triangle

Name ______________________

Shapes: Rectangle

A rectangle is a figure with four corners and four sides. Sides opposite each other are the same length. This is a rectangle .

Directions: Find the rectangles and put a circle around them.

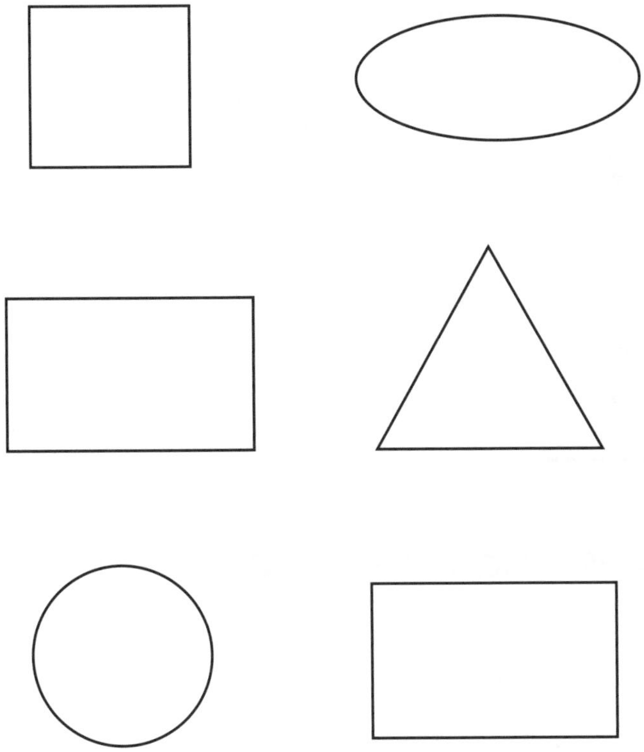

Directions: Trace the word. Write the word.

rectangle

Shapes: Triangle and Rectangle

Directions: Practice drawing triangles. Trace the samples and make four of your own.

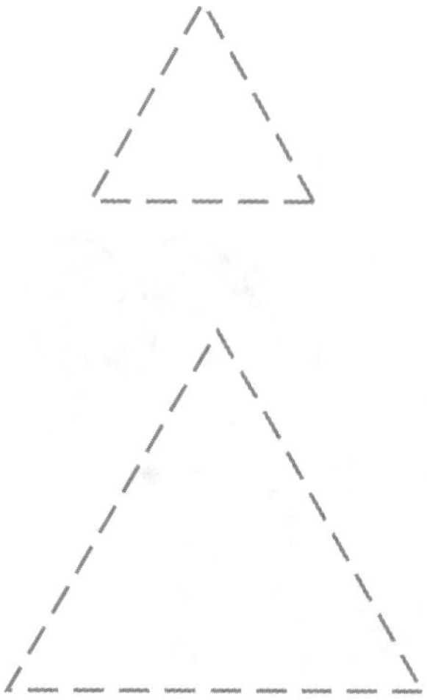

Directions: Practice drawing rectangles. Trace the samples and make four of your own.

Shapes: Oval and Rhombus

An oval is an egg-shaped figure. A rhombus is a figure with four sides of the same length. Its corners form points at the top, sides and bottom. This is an oval ⬭. This is a rhombus ◇.

Directions: Color the ovals red. Color the rhombuses blue.

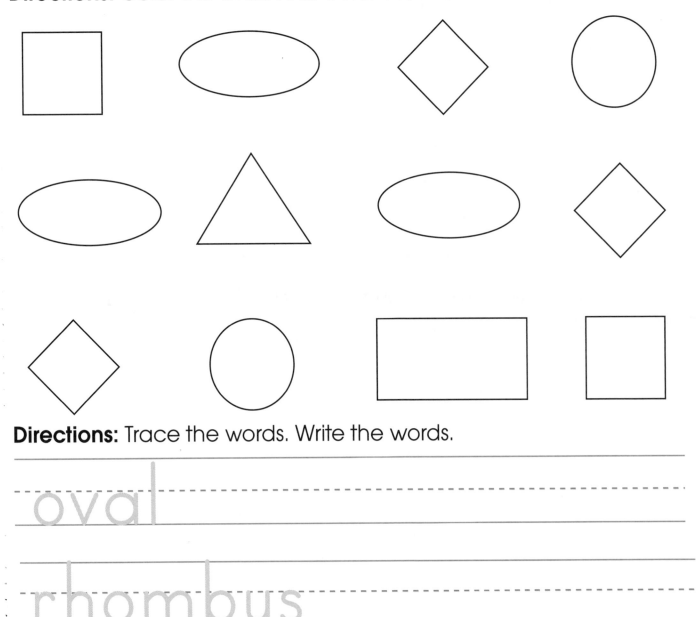

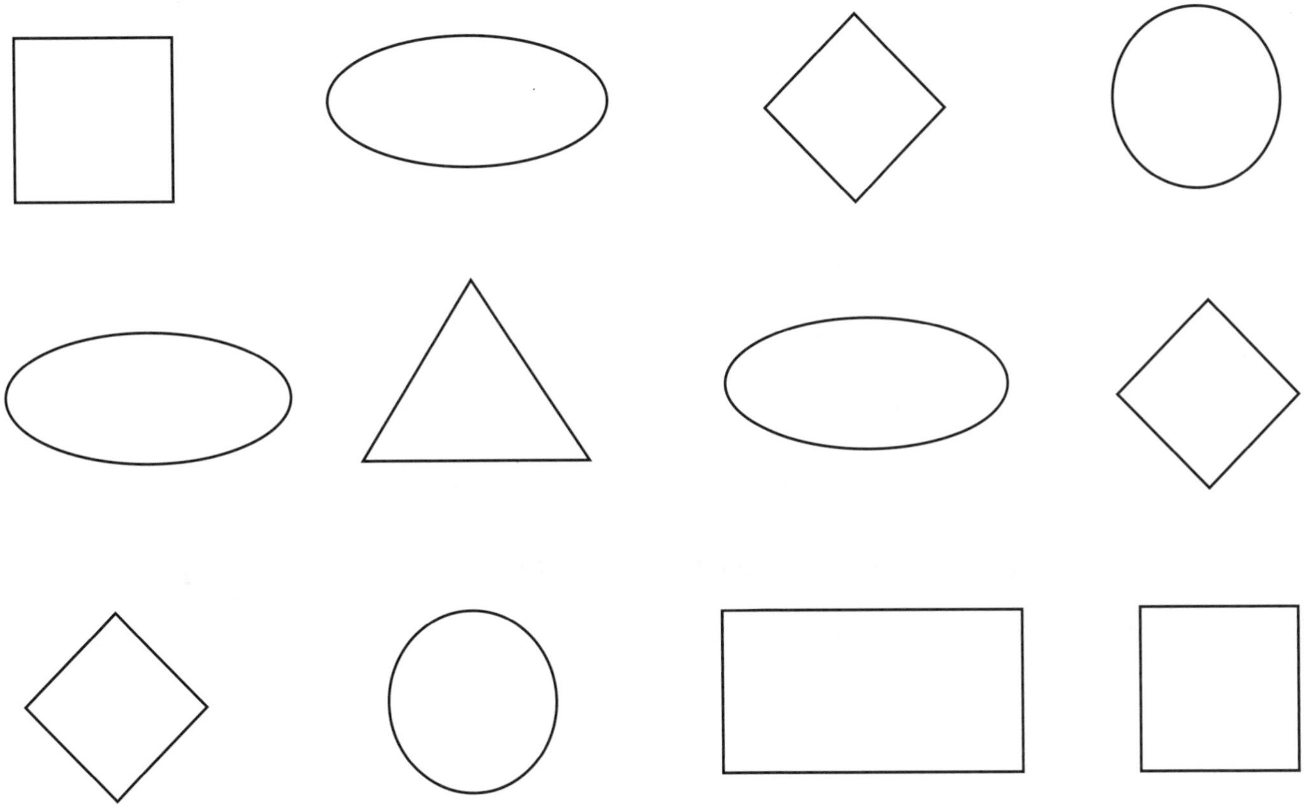

Directions: Trace the words. Write the words.

oval

rhombus

Name ______________________________

Shapes: Oval and Rhombus

Directions: Practice drawing rhombuses. Trace the samples and make four of your own.

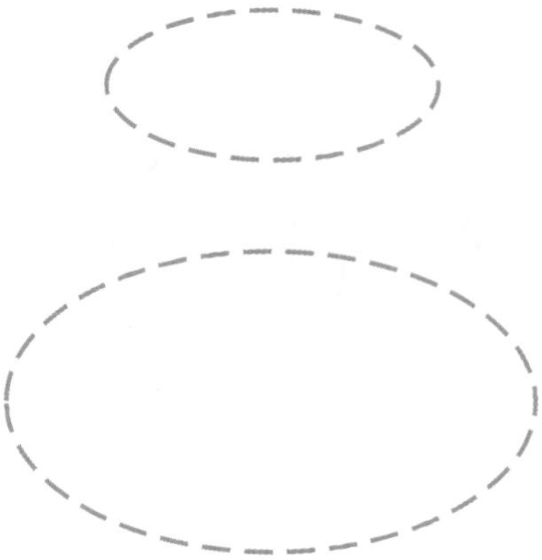

Directions: Practice drawing rhombuses. Trace the samples and make four of your own.

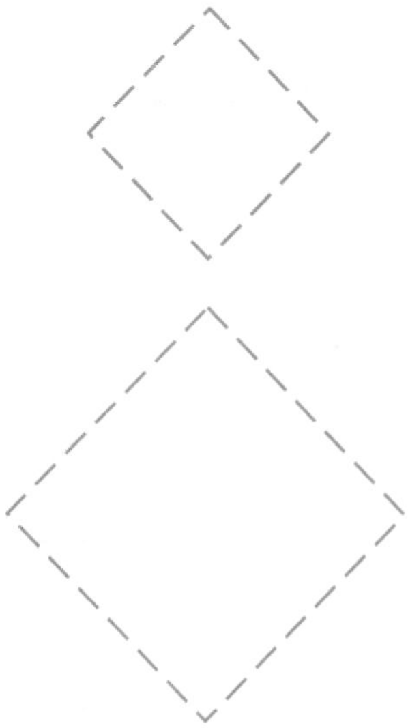

Name ______________________________

Shapes and Colors

Directions: Color the squares □ purple.

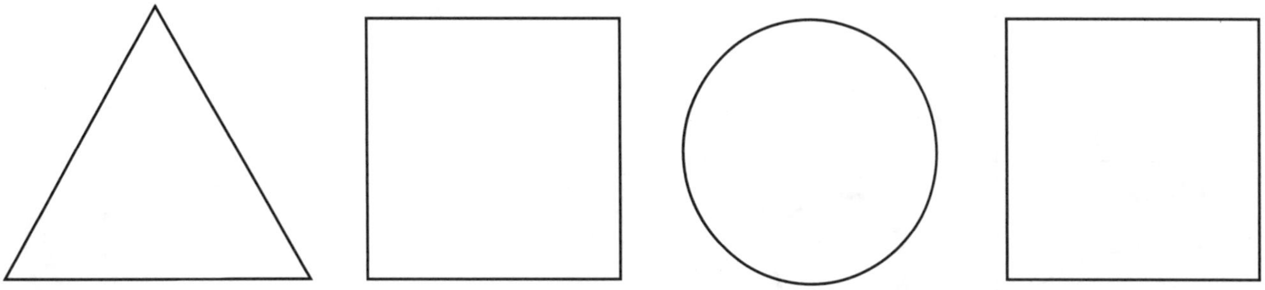

Directions: Color the heart ♡ blue.

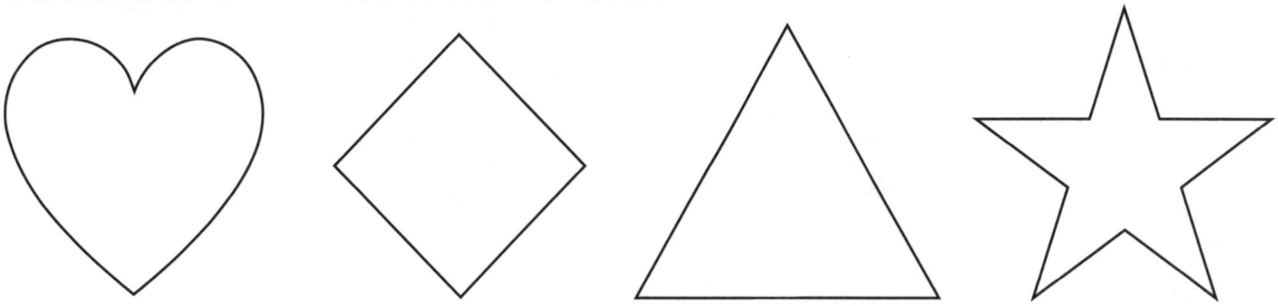

Directions: Color the rhombuses ◇ yellow.

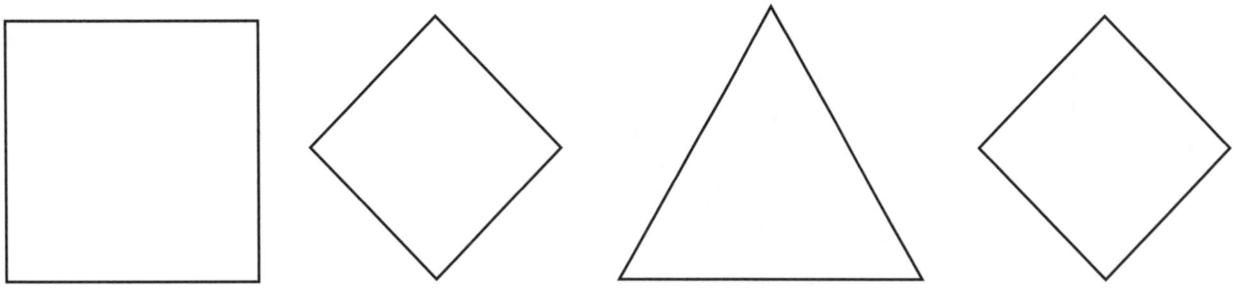

Directions: Color the star ☆ red.

Name ______________________________

Shape Review

Directions: Color the shapes in the picture as shown.

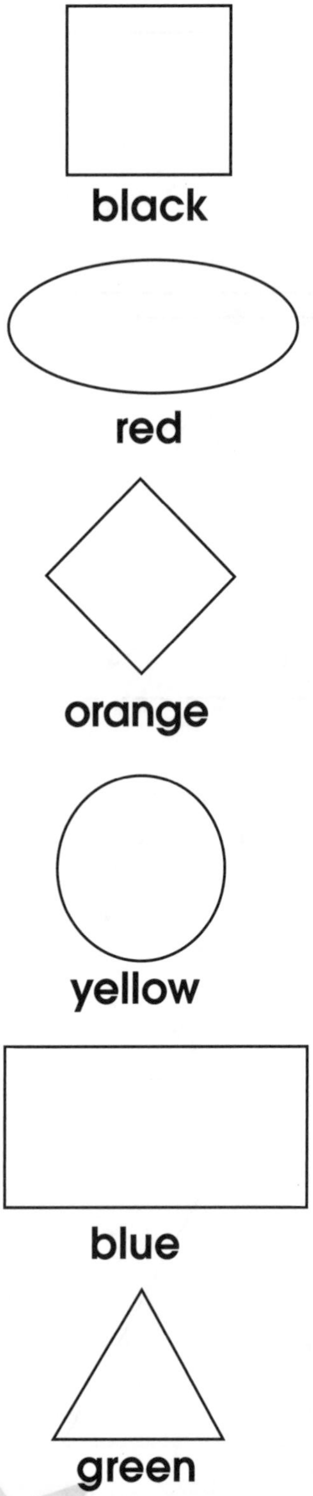

Name ________________________________

Classifying: Stars

Help Bob find the stars.

Directions: Color all the stars blue.

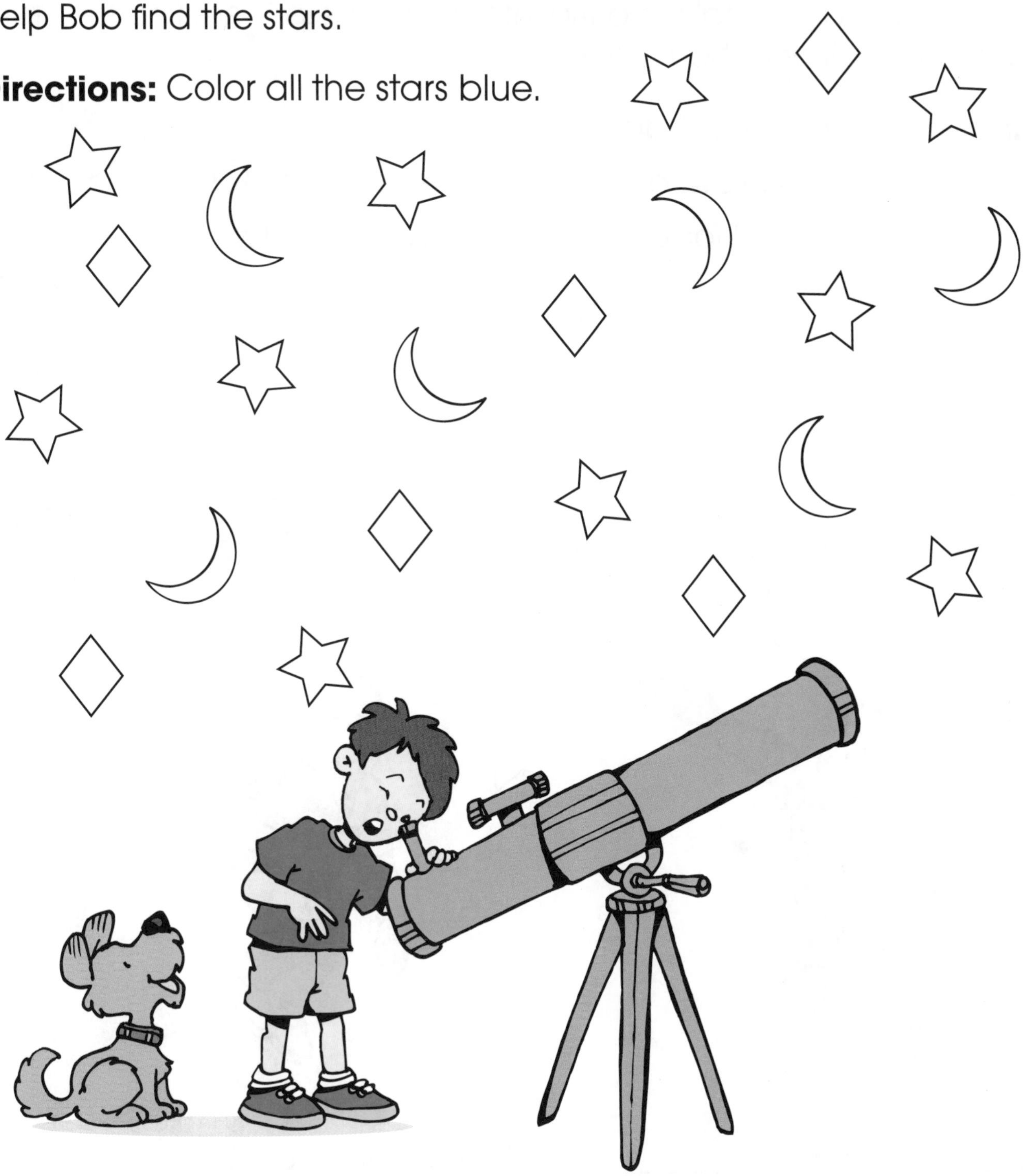

How many stars did you and Bob find?________

Name ______________________________

Classifying: Shapes

Mary and Rudy are taking a trip into space. Help them find the stars, moons, circles and rhombuses.

Directions: Color the shapes.

Use yellow for ☆'s. Use blue for ☾'s.

Use red for ○'s. Use purple for ◇'s.

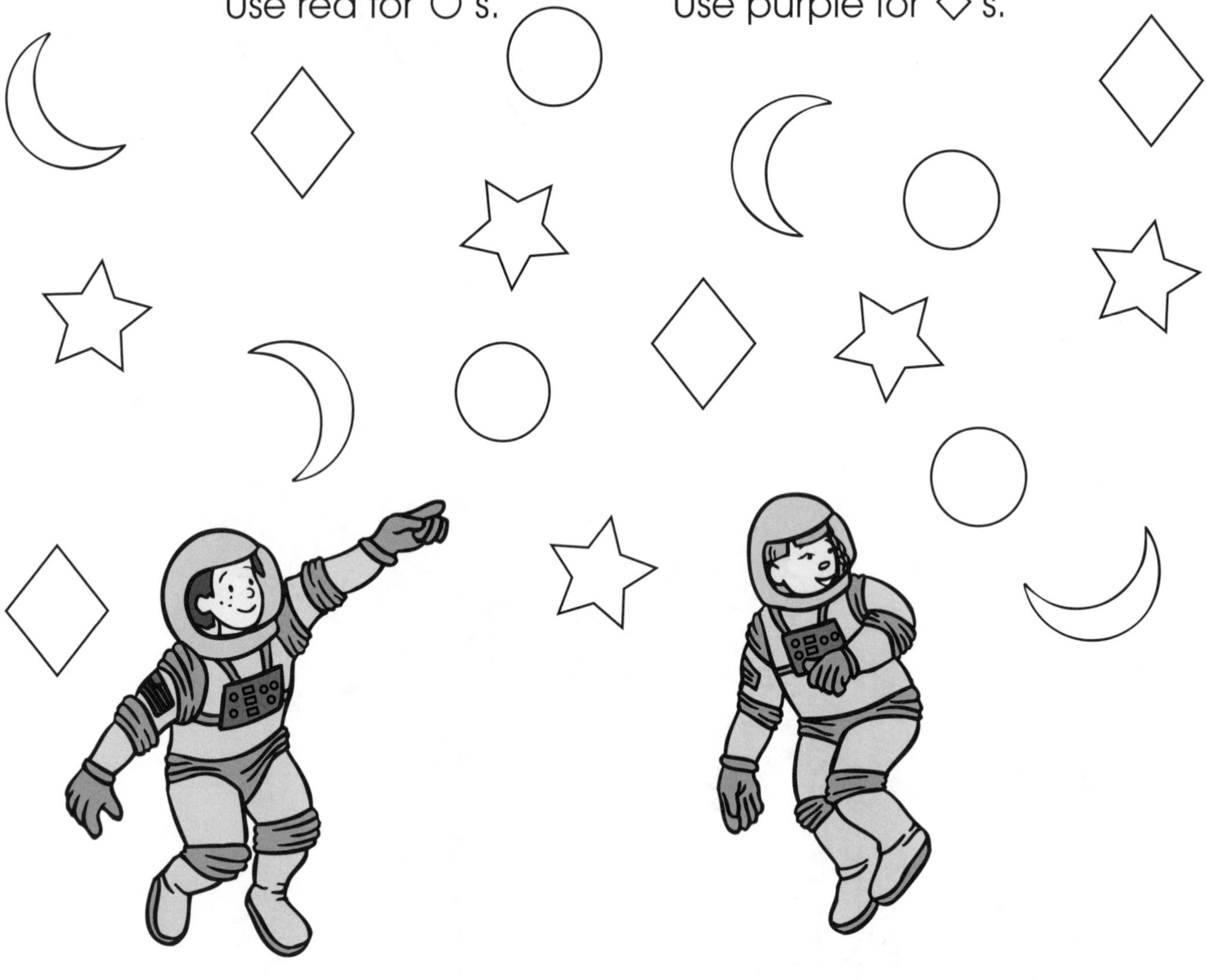

How many stars? ________ How many moons? ________

How many circles? ________ How many rhombuses? ________

Name ______________________________

Classifying: Shapes

Directions: Look at the shapes. Answer the questions.

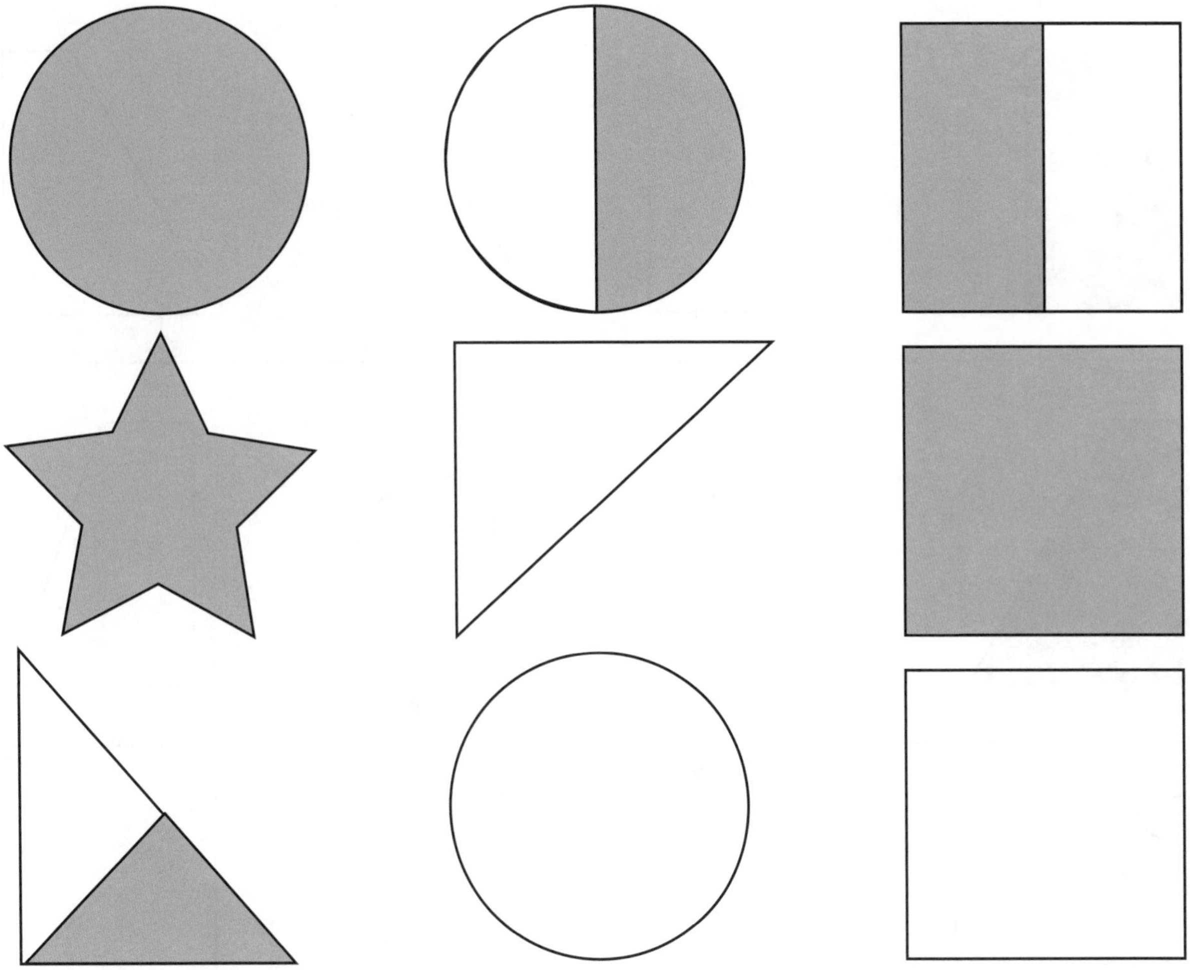

1. How many all-white shapes? ______
2. How many all-blue shapes? ______
3. How many half-white shapes? ______
4. How many all-blue stars? ______
5. How many all-white circles? ______
6. How many half-blue shapes? ______

Name ______________________________

Same and Different: Shapes

Directions: Color the shape that looks the same as the first shape in each row.

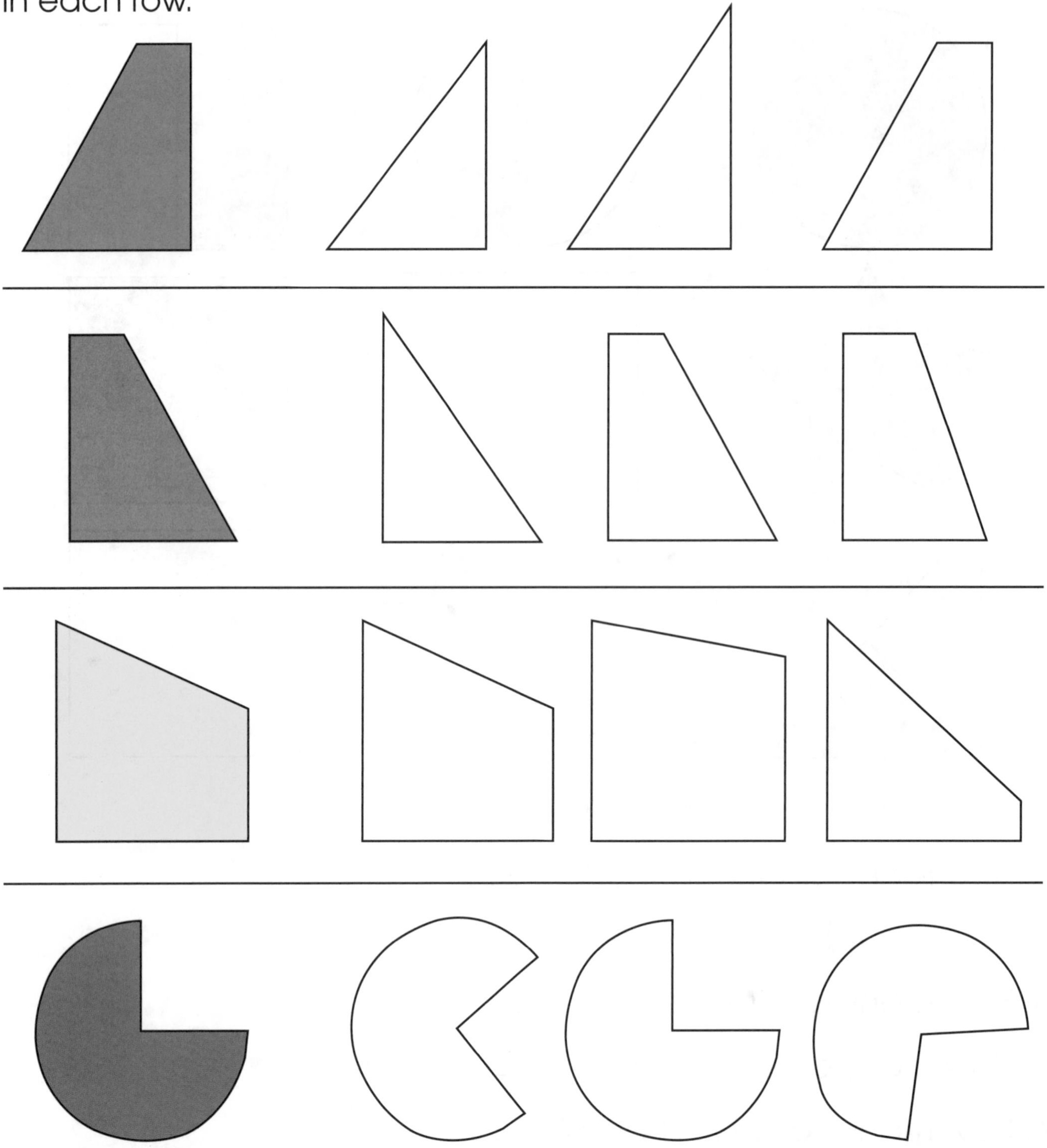

Same and Different: Shapes

Directions: Draw an **X** on the shapes in each row that do not match the first shape.

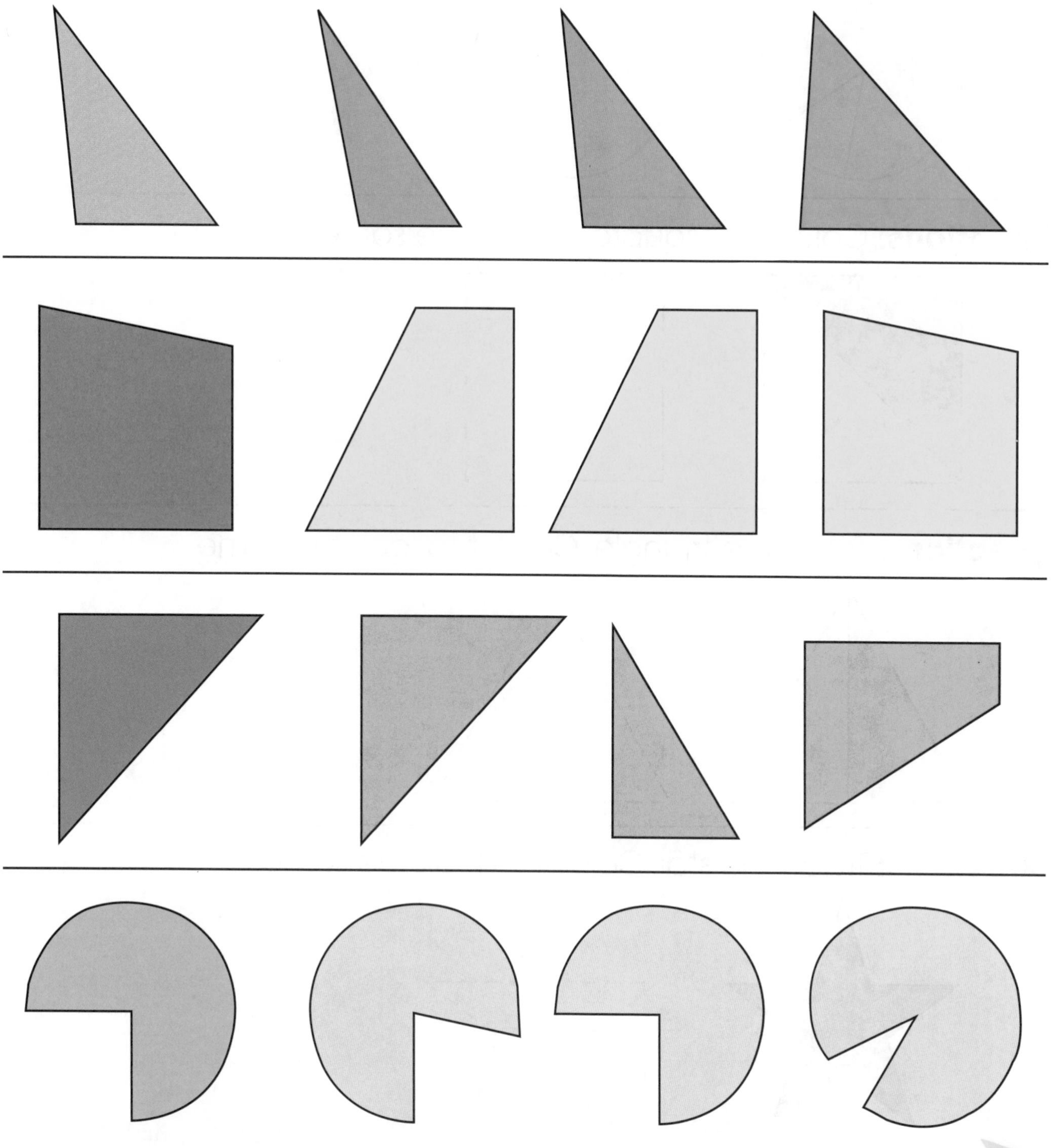

Name ______________________________

Copying: Shapes

Directions: Color your circle to look the same.

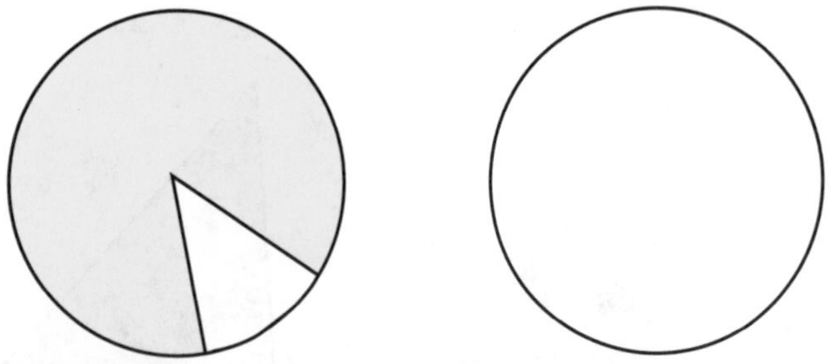

Directions: Color your square to look the same.

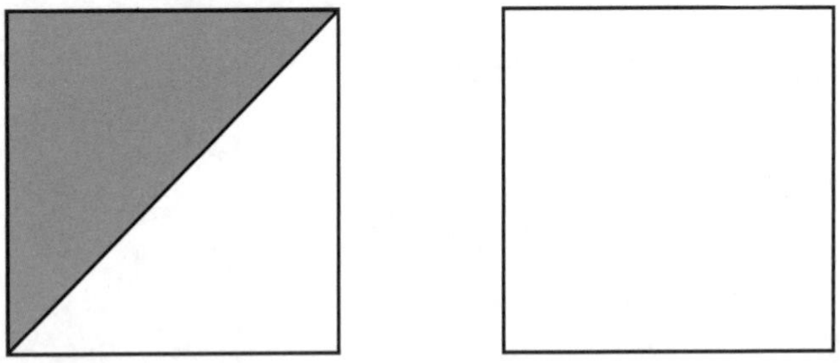

Directions: Trace the triangle. Color it to look the same.

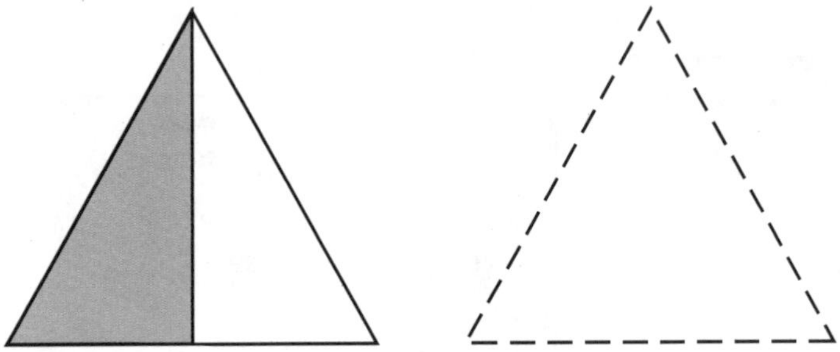

Directions: Trace the star. Color it to look the same.

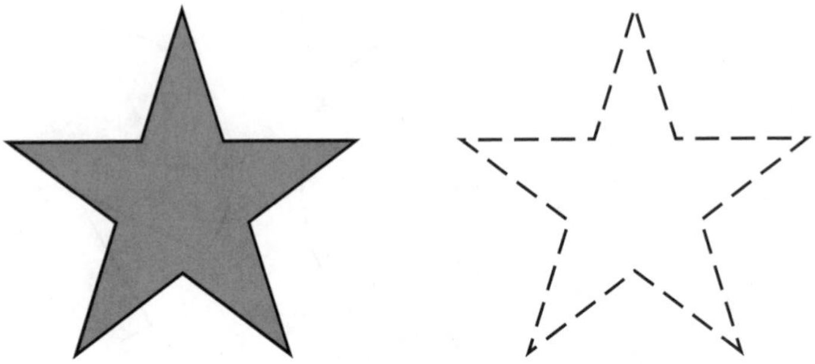

Name ____________________

Copying: Shapes

Directions: Color the second shape the same as the first one. Then draw and color the shape two more times.

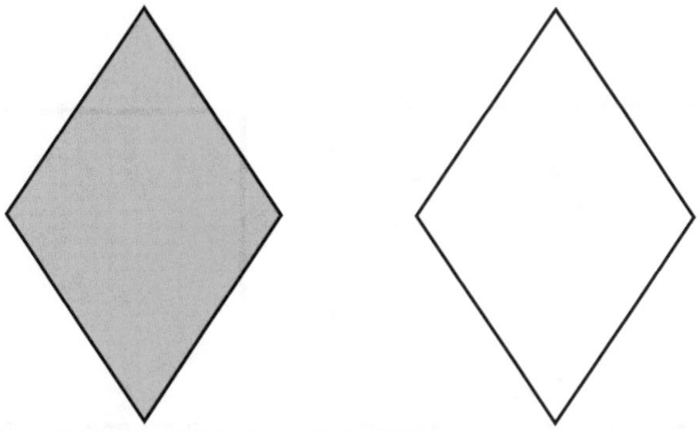

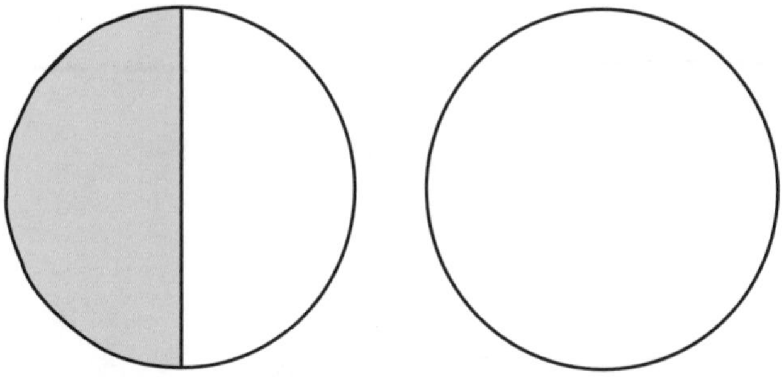

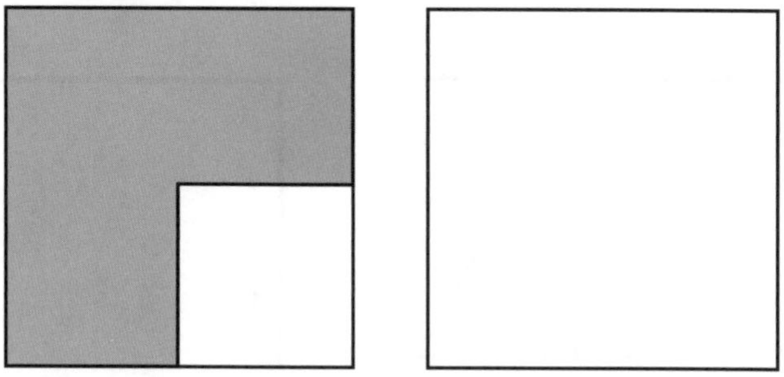

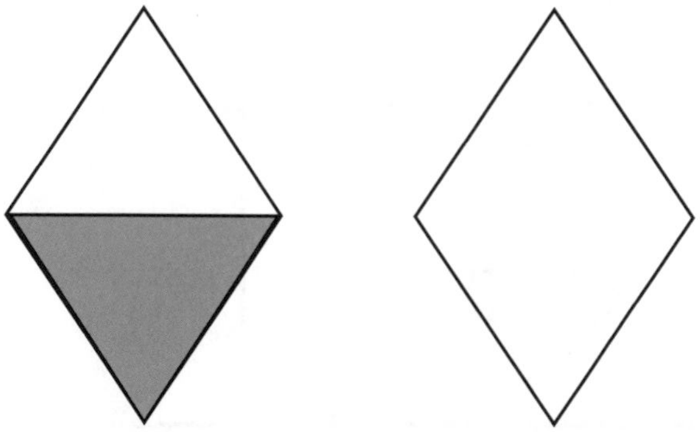

Name ______________________________

Patterns: Find and Copy

Directions: Circle the shape in the middle box that matches the one on the left. Draw another shape with the same pattern in the box on the right.

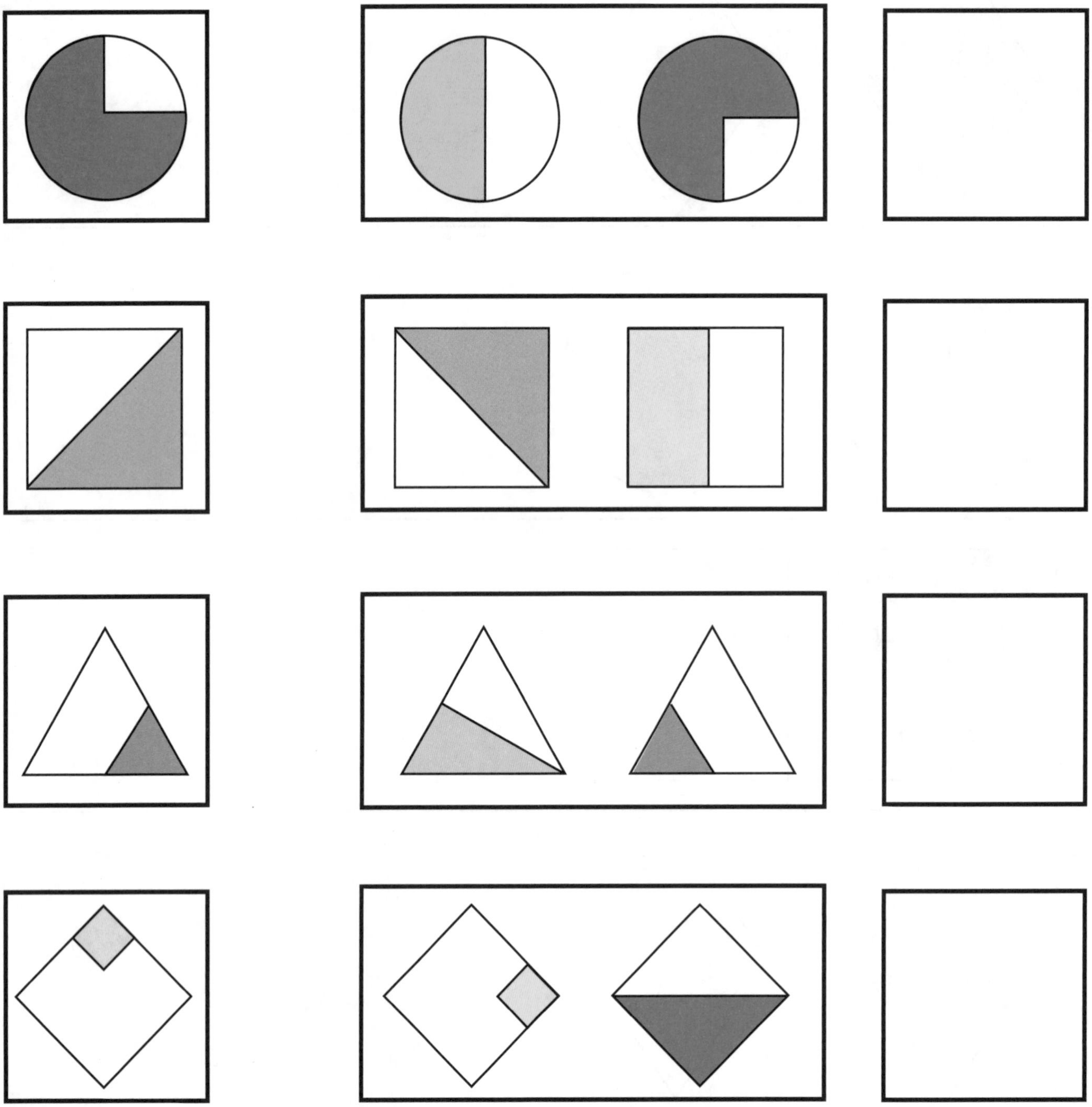

Name ______________________________

Patterns

Directions: Fill in the missing shape in each row.

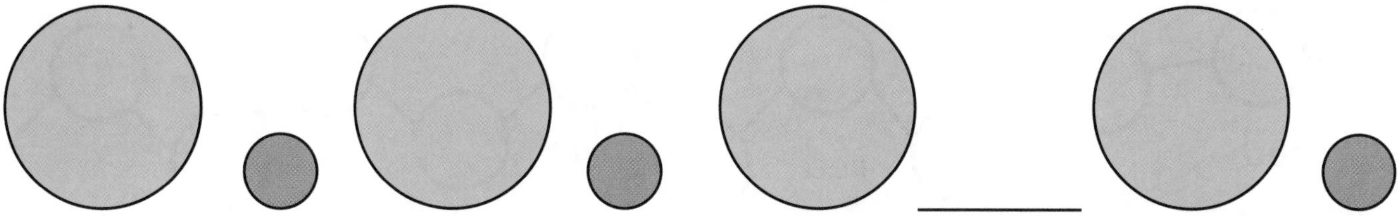

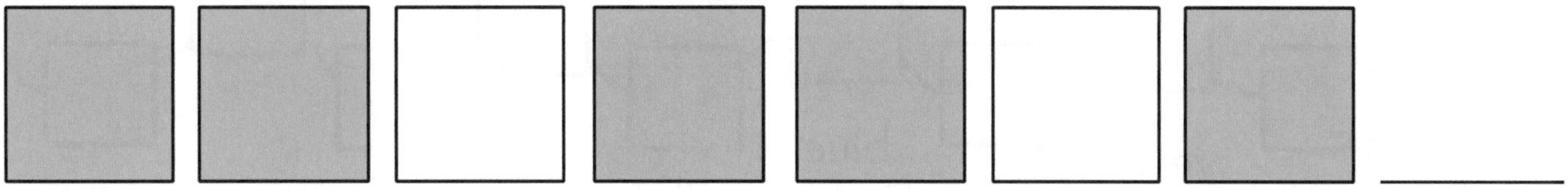

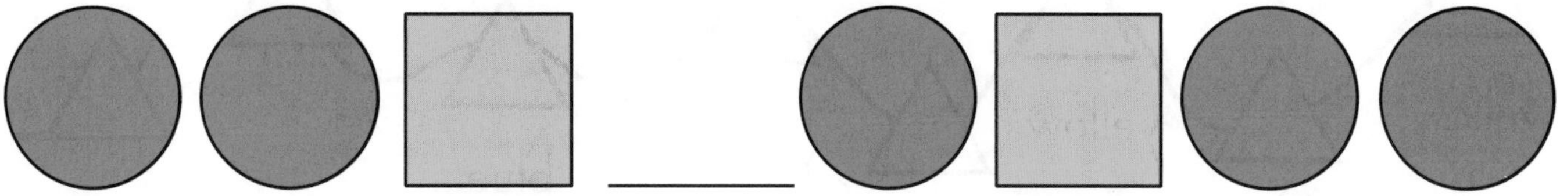

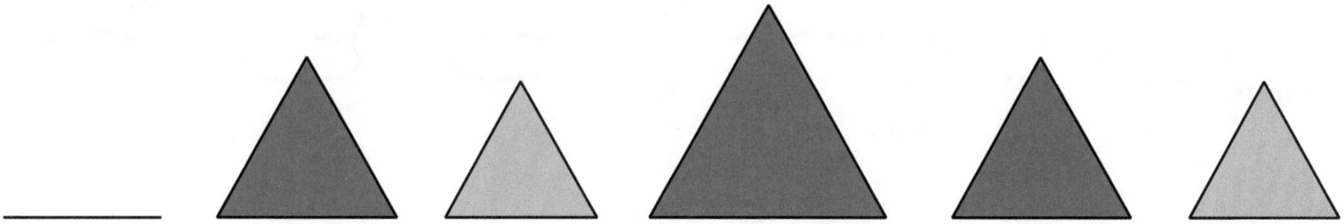

Name ______________________

Patterns

Directions: Color to complete the patterns.

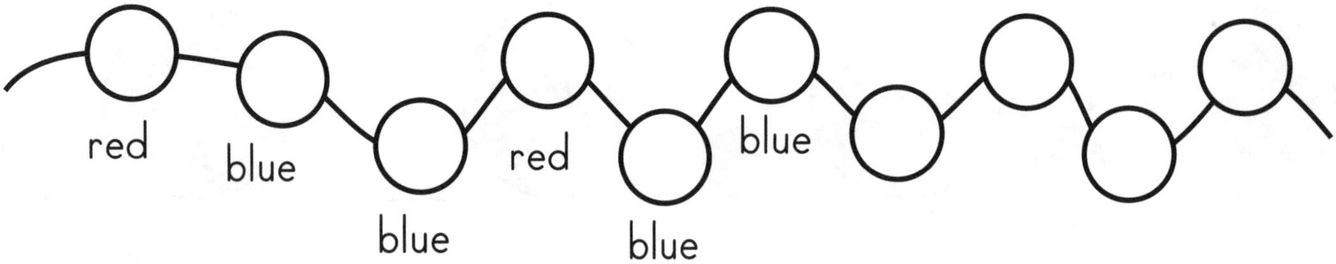

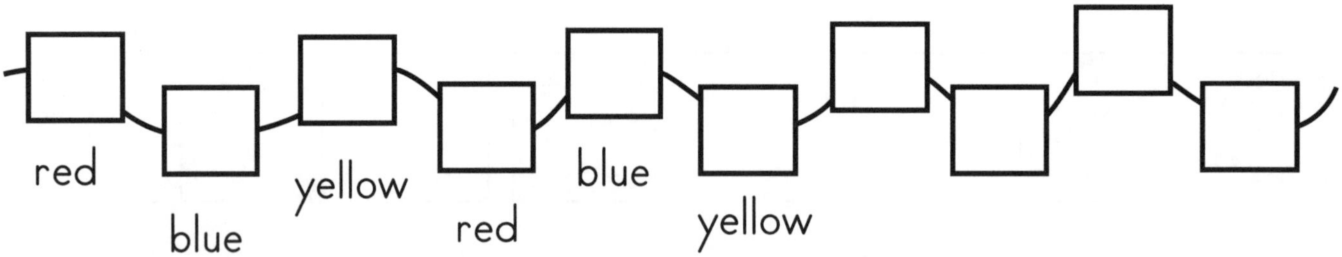

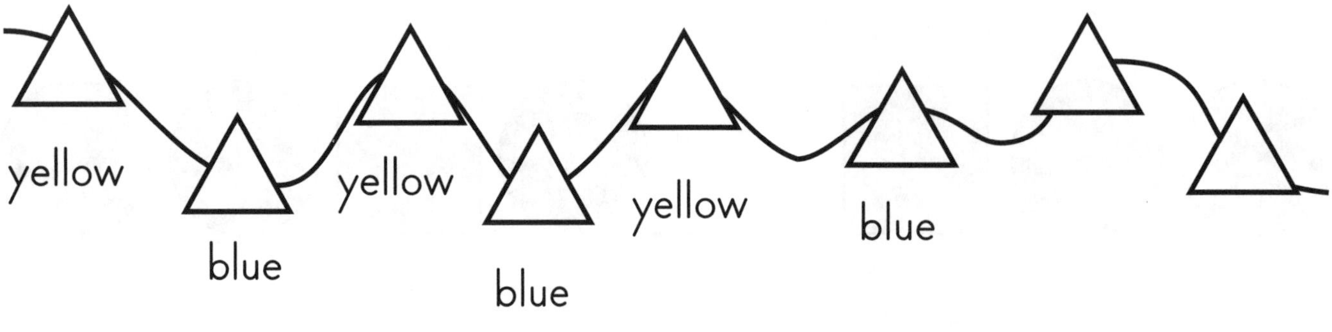

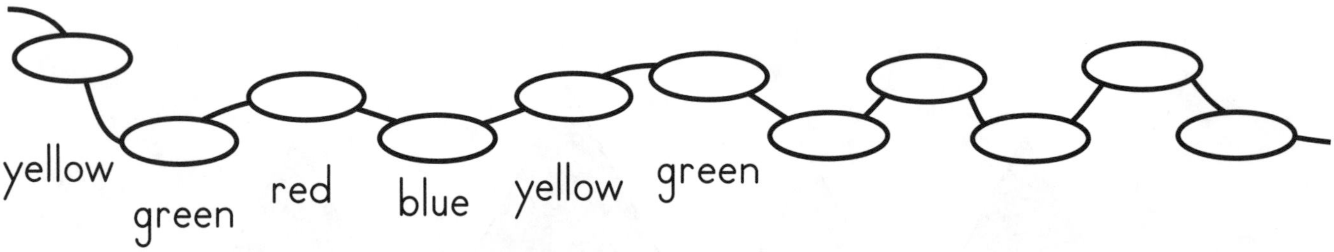

Name ______________________________

Fractions: Whole and Half

A fraction is a number that names part of a whole, such as $\frac{1}{2}$ or $\frac{3}{4}$.

Directions: Color half of each object.

Example:

Whole apple

Half an apple

$$\frac{1}{2}$$

Name ______________________________

Fractions: Halves $\frac{1}{2}$

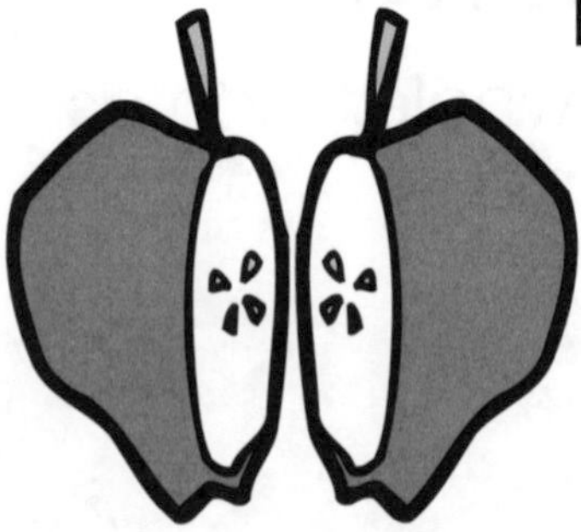

$\frac{1}{2}$ $\frac{\text{Part shaded or divided}}{\text{Number of equal parts}}$

Directions: Color only the shapes that show halves.

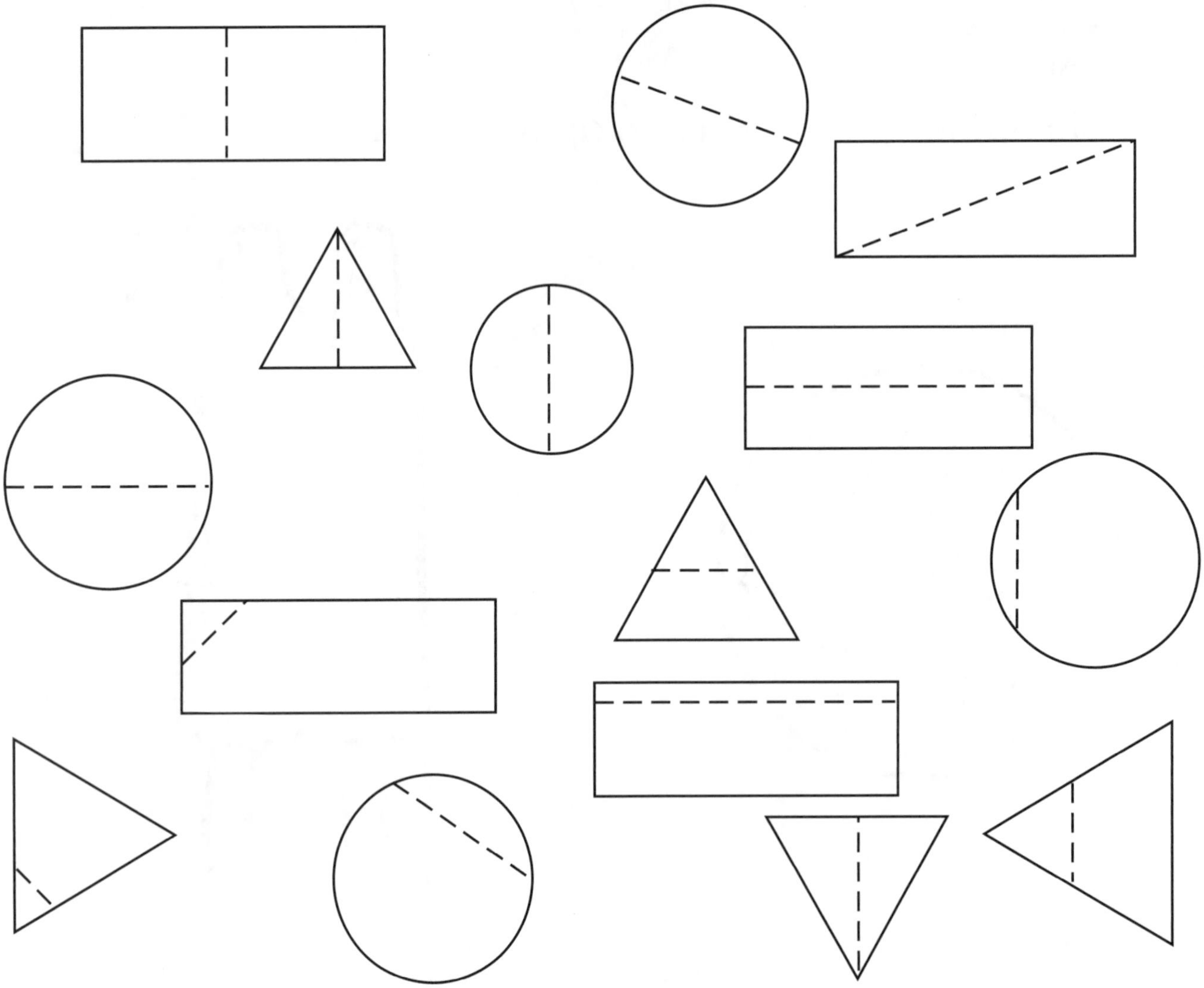

Name ______________________________

Fractions: Thirds $\frac{1}{3}$

Directions: Circle the objects that have 3 equal parts.

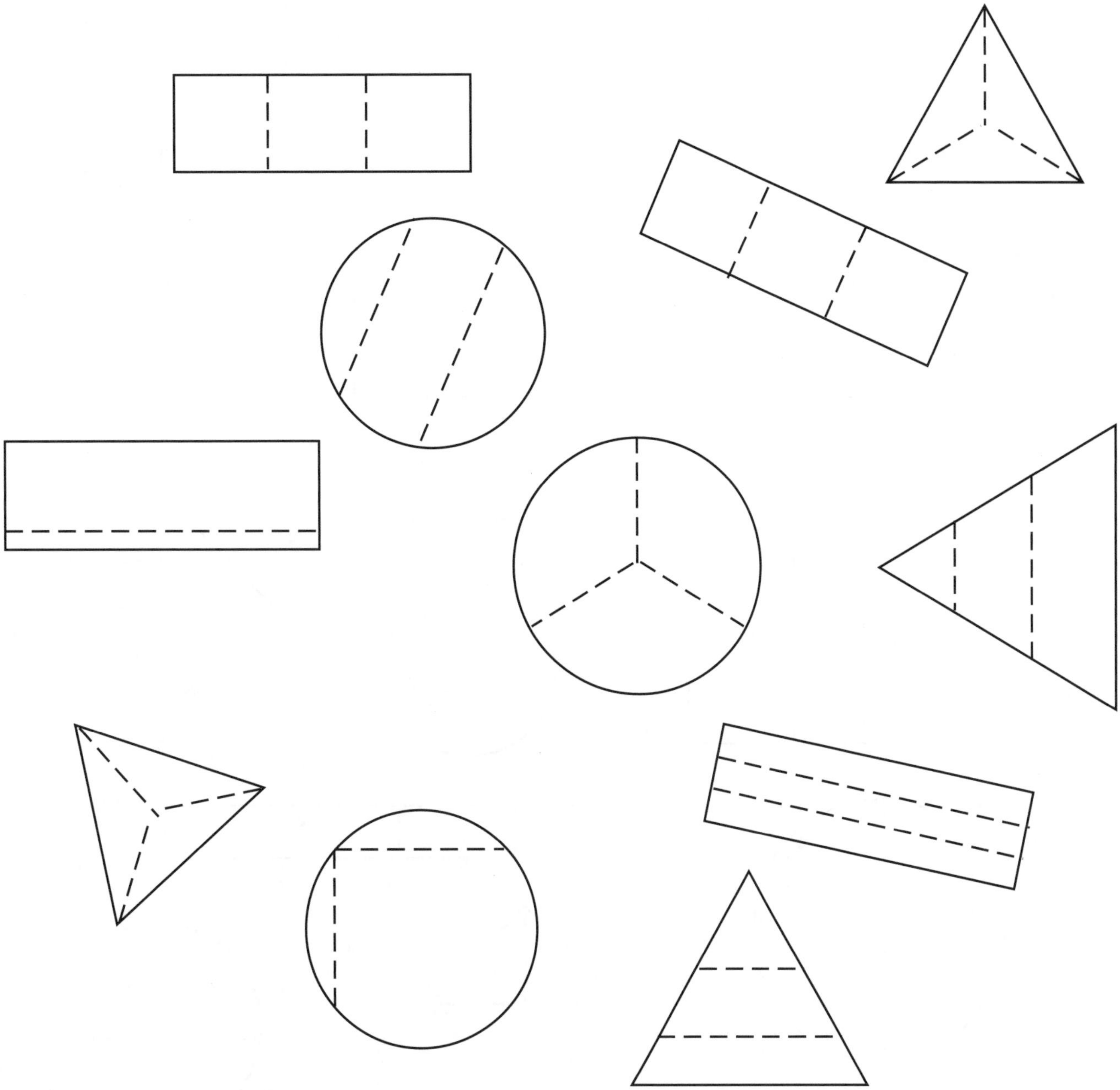

Name ____________________

Fractions: Fourths $\frac{1}{4}$

Directions: Circle the objects that have four equal parts.

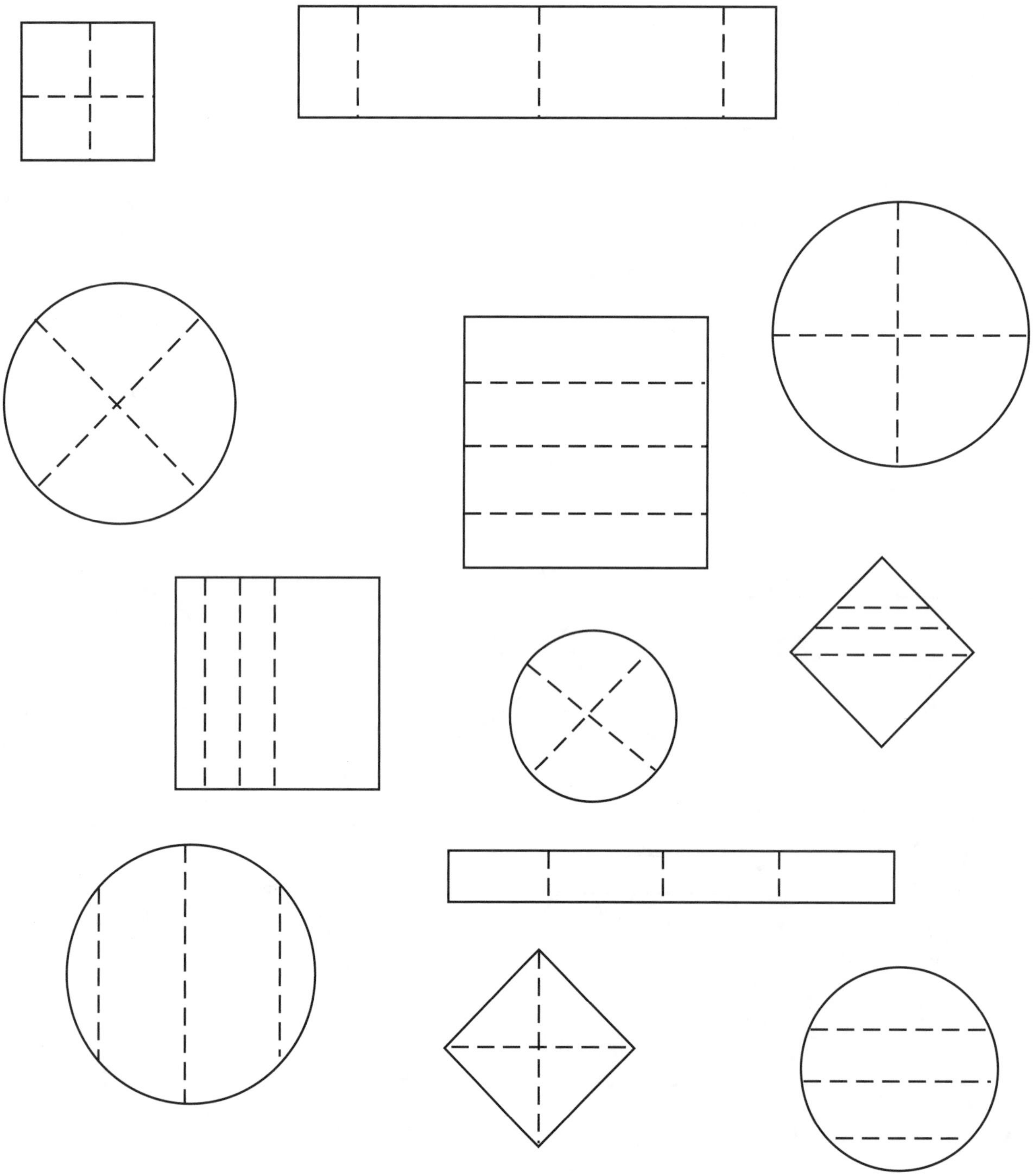

Name ____________________

Fractions: Thirds and Fourths

Directions: Each object has 3 equal parts. Color one section.

Directions: Each object has 4 equal parts. Color one section.

Name ______________________________

Review: Fractions

Directions: Count the equal parts, then write the fraction.

Example:

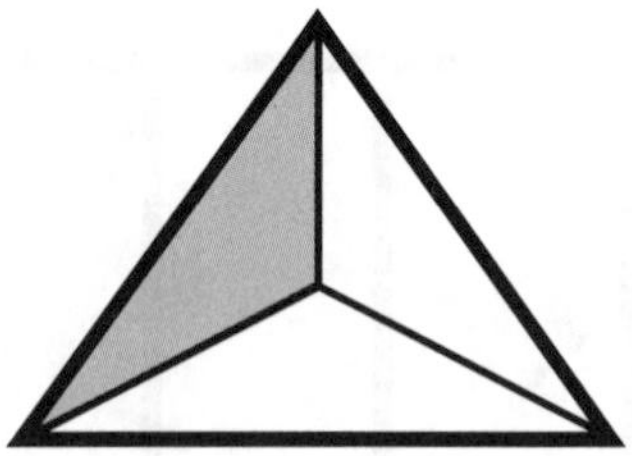

Shaded part = 1 Write $\frac{1}{3}$

Equal parts = 3

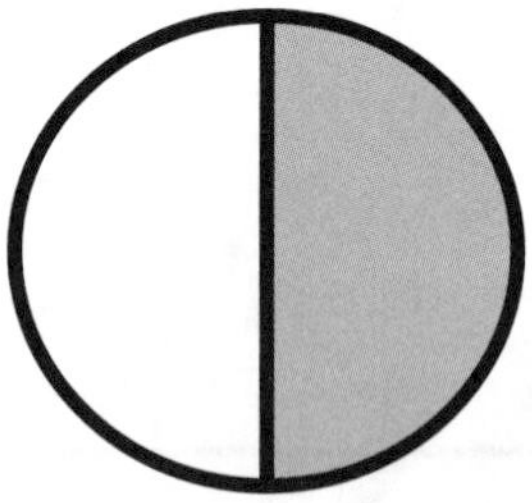

Shaded part = 1 Write ____

Equal parts = ____

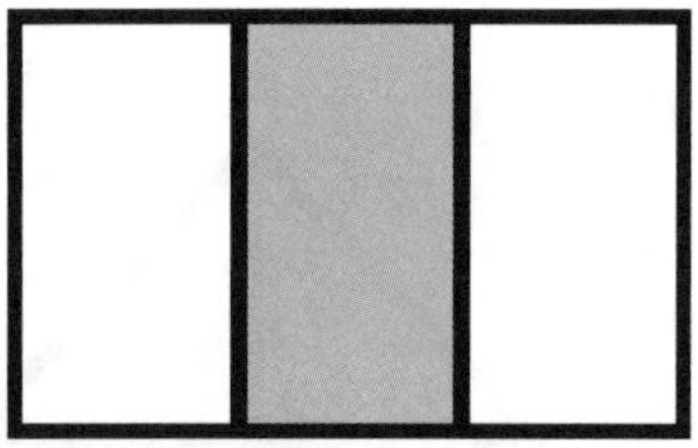

Shaded part = 1 Write ____

Equal parts = ____

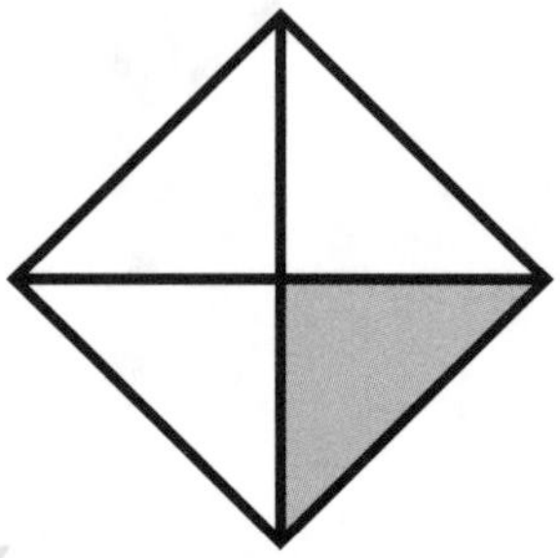

Shaded part = 1 Write ____

Equal parts = ____

Name ______________________________

Review

Directions: Write the missing numbers by counting by tens and fives.

_____ , 20, _____ , _____ , _____ , _____ , 70, _____ , _____ , 100

5, _____ , 15, _____ , _____ , 30, _____ , _____ , _____ , _____

Directions: Color the object with thirds red. Color the object with halves blue. Color the object with fourths green.

Directions: Draw a line to the correct equal part.

$\frac{1}{3}$

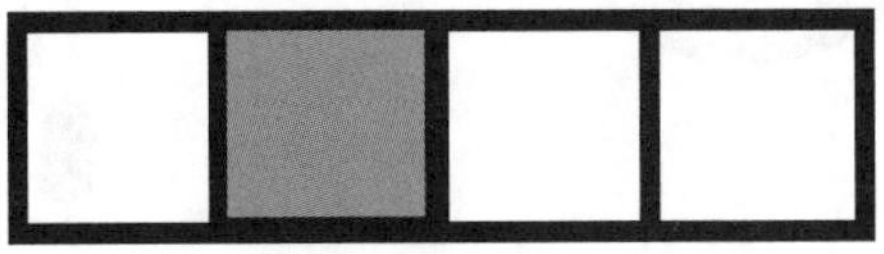

$\frac{1}{4}$

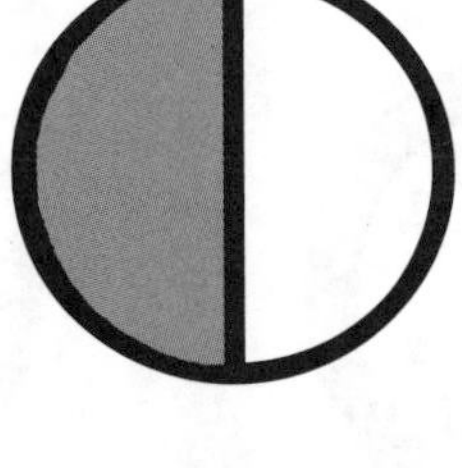

$\frac{1}{2}$

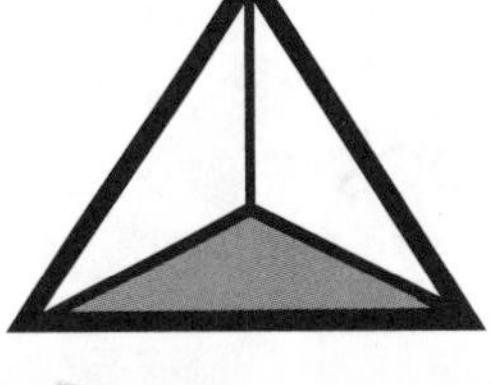

Name ______________________________

Time: Hour

The short hand of the clock tells the hour. The long hand tells how many minutes after the hour. When the minute hand is on the **12**, it is the beginning of the hour.

Directions: Look at each clock. Write the time.

Example:

__3__ o'clock

____ o'clock

____ o'clock

____ o'clock

____ o'clock

____ o'clock

____ o'clock

____ o'clock

____ o'clock

Name ______________________________

Time: Hour, Half-Hour

The short hand of the clock tells the hour. The long hand tells how many minutes after the hour. When the minute hand is on the **6**, it is on the half-hour. A half-hour is thirty minutes. It is written **:30**, such as **5:30.**

Directions: Look at each clock. Write the time.

Example:

hour **half-hour**

1 : 30

____ : ____

____ : ____

____ : ____

____ : ____

____ : ____

____ : ____

____ : ____

____ : ____

Name ____________________

Time: Hour, Half-Hour

Directions: Draw the hands on each clock to show the correct time.

2:30

9:00

7:00

4:30

3:00

1:30

Name ____________________

Time: Counting by Fives

Directions: Fill in the numbers on the clock face. Count by fives around the clock.

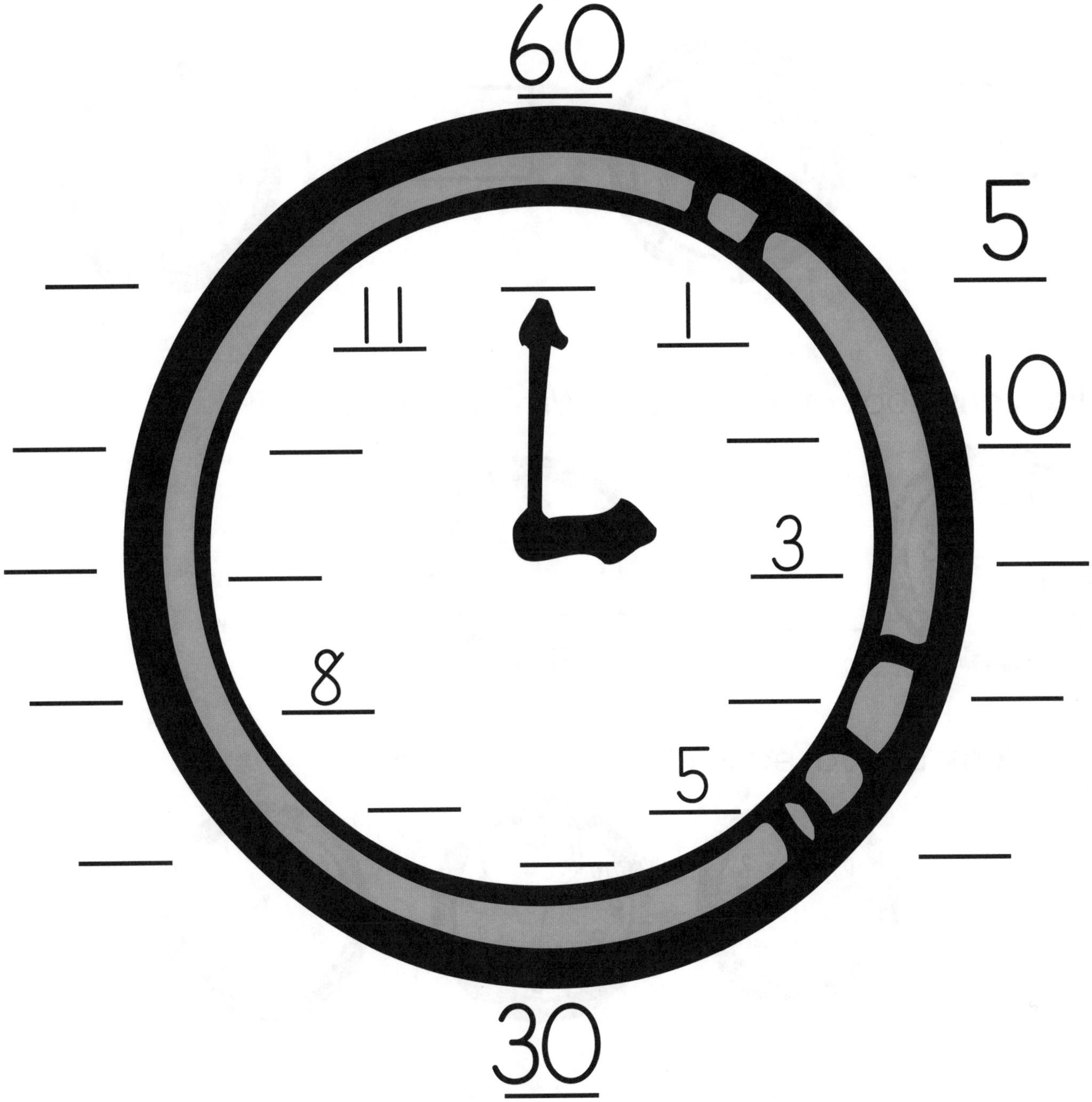

There are 60 minutes in one hour.

Review: Time

Directions: Look at the time on the digital clocks and draw the hands on the clocks.

10:00

5:00

Directions: Look at each clock. Write the time.

_____o'clock

_____o'clock

Directions: Look at each clock. Write the time.

_____:_____ _____:_____ _____:_____

Name ______________________________

Review: Time

Directions: Tell what time it is on the clocks.

 ____________

 ____________

 ____________

 ____________

 ____________

 ____________

Name ______________________________

Review: Time

Directions: Match the time on the clock with the digital time.

10:00

5:00

3:00

9:00

2:00

Name ______________________________

Money: Penny and Nickel

A penny is worth one cent. It is written **1¢** or **$.01**. A nickel is worth five cents. It is written **5¢** or **$.05**.

Directions: Count the money and write the answers.

penny

1 penny = 1¢

nickel

1 nickel = 5¢

= __3__ ¢

= __15__ ¢

= ______ ¢

= ______ ¢

= ______ ¢

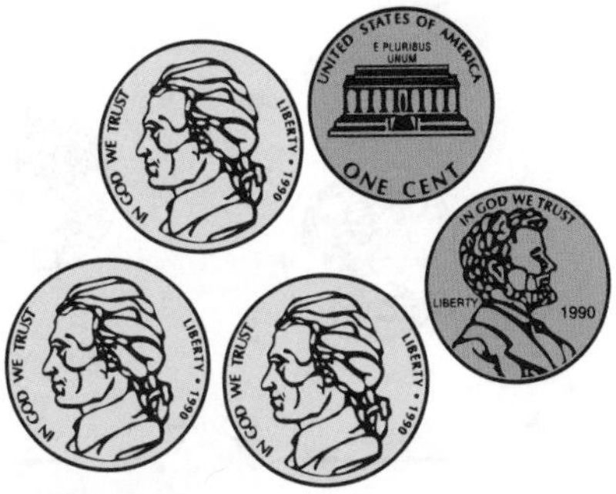

= ______ ¢

Name ______________________

Money: Penny, Nickel, Dime

A penny is worth one cent. It is written **1¢** or **$.01**. A nickel is worth five cents. It is written **5¢** or **$.05**. A dime is worth ten cents. It is written **10¢** or **$.10**.

Directions: Add the coins pictured and write the total amounts in the blanks.

Example:

dime 10¢ = **nickel** 5¢ + **nickel** 5¢ = **pennies** 10¢

10¢ + 1¢ = ______ ¢

10¢ + ______ ¢ = ______ ¢

______ ¢ + ______ ¢ + ______ ¢ = ______ ¢

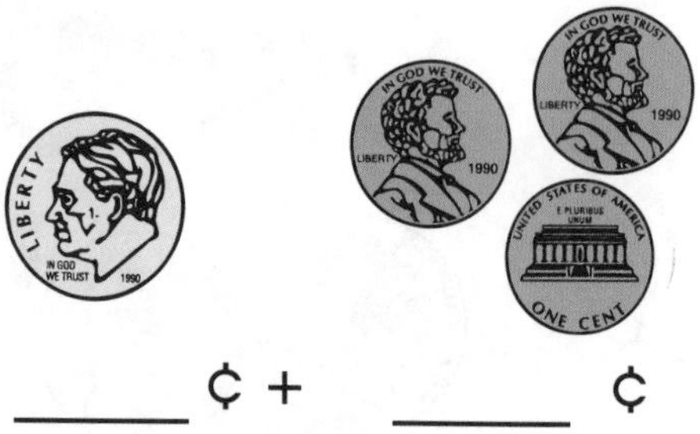

______ ¢ + ______ ¢ = ______ ¢

Name ____

Money: Penny, Nickel, Dime

Directions: Match the amounts in each purse to the price tags.

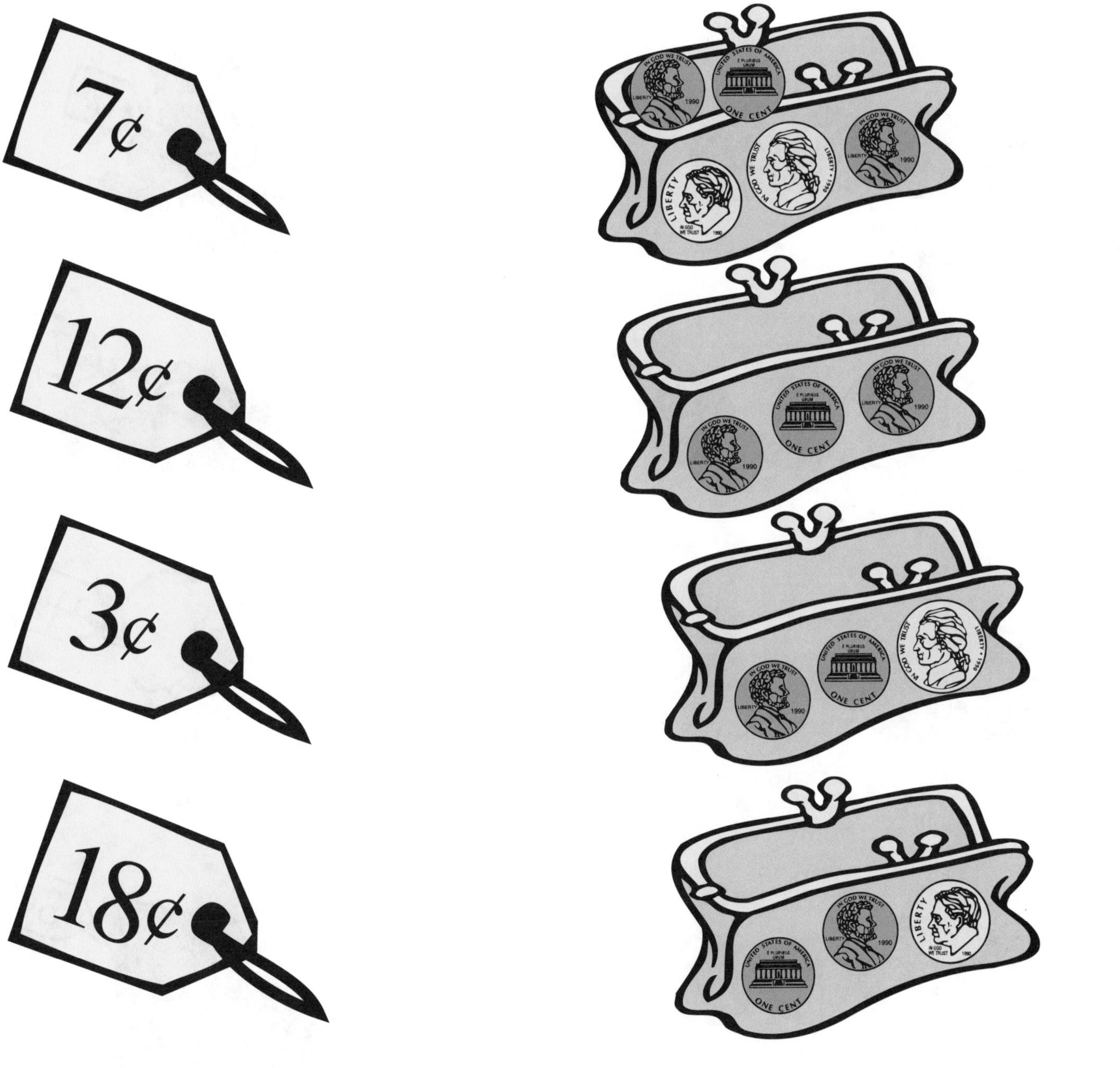

Name ______________________________

Money: Penny, Nickel, Dime

Directions: Match the correct amount of money with the price of the object.

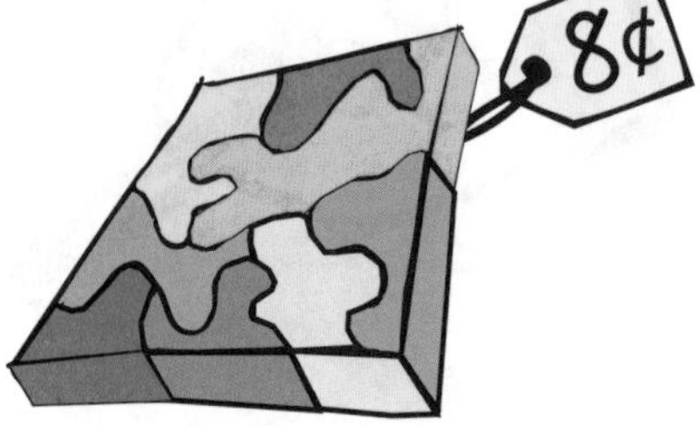

Name ____

Review

Directions: What time is it?

_____ o'clock

Directions: Draw the hands on each clock.

2:30

7:30

11:00

Directions: How much money?

= ________ ¢

= ________ ¢

Directions: Add or subtract.

9 + 3 = _____ 6 + 8 = _____ 15 - 9 = _____

12 - 8 = _____ 12 + 2 = _____ 7 + 6 = _____

Name ______________________________

Review

Directions: Follow the instructions.

1. How much money?

_____ ¢

	Tens	Ones		Tens	Ones
2. 57 =	_____	_____	28 =	_____	_____

3. What is this shape? Circle the answer.

Square

Triangle

Circle

What is this shape? __________

4.

Shaded part = _____ Write

Equal parts = _____ _____

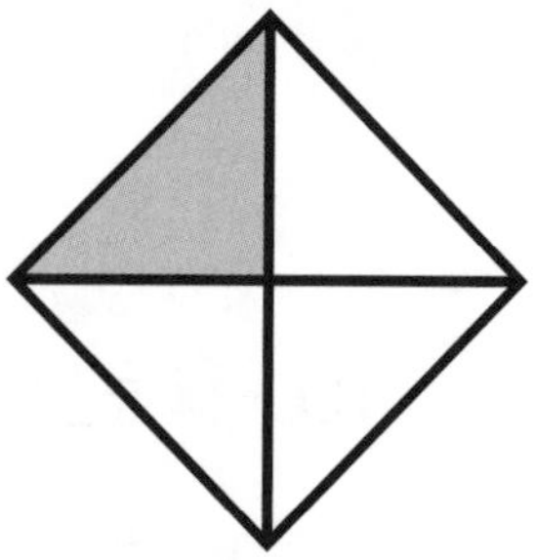

Shaded part = _____ Write

Equal parts = _____ _____

5. 12 + 3 = _____ 9 + 6 = _____ 15 - 7 = _____

Name ______________________________

Measurement

A ruler has 12 inches. 12 inches equal 1 foot.

Directions: Cut out the ruler at the bottom of the page. Measure the objects to the nearest inch.

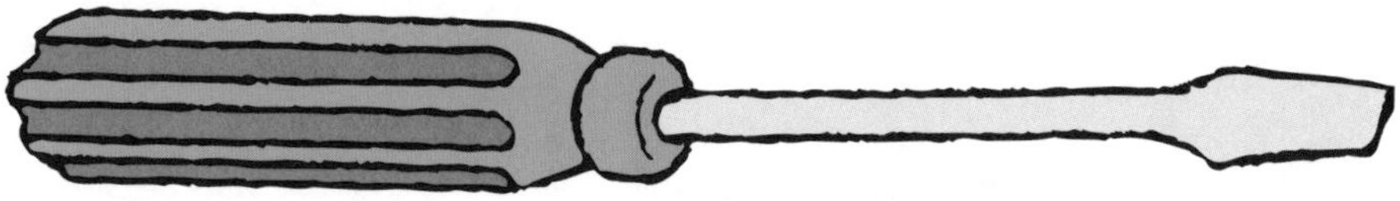

The screwdriver is ______ inches long.

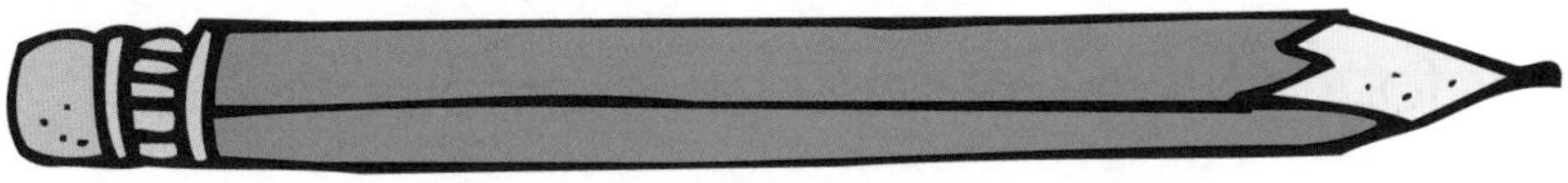

The pencil is ______ inches long.

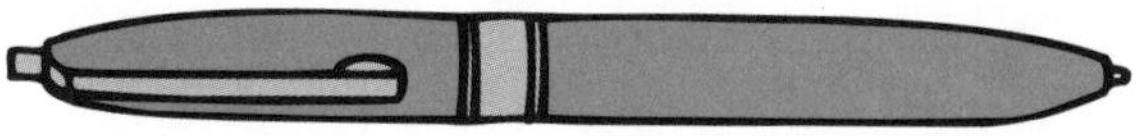

The pen is ______ inches long.

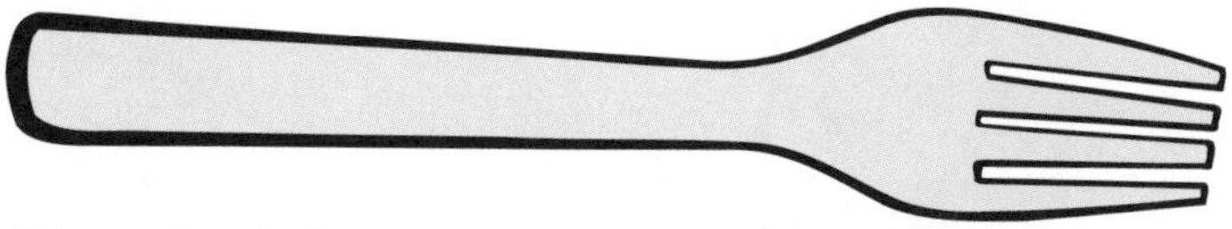

The fork is ______ inches long.

Cut ✂ -

Page is blank for cutting exercise on previous page.

Answer Key

Page 6

Name, Address, Phone

This book belongs to

Answers will vary.

I live at

Answers will vary.

The city I live in is

Answers will vary.

The state I live in is

Answers will vary.

My phone number is

Answers will vary.

Page 7

Review the Alphabet

Directions: Practice writing the letters.

Aa Bb Cc Dd Ee Ff Gg Hh Ii

Child will write letters as shown.

Page 8

Review the Alphabet

Directions: Practice writing the letters.

Jj Kk Ll Mm Nn Oo Pp Qq Rr

Child will write letters as shown.

Page 9

Review the Alphabet

Directions: Practice writing the letters.

Ss Tt Uu Vv Ww Xx Yy Zz

Child will write letters as shown.

Page 10

Letter Recognition

Directions: In each set, match the lower-case letter to the upper-case letter.

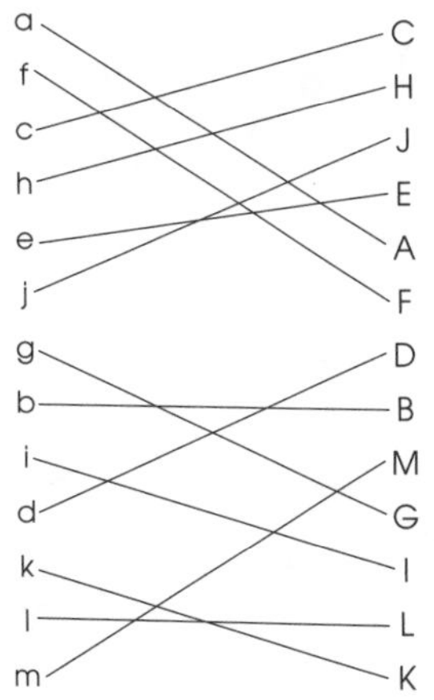

Page 11

Letter Recognition

Directions: In each set, match the lower-case letter to the upper-case letter.

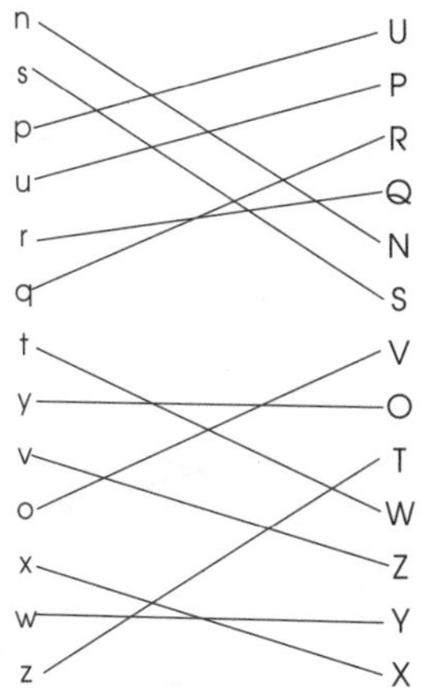

Answer Key

Page 12

Beginning Consonants: Bb, Cc, Dd, Ff

Beginning consonants are the sounds that come at the beginning of words. Consonants are the letters b, c, d, f, g, h, j, k, l, m, n, p, q, r, s, t, v, w, x, y and z.

Directions: Say the name of each letter. Say the sound each letter makes. Circle the letters that make the beginning sound for each picture.

Page 13

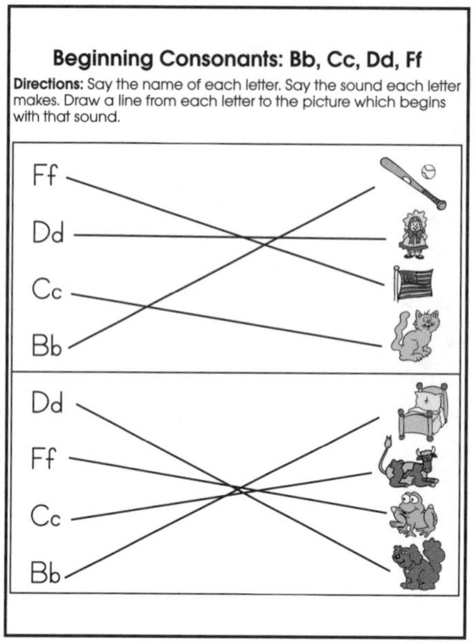

Beginning Consonants: Bb, Cc, Dd, Ff

Directions: Say the name of each letter. Say the sound each letter makes. Draw a line from each letter to the picture which begins with that sound.

Page 14

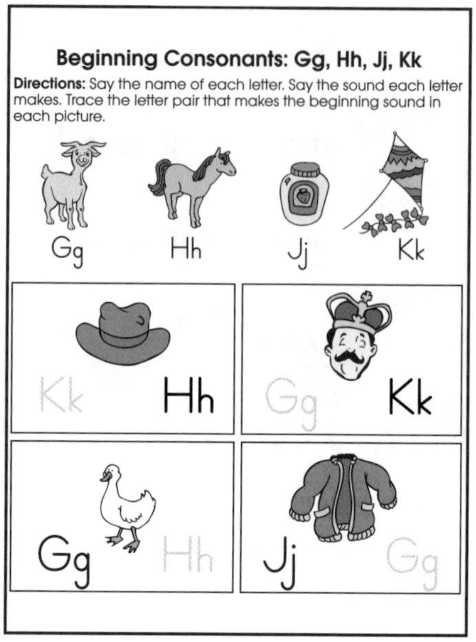

Beginning Consonants: Gg, Hh, Jj, Kk

Directions: Say the name of each letter. Say the sound each letter makes. Trace the letter pair that makes the beginning sound in each picture.

Page 15

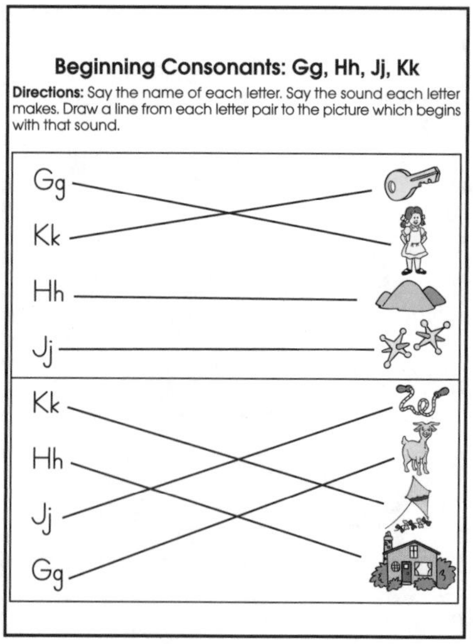

Beginning Consonants: Gg, Hh, Jj, Kk

Directions: Say the name of each letter. Say the sound each letter makes. Draw a line from each letter pair to the picture which begins with that sound.

Page 16

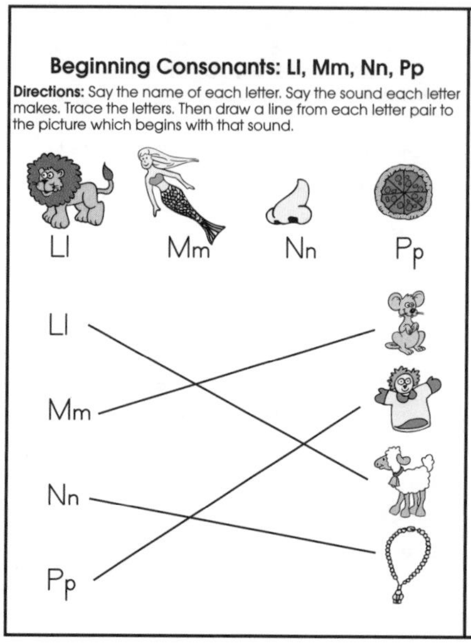

Beginning Consonants: Ll, Mm, Nn, Pp

Directions: Say the name of each letter. Say the sound each letter makes. Trace the letters. Then draw a line from each letter pair to the picture which begins with that sound.

Page 17

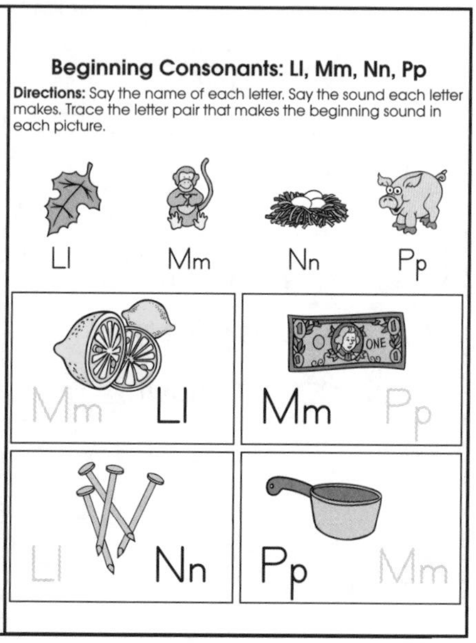

Beginning Consonants: Ll, Mm, Nn, Pp

Directions: Say the name of each letter. Say the sound each letter makes. Trace the letter pair that makes the beginning sound in each picture.

Answer Key

Page 18

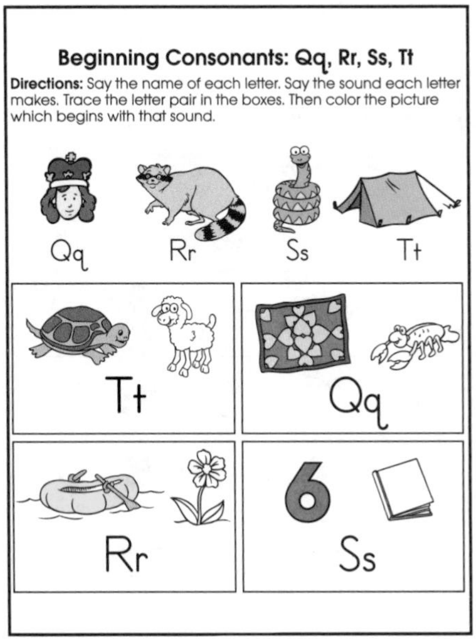

Beginning Consonants: Qq, Rr, Ss, Tt

Directions: Say the name of each letter. Say the sound each letter makes. Trace the letter pair in the boxes. Then color the picture which begins with that sound.

Page 19

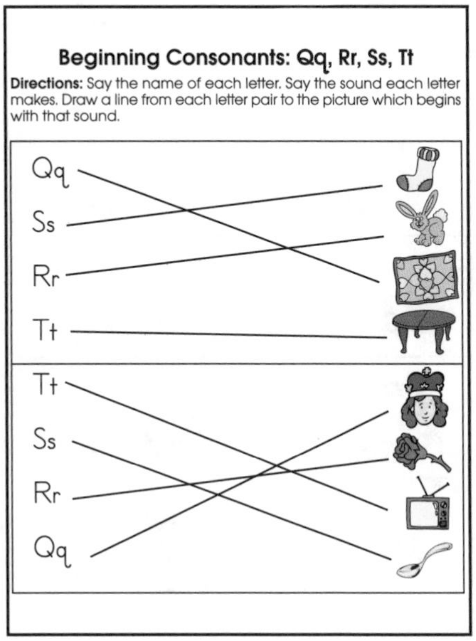

Beginning Consonants: Qq, Rr, Ss, Tt

Directions: Say the name of each letter. Say the sound each letter makes. Draw a line from each letter pair to the picture which begins with that sound.

Page 20

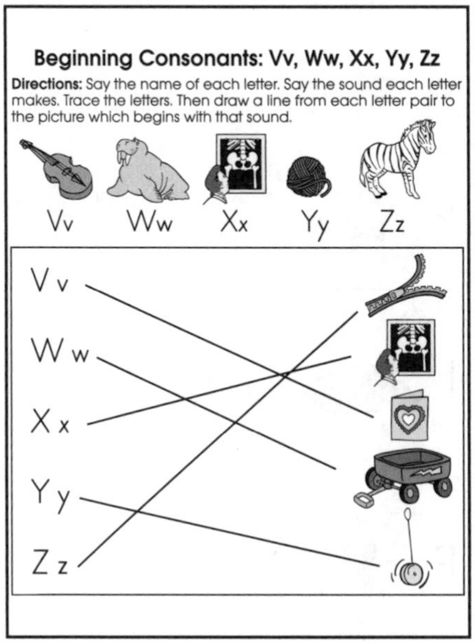

Beginning Consonants: Vv, Ww, Xx, Yy, Zz

Directions: Say the name of each letter. Say the sound each letter makes. Trace the letters. Then draw a line from each letter pair to the picture which begins with that sound.

Page 21

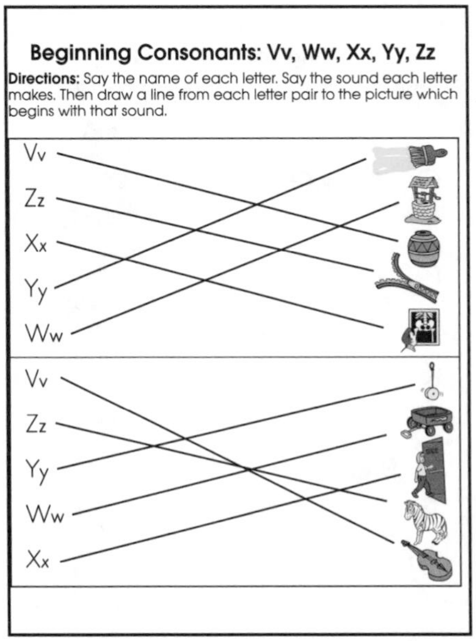

Beginning Consonants: Vv, Ww, Xx, Yy, Zz

Directions: Say the name of each letter. Say the sound each letter makes. Then draw a line from each letter pair to the picture which begins with that sound.

Page 22

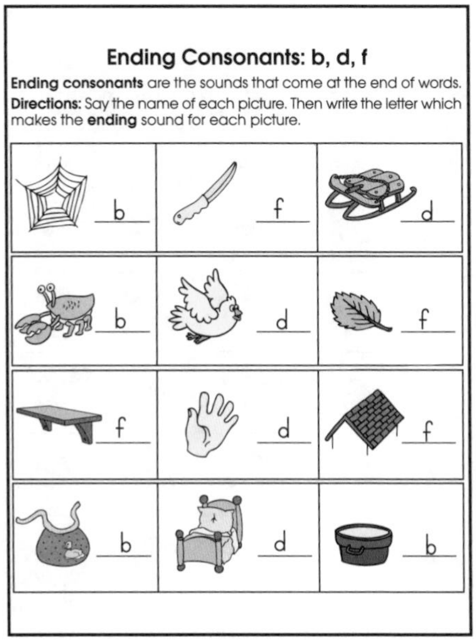

Ending Consonants: b, d, f

Ending consonants are the sounds that come at the end of words.

Directions: Say the name of each picture. Then write the letter which makes the **ending** sound for each picture.

Page 23

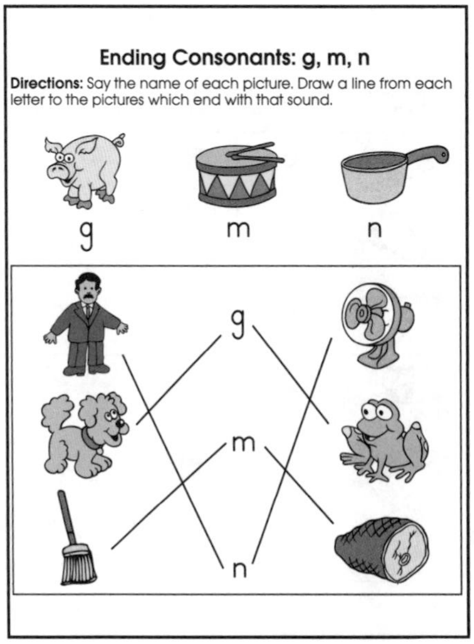

Ending Consonants: g, m, n

Directions: Say the name of each picture. Draw a line from each letter to the pictures which end with that sound.

Answer Key

Page 24

Ending Consonants: k, l, p

Directions: Trace the letters in each row. Say the name of each picture. Then color the pictures in each row which end with that sound.

k

l

p

Page 25

Ending Consonants: r, s, t, x

Directions: Say the name of each picture. Then circle the ending sound for each picture.

(r) s t x | r (s) t x

(r) s t x | r s (t) x

r s (t) x | r (s) t x

r s t (x) | r s (t) x

Page 26

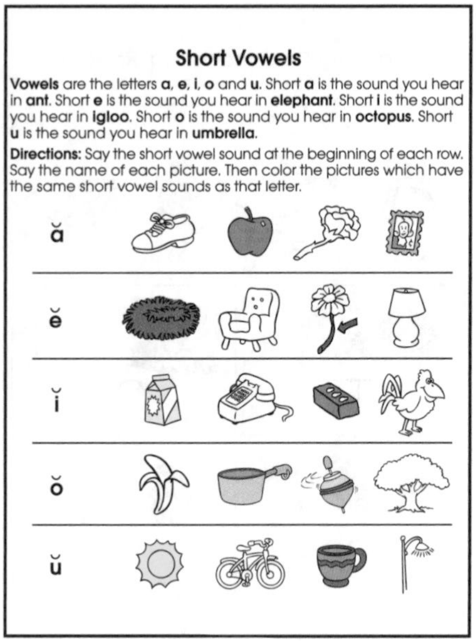

Short Vowels

Vowels are the letters **a**, **e**, **i**, **o** and **u**. Short **a** is the sound you hear in **ant**. Short **e** is the sound you hear in **elephant**. Short **i** is the sound you hear in **igloo**. Short **o** is the sound you hear in **octopus**. Short **u** is the sound you hear in **umbrella**.

Directions: Say the short vowel sound at the beginning of each row. Say the name of each picture. Then color the pictures which have the same short vowel sounds as that letter.

ă

ĕ

ĭ

ŏ

ŭ

Page 27

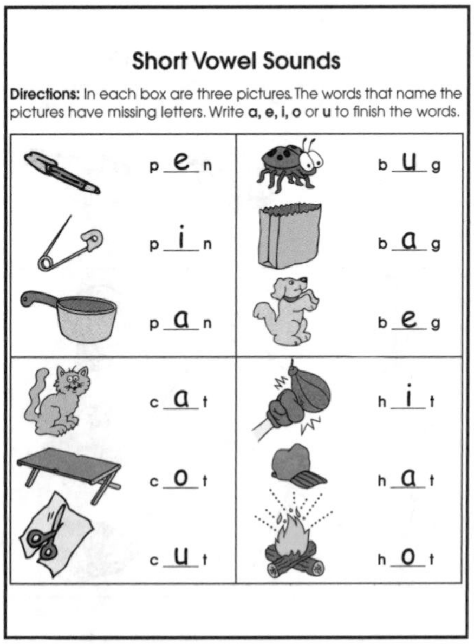

Short Vowel Sounds

Directions: In each box are three pictures. The words that name the pictures have missing letters. Write **a**, **e**, **i**, **o** or **u** to finish the words.

p e n | b u g

p i n | b a g

p a n | b e g

c a t | h i t

c o t | h a t

c u t | h o t

Page 28

Long Vowels

Vowels are the letters **a**, **e**, **i**, **o** and **u**. Long vowel sounds say their own names. Long **a** is the sound you hear in **hay**. Long **e** is the sound you hear in **me**. Long **i** is the sound you hear in **pie**. Long **o** is the sound you hear in **no**. Long **u** is the sound you hear in **cute**.

Directions: Say the long vowel sound at the beginning of each row. Say the name of each picture. Color the pictures in each row that have the same long vowel sound as that letter.

ā

ē

ī

ō

ū

Page 29

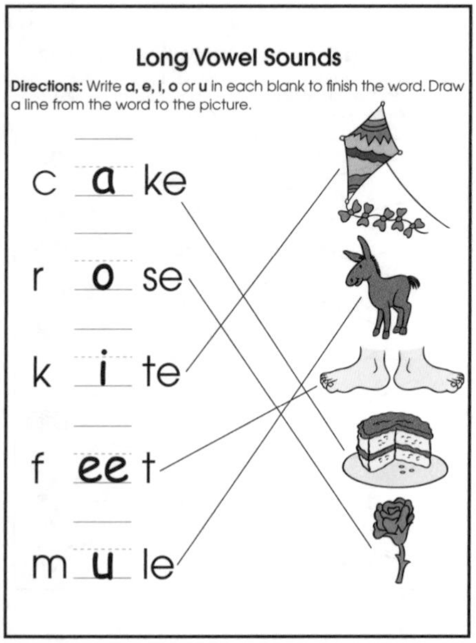

Long Vowel Sounds

Directions: Write **a**, **e**, **i**, **o** or **u** in each blank to finish the word. Draw a line from the word to the picture.

c a ke

r o se

k i te

f ee t

m u le

Answer Key

Page 30

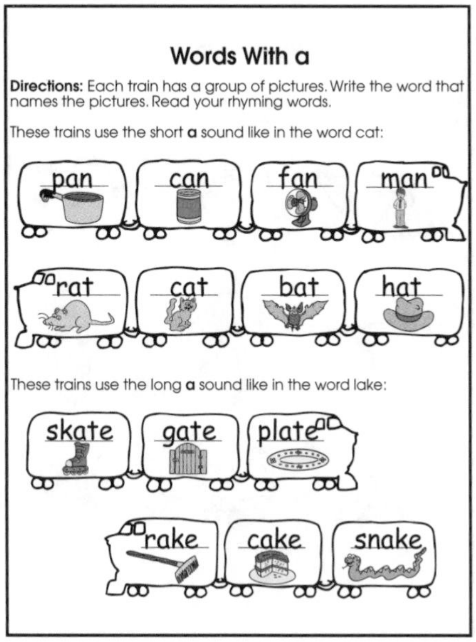

Words With a

Directions: Each train has a group of pictures. Write the word that names the pictures. Read your rhyming words.

These trains use the short **a** sound like in the word cat:

pan can fan man

rat cat bat hat

These trains use the long **a** sound like in the word lake:

skate gate plate

rake cake snake

Page 31

Short and Long Aa

Directions: Say the name of each picture. If it has the short **a** sound, color it **red**. If it has the long **a** sound, color it **yellow**.

Page 32

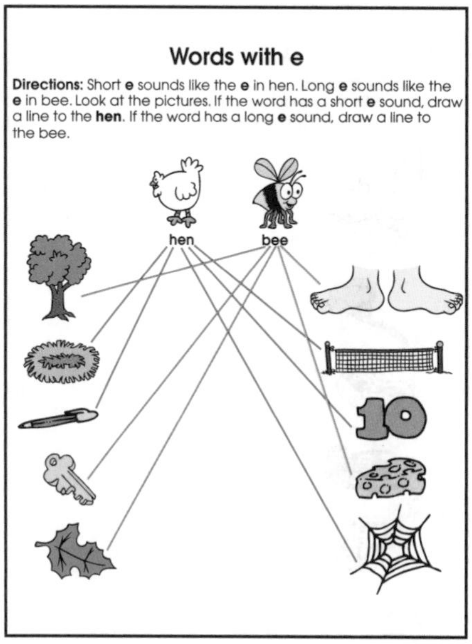

Words with e

Directions: Short **e** sounds like the **e** in hen. Long **e** sounds like the **e** in bee. Look at the pictures. If the word has a short **e** sound, draw a line to the **hen**. If the word has a long **e** sound, draw a line to the bee.

Page 33

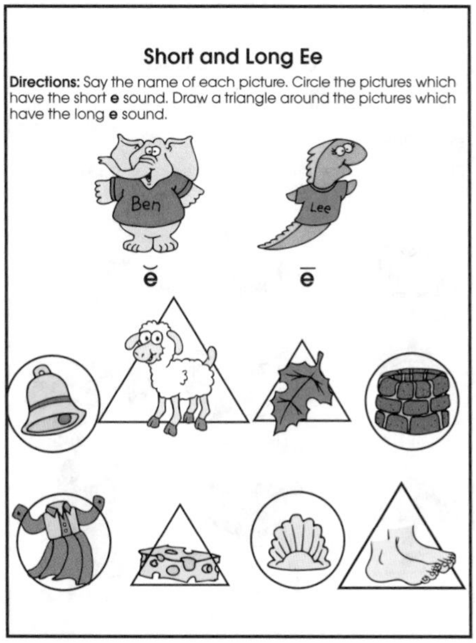

Short and Long Ee

Directions: Say the name of each picture. Circle the pictures which have the short **e** sound. Draw a triangle around the pictures which have the long **e** sound.

Page 34

Words with i

Directions: Short **i** sounds like the **i** in pig. Long **i** sounds like the **i** in kite. Draw a circle around the words with the short **i** sound. Draw an **X** on the words with the long **i** sound.

Page 35

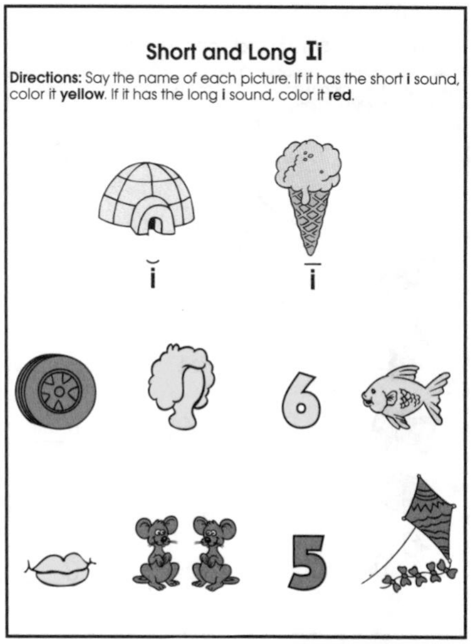

Short and Long Ii

Directions: Say the name of each picture. If it has the short **i** sound, color it **yellow**. If it has the long **i** sound, color it **red**.

Answer Key

Page 36

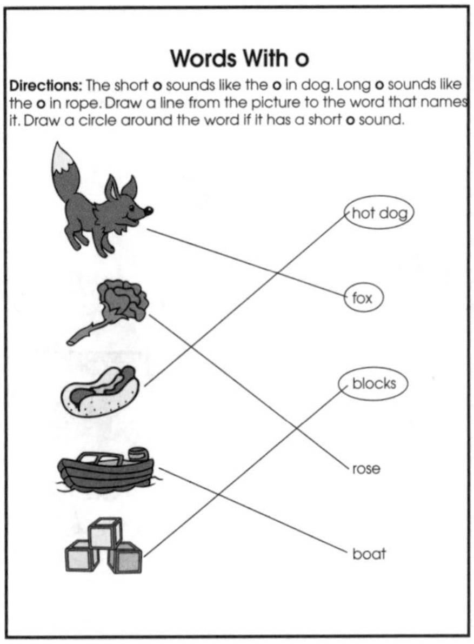

Words With o

Directions: The short **o** sounds like the **o** in dog. Long **o** sounds like the **o** in rope. Draw a line from the picture to the word that names it. Draw a circle around the word if it has a short **o** sound.

hot dog
fox
blocks
rose
boat

Page 37

Short and Long Oo

Directions: Say the name of each picture. If the picture has the long **o** sound write an **L** on the blank. If the picture has the short **o** sound, write an **S** on the blank.

L S
S S L
L S L

Page 38

Words With u

Directions: The short **u** sounds like the **u** in bug. The long **u** sounds like the **u** in blue. Draw a circle around the words with short **u**. Draw an **X** on the words with long **u**.

rug cup music
tub suit glue
bug puppy gum

Page 39

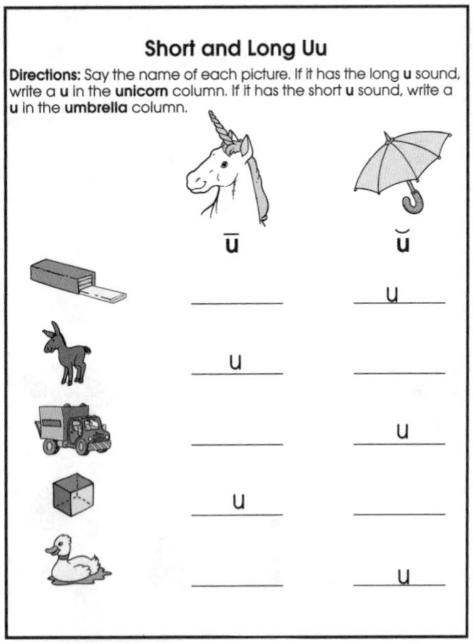

Short and Long Uu

Directions: Say the name of each picture. If it has the long **u** sound, write a **u** in the **unicorn** column. If it has the short **u** sound, write a **u** in the **umbrella** column.

ū	ŭ
	u
u	
	u
u	
	u

Page 40

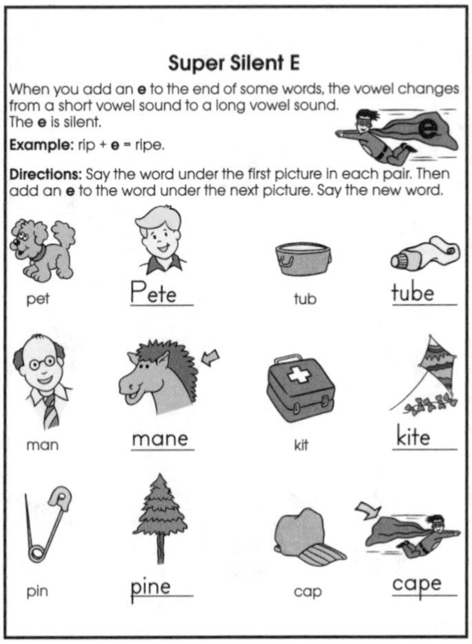

Super Silent E

When you add an **e** to the end of some words, the vowel changes from a short vowel sound to a long vowel sound. The **e** is silent.

Example: rip + **e** = ripe.

Directions: Say the word under the first picture in each pair. Then add an **e** to the word under the next picture. Say the new word.

pet Pete tub tube
man mane kit kite
pin pine cap cape

Page 41

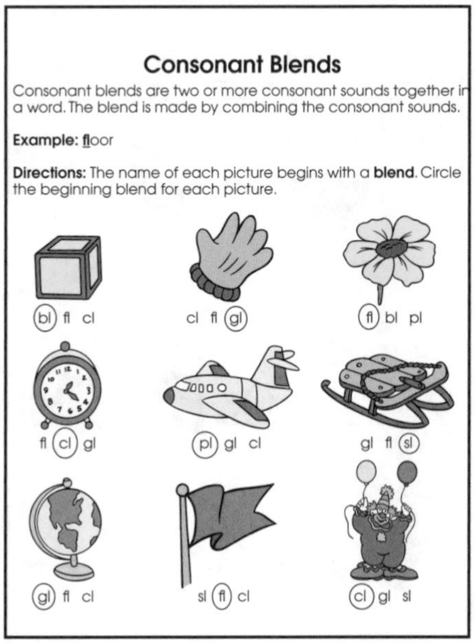

Consonant Blends

Consonant blends are two or more consonant sounds together in a word. The blend is made by combining the consonant sounds.

Example: floor

Directions: The name of each picture begins with a **blend**. Circle the beginning blend for each picture.

bl fl cl — cl fl gl — fl bl pl
fl cl gl — pl gl cl — gl fl sl
gl fl cl — sl fl cl — cl gl sl

Answer Key

Page 42

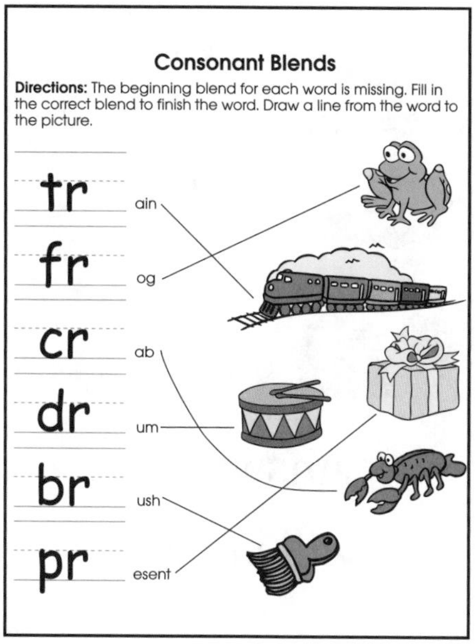

Consonant Blends

Directions: The beginning blend for each word is missing. Fill in the correct blend to finish the word. Draw a line from the word to the picture.

tr ain
fr og
cr ab
dr um
br ush
pr esent

Page 43

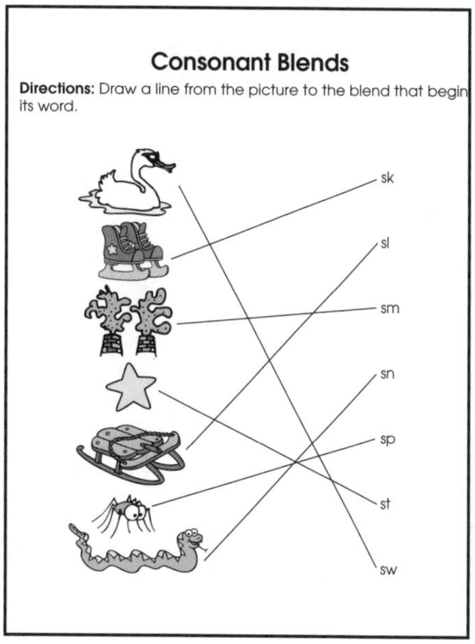

Consonant Blends

Directions: Draw a line from the picture to the blend that begin its word.

sk
sl
sm
sn
sp
st
sw

Page 44

Consonant Teams

Consonant teams are two or more consonants that work together to make a single sound. **Example:** show

Directions: Look at the first picture in each row. Circle the pictures in the row that begin with the same sound.

chair
shell
thumb
wheel

Page 45

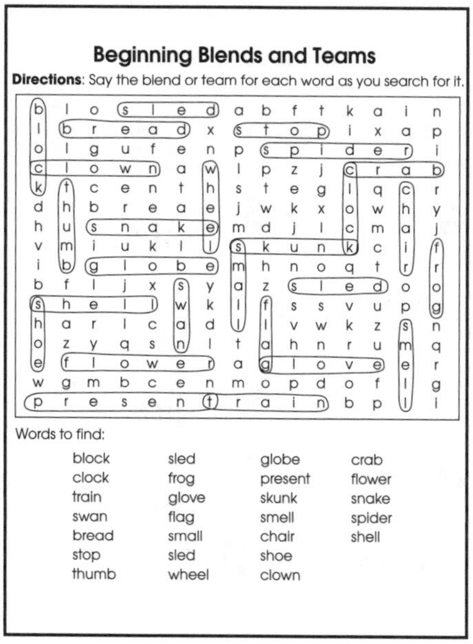

Beginning Blends and Teams

Directions: Say the blend or team for each word as you search for it.

b	l	o	s	l	e	d	a	b	f	t	k	a	i	n
l	b	r	e	a	d	x	s	t	o	p	i	x	a	p
o	l	g	u	f	e	n	p	s	p	i	d	e	r	i
c	l	o	w	n	a	w	l	p	z	j	c	r	a	b
k	t	c	e	n	t	h	s	t	e	g	l	q	c	r
d	h	b	r	e	a	e	j	w	k	x	o	w	h	y
h	u	s	n	a	k	e	m	d	j	l	c	m	a	j
v	m	i	u	k	l	l	s	k	u	n	k	c	i	f
i	b	g	l	o	b	e	m	h	n	o	q	t	r	r
b	f	l	j	x	s	y	a	z	s	l	e	d	o	o
s	h	e	l	l	w	k	l	f	s	s	v	u	p	g
h	a	r	l	c	a	d	l	l	v	w	k	z	s	n
o	z	y	q	s	n	l	t	a	h	n	r	u	m	q
e	f	l	o	w	e	r	a	g	l	o	v	e	e	r
w	g	m	b	c	e	n	m	o	p	d	o	f	l	g
p	r	e	s	e	n	t	r	a	i	n	b	p	l	i

Words to find:

block	sled	globe	crab
clock	frog	present	flower
train	glove	skunk	snake
swan	flag	smell	spider
bread	small	chair	shell
stop	sled	shoe	
thumb	wheel	clown	

Page 46

Ending Consonant Blends

Directions: Write **lt** or **ft** to complete the words.

be lt
ra ft
sa lt
qui lt
le ft

Page 47

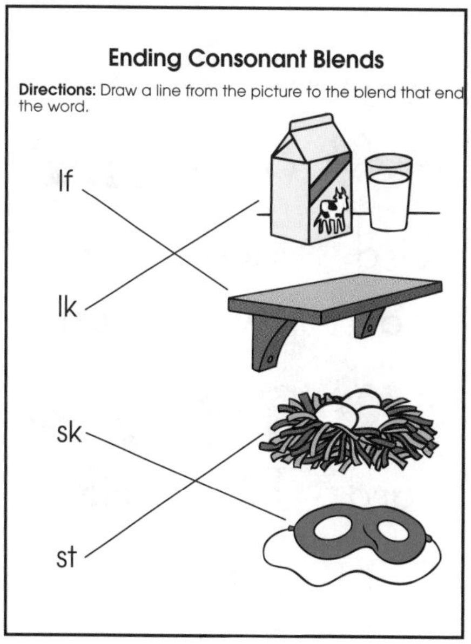

Ending Consonant Blends

Directions: Draw a line from the picture to the blend that end the word.

lf
lk
sk
st

Page 48

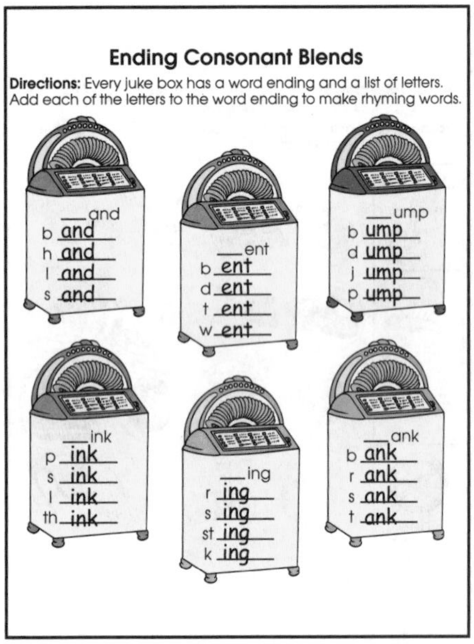

Ending Consonant Blends

Directions: Every juke box has a word ending and a list of letters. Add each of the letters to the word ending to make rhyming words.

___and: b and, h and, l and, s and

___ent: b ent, d ent, t ent, w ent

___ump: b ump, d ump, j ump, p ump

___ink: p ink, s ink, l ink, th ink

___ing: r ing, s ing, st ing, k ing

___ank: b ank, r ank, s ank, t ank

Page 49

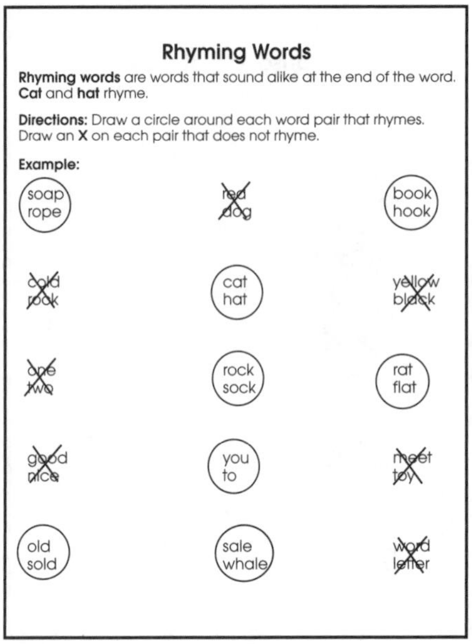

Rhyming Words

Rhyming words are words that sound alike at the end of the word. **Cat** and **hat** rhyme.

Directions: Draw a circle around each word pair that rhymes. Draw an **X** on each pair that does not rhyme.

Example:

soap rope (circled) — red dog (X) — book hook (circled)

cold rock (X) — cat hat (circled) — yellow black (X)

one two (X) — rock sock (circled) — rat flat (circled)

good nice (X) — you to (circled) — meet toy (X)

old sold (circled) — sale whale (circled) — word letter (X)

Page 50

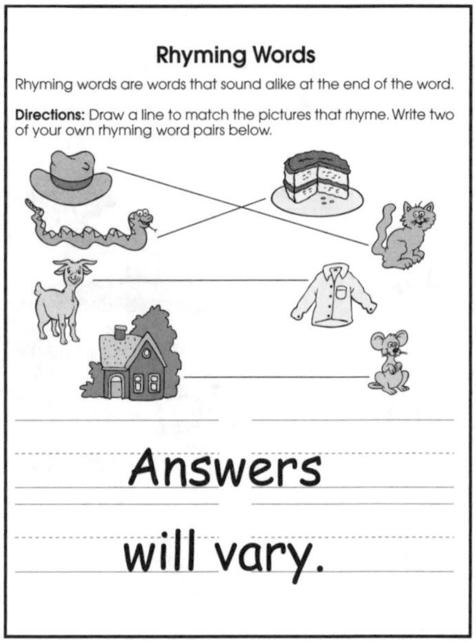

Rhyming Words

Rhyming words are words that sound alike at the end of the word.

Directions: Draw a line to match the pictures that rhyme. Write two of your own rhyming word pairs below.

Answers will vary.

Page 51

ABC Order

Directions: Circle the first letter of each word. Then put each pair of words in abc order.

car bird — moon two — nest fan

bird, car — moon, two — fan, nest

card dog — pig bike — sun pie

card, dog — bike, pig — pie, sun

Page 52

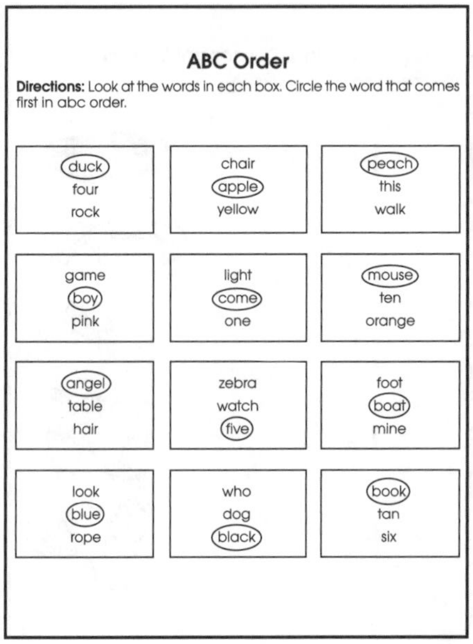

ABC Order

Directions: Look at the words in each box. Circle the word that comes first in abc order.

(duck) four rock	chair (apple) yellow	(peach) this walk
game (boy) pink	light (come) one	(mouse) ten orange
(angel) table hair	zebra watch (five)	foot (boat) mine
look (blue) rope	who dog (black)	(book) tan six

Page 53

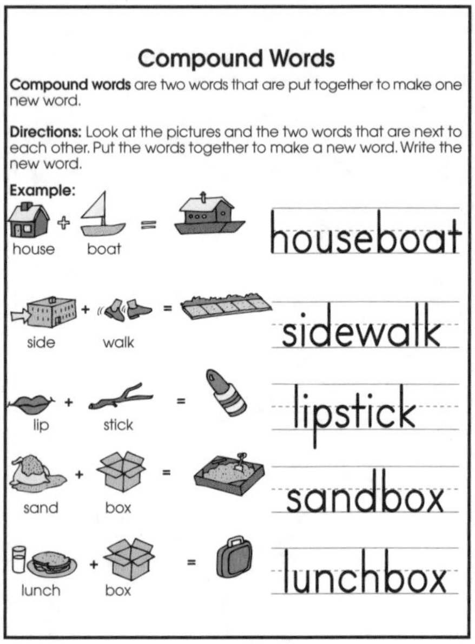

Compound Words

Compound words are two words that are put together to make one new word.

Directions: Look at the pictures and the two words that are next to each other. Put the words together to make a new word. Write the new word.

Example:

house + boat = houseboat

side + walk = sidewalk

lip + stick = lipstick

sand + box = sandbox

lunch + box = lunchbox

Answer Key

Page 54

Compound Words

Directions: Circle the compound word which completes each sentence. Write each word on the lines.

1. The **mailman** brings us letters. (mailman) snowman
2. A **sunflower** grows tall. sunlight (sunflower)
3. The snow falls **outside**. (outside) inside
4. A **raindrop** fell on my head. (raindrop) rainbow
5. I put the letter in a **mailbox**. (mailbox) shoebox

Page 55

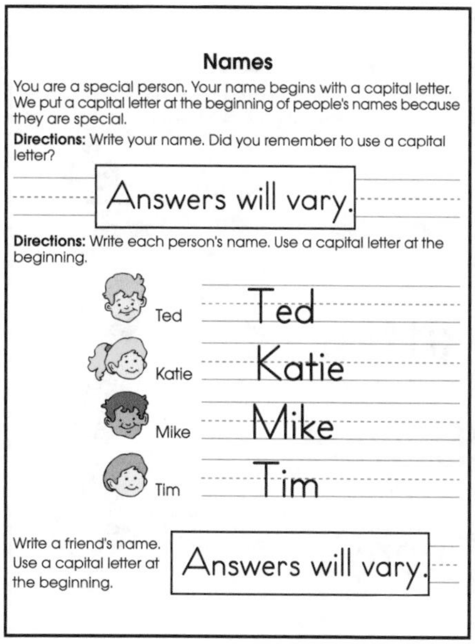

Names

You are a special person. Your name begins with a capital letter. We put a capital letter at the beginning of people's names because they are special.

Directions: Write your name. Did you remember to use a capital letter?

Answers will vary.

Directions: Write each person's name. Use a capital letter at the beginning.

Ted — Ted
Katie — Katie
Mike — Mike
Tim — Tim

Write a friend's name. Use a capital letter at the beginning. Answers will vary.

Page 56

Names: Days of the Week

The days of the week begin with capital letters.

Directions: Write the days of the week in the spaces below. Put them in order. Be sure to start with capital letters.

Tuesday
Saturday
Monday
Friday
Thursday
Sunday
Wednesday

Sunday
Monday
Tuesday
Wednesday
Thursday
Friday
Saturday

Page 57

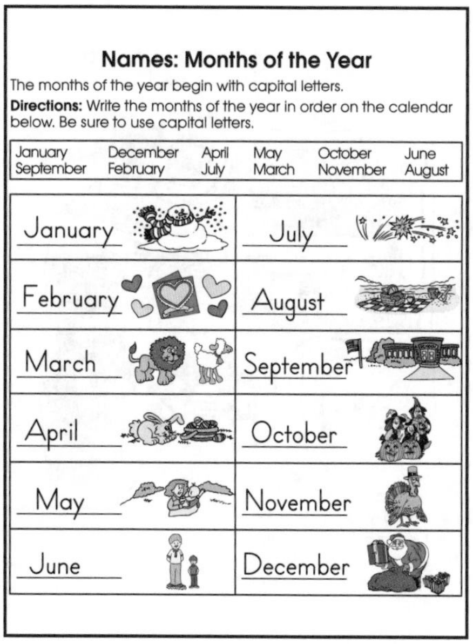

Names: Months of the Year

The months of the year begin with capital letters.

Directions: Write the months of the year in order on the calendar below. Be sure to use capital letters.

January	December	April	May	October	June
September	February	July	March	November	August

January	July
February	August
March	September
April	October
May	November
June	December

Page 58

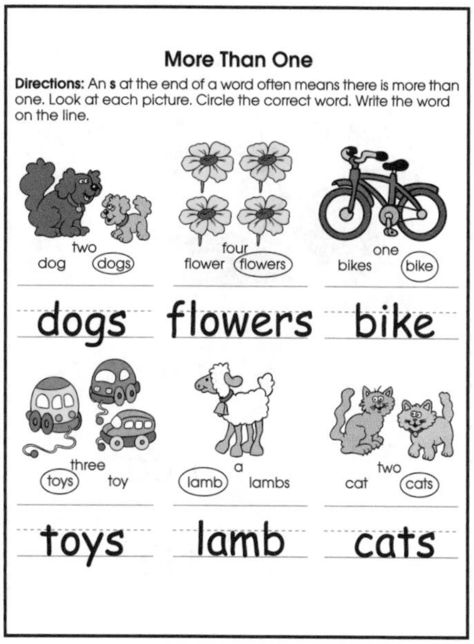

More Than One

Directions: An **s** at the end of a word often means there is more than one. Look at each picture. Circle the correct word. Write the word on the line.

two: dog (dogs) — **dogs**
four: flower (flowers) — **flowers**
one: bikes (bike) — **bike**
three: (toys) toy — **toys**
a: (lamb) lambs — **lamb**
two: cat (cats) — **cats**

Page 60

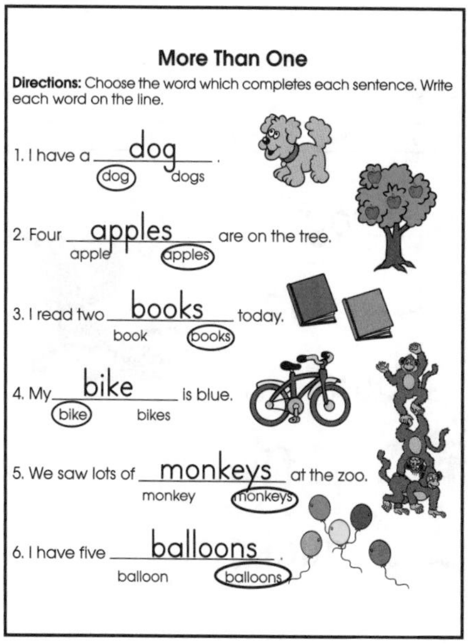

More Than One

Directions: Choose the word which completes each sentence. Write each word on the line.

1. I have a **dog**. (dog) dogs
2. Four **apples** are on the tree. apple (apples)
3. I read two **books** today. book (books)
4. My **bike** is blue. (bike) bikes
5. We saw lots of **monkeys** at the zoo. monkey (monkeys)
6. I have five **balloons**. balloon (balloons)

Answer Key

Page 61

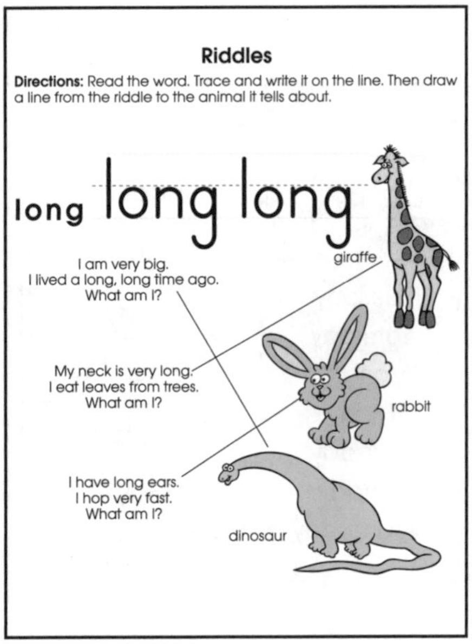

Riddles

Directions: Read the word. Trace and write it on the line. Then draw a line from the riddle to the animal it tells about.

long long long

I am very big.
I lived a long, long time ago.
What am I?

My neck is very long.
I eat leaves from trees.
What am I?

I have long ears.
I hop very fast.
What am I?

giraffe

rabbit

dinosaur

Page 62

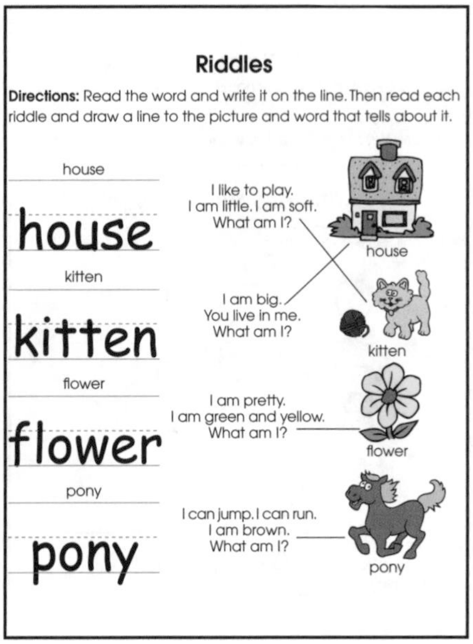

Riddles

Directions: Read the word and write it on the line. Then read each riddle and draw a line to the picture and word that tells about it.

house

house

kitten

kitten

flower

flower

pony

pony

I like to play.
I am little. I am soft.
What am I?

I am big.
You live in me.
What am I?

I am pretty.
I am green and yellow.
What am I?

I can jump. I can run.
I am brown.
What am I?

house

kitten

flower

pony

Page 63

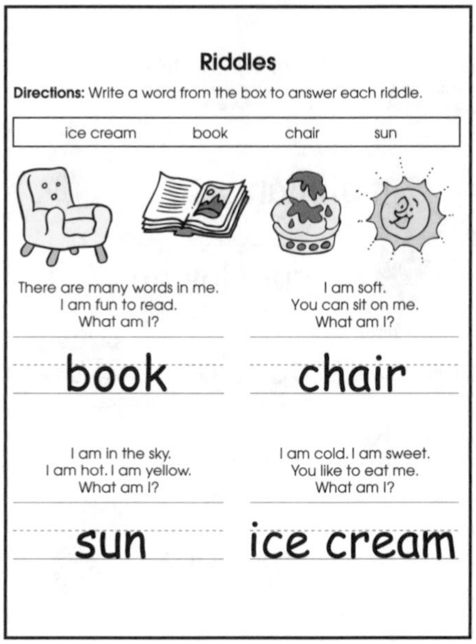

Riddles

Directions: Write a word from the box to answer each riddle.

ice cream	book	chair	sun

There are many words in me.
I am fun to read.
What am I?

book

I am soft.
You can sit on me.
What am I?

chair

I am in the sky.
I am hot. I am yellow.
What am I?

sun

I am cold. I am sweet.
You like to eat me.
What am I?

ice cream

Page 64

Comprehension

Directions: Look at the picture. Write the words from the box to finish the sentences.

frog	log	bird	fish	ducks

The frog can jump.

The turtle is on a log.

A bird is in the tree.

The boy wants a fish.

I see three ducks.

Page 65

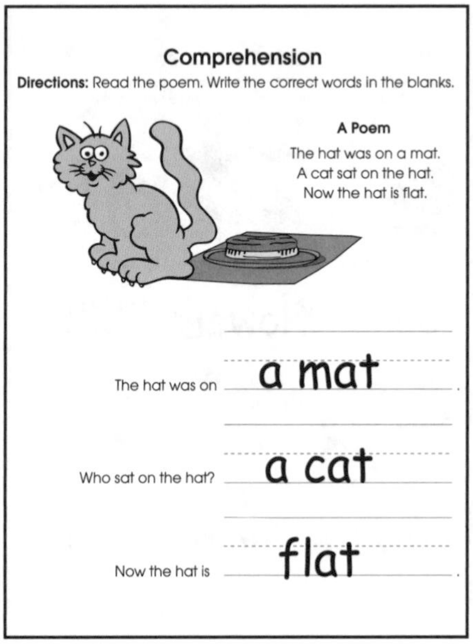

Comprehension

Directions: Read the poem. Write the correct words in the blanks.

A Poem

The hat was on a mat.
A cat sat on the hat.
Now the hat is flat.

The hat was on a mat.

Who sat on the hat? a cat

Now the hat is flat.

Page 66

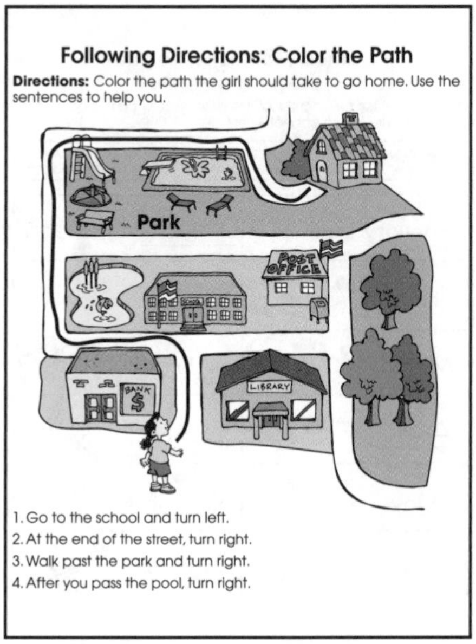

Following Directions: Color the Path

Directions: Color the path the girl should take to go home. Use the sentences to help you.

1. Go to the school and turn left.
2. At the end of the street, turn right.
3. Walk past the park and turn right.
4. After you pass the pool, turn right.

Answer Key

Page 67

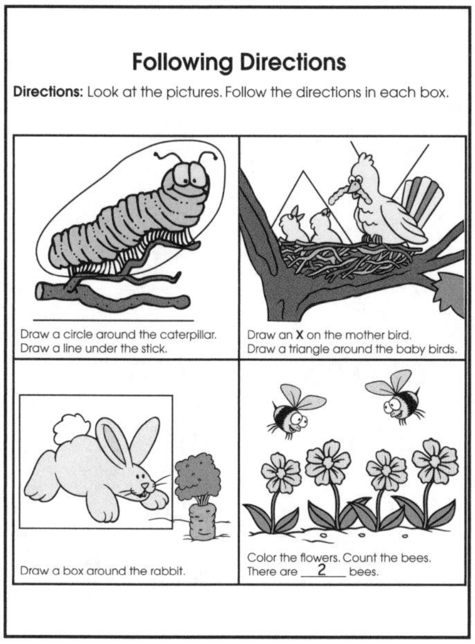
Following Directions

Directions: Look at the pictures. Follow the directions in each box.

Draw a circle around the caterpillar. Draw a line under the stick.

Draw an **X** on the mother bird. Draw a triangle around the baby birds.

Draw a box around the rabbit.

Color the flowers. Count the bees. There are 2 bees.

Page 68

Classifying

Directions: Classifying is sorting things into groups. Draw a circle around the pictures that answer the question.

What Can Swim?

What Can Fly?

Page 69

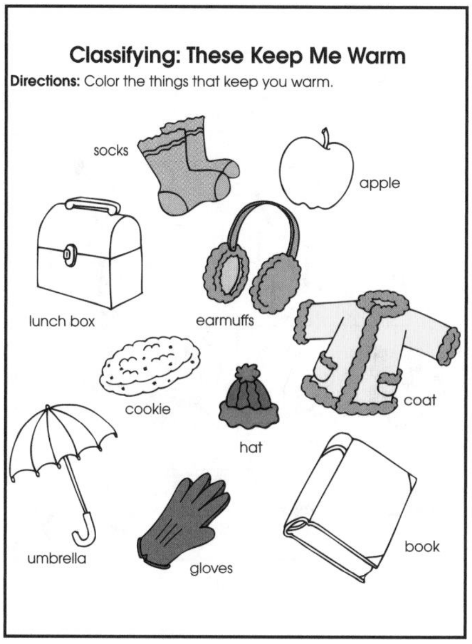
Classifying: These Keep Me Warm

Directions: Color the things that keep you warm.

socks

apple

lunch box

earmuffs

coat

cookie

hat

umbrella

gloves

book

Page 70

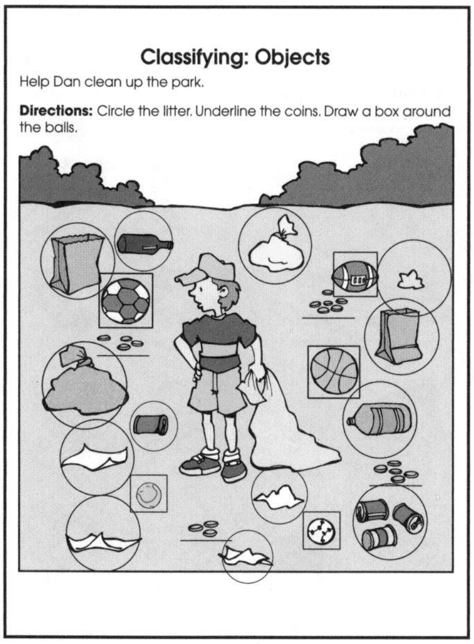
Classifying: Objects

Help Dan clean up the park.

Directions: Circle the litter. Underline the coins. Draw a box around the balls.

Page 71

Classifying: Things to Drink

Directions: Circle the pictures of things you can drink. Write the names of those things in the blanks.

milk

ice

soup and crackers

juice

soda

ice-cream bar

milk

juice

soda

Page 72

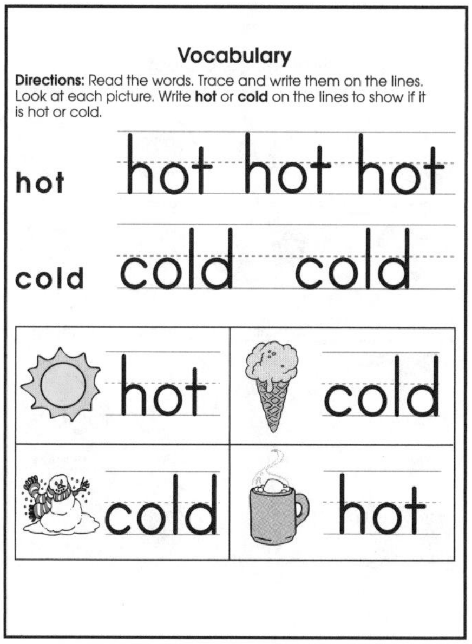
Vocabulary

Directions: Read the words. Trace and write them on the lines. Look at each picture. Write **hot** or **cold** on the lines to show if it is hot or cold.

hot hot hot hot

cold cold cold

hot

cold

cold

hot

Page 73

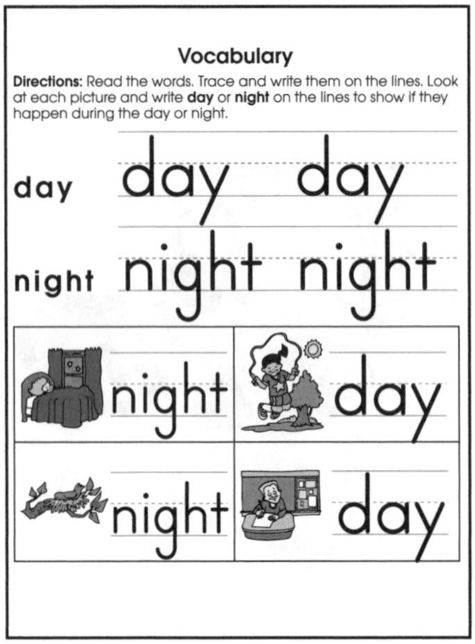

Vocabulary

Directions: Read the words. Trace and write them on the lines. Look at each picture and write **day** or **night** on the lines to show if they happen during the day or night.

day — day day

night — night night

night | day

night | day

Page 74

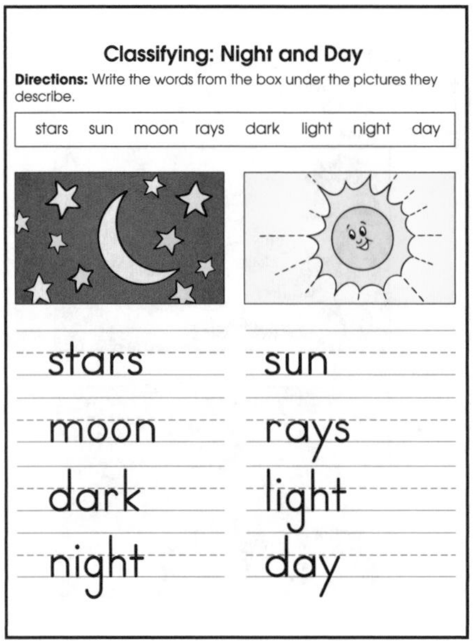

Classifying: Night and Day

Directions: Write the words from the box under the pictures they describe.

stars sun moon rays dark light night day

stars	sun
moon	rays
dark	light
night	day

Page 75

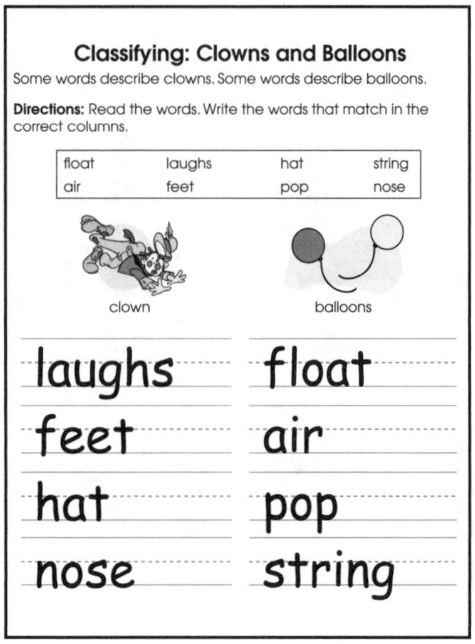

Classifying: Clowns and Balloons

Some words describe clowns. Some words describe balloons.

Directions: Read the words. Write the words that match in the correct columns.

float laughs hat string air feet pop nose

clown	balloons
laughs	float
feet	air
hat	pop
nose	string

Page 76

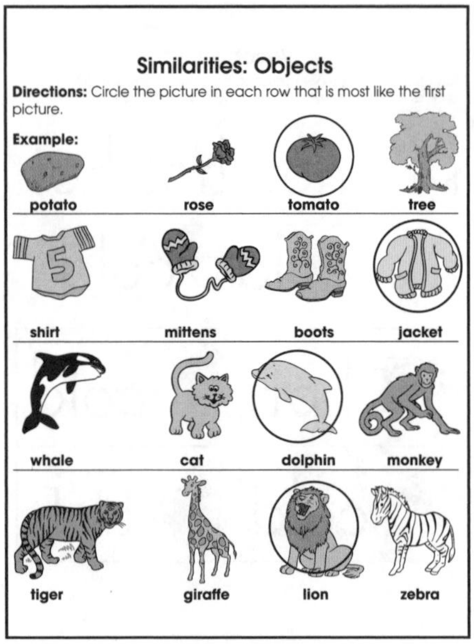

Similarities: Objects

Directions: Circle the picture in each row that is most like the first picture.

Example:

potato rose tomato tree

shirt mittens boots jacket

whale cat dolphin monkey

tiger giraffe lion zebra

Page 77

Similarities: Objects

Directions: Circle the picture in each row that is most like the first picture.

Example:

carrot jacks bread pea

baseball sneakers basketball bat

store school home bakery

kitten dog fox cat

Page 78

Classifying: Food Groups

Directions: Color the meats and eggs blue. Color the fruits and vegetables green. Color the breads tan. Color the dairy foods (milk and cheese) yellow.

fish bread apple cheese

crackers carrot orange eggs

steaks pear milk yogurt

ice cream chicken potato pretzel

Answer Key

Page 79

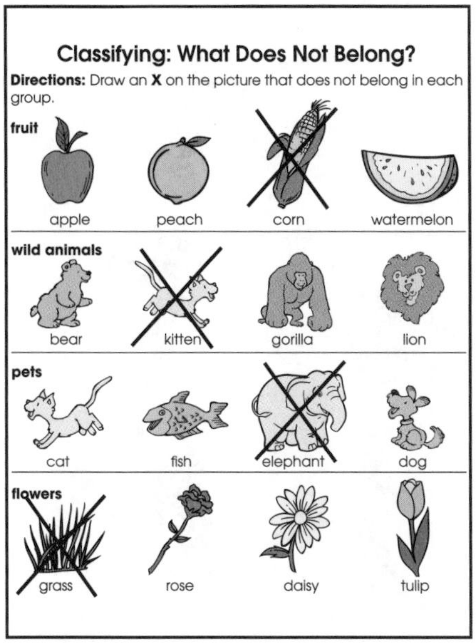

Classifying: What Does Not Belong?

Directions: Draw an **X** on the picture that does not belong in each group.

Page 80

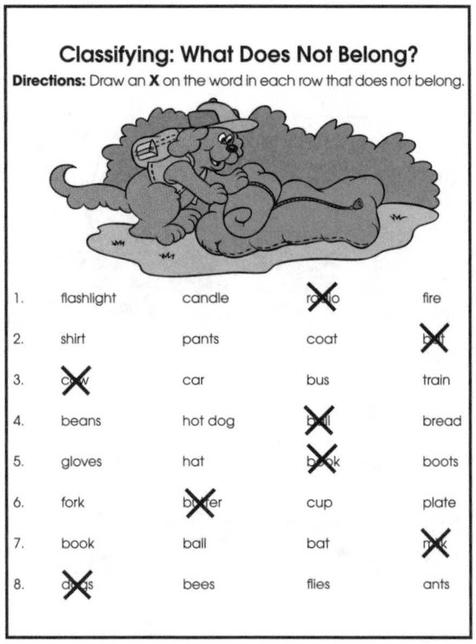

Classifying: What Does Not Belong?

Directions: Draw an **X** on the word in each row that does not belong.

1.	flashlight	candle	radio	fire
2.	shirt	pants	coat	belt
3.	cow	car	bus	train
4.	beans	hot dog	ball	bread
5.	gloves	hat	book	boots
6.	fork	butter	cup	plate
7.	book	ball	bat	milk
8.	dogs	bees	flies	ants

Page 81

Classifying: Objects

Directions: Write each word in the correct row at the bottom of the page.

Things we ride in:

airplane, car, boat

Things we eat with:

plate, spoon, fork

Things we draw with:

pencil, crayon, chalk

Things we listen to:

drum, radio, television

Page 82

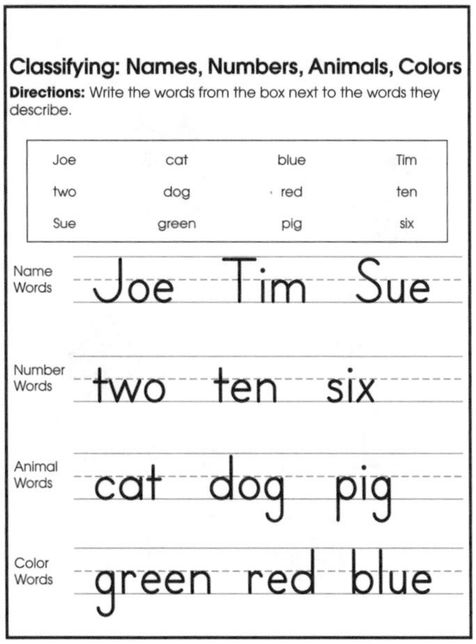

Classifying: Names, Numbers, Animals, Colors

Directions: Write the words from the box next to the words they describe.

Joe	cat	blue	Tim
two	dog	red	ten
Sue	green	pig	six

Name Words: Joe Tim Sue

Number Words: two ten six

Animal Words: cat dog pig

Color Words: green red blue

Page 83

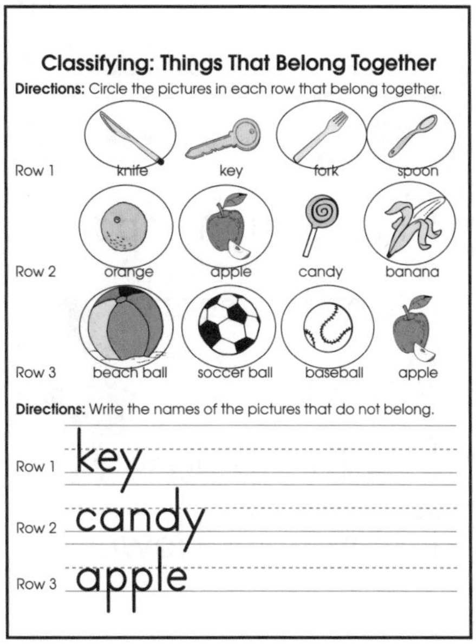

Classifying: Things That Belong Together

Directions: Circle the pictures in each row that belong together.

Directions: Write the names of the pictures that do not belong.

Row 1 key

Row 2 candy

Row 3 apple

Page 84

Classifying: Why They Are Different

Directions: Look at your answers on page 83. Write why each object does not belong.

You don't eat with a key.
A candy is not a fruit.
An apple is not a ball.

Directions: For each object, draw a group of pictures that belong with it.

candy bar

Drawings will vary.

lettuce

Drawings will vary.

Page 85

Sequencing: Fill the Glasses

Directions: Follow the instructions to fill each glass. Use crayons to draw your favorite drink in the ones that are full and half-full.

full
half-full
empty
empty
half-full
full

Page 86

Sequencing: Raking Leaves

Directions: Write a number in each box to show the order of the story.

1
4
3
2

Page 87

Sequencing: Make a Snowman!

Directions: Write the number of the sentence that goes with each picture in the box.

1. Roll a large snowball for the snowman's bottom.
2. Make another snowball and put it on top of the first.
3. Put the last snowball on top.
4. Dress the snowman.

1
3
2
4

Page 88

Sequencing: A Recipe

Directions: Look at the recipe below. Put each step in order. Write **1, 2, 3** or **4** in the box.

HOW TO MAKE BREAD BUDDIES

3 Roll dough into balls and shapes. Connect pieces with a drop of water.

1 Mix 1 cup of water, 1 cup of salt and 3 cups of flour.

2 Knead the dough.

4 Have an adult bake your bread buddy for 2-3 hours at 300°. Let it cool. Then paint it!

What kind of bread buddy did you make?

Answers will vary.

Page 89

Sequencing: How Flowers Grow

Directions: Read the story. Then write the steps to grow a flower.

First find a sunny spot. Then plant the seed. Water it. The flower will start to grow. Pull the weeds around it. Remember to keep giving the flower water. Enjoy your flower.

1. Find a sunny spot.
2. Plant the seed.
3. Water it.
4. Pull the weeds.
5. Enjoy your flower.

Page 90

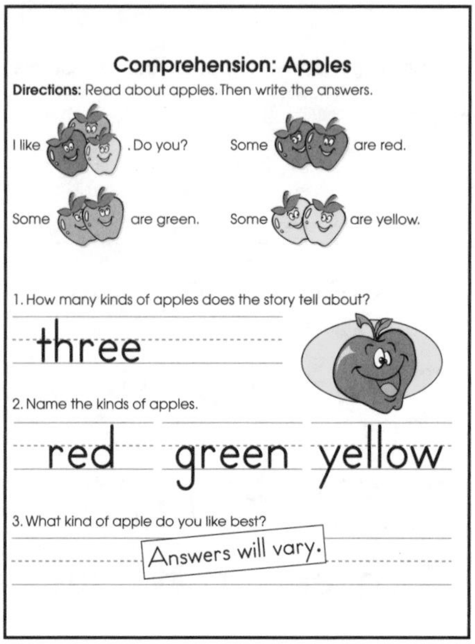

Comprehension: Apples

Directions: Read about apples. Then write the answers.

I like apples. Do you? Some are red. Some are green. Some are yellow.

1. How many kinds of apples does the story tell about?

three

2. Name the kinds of apples.

red green yellow

3. What kind of apple do you like best?

Answers will vary.

Answer Key

Page 91

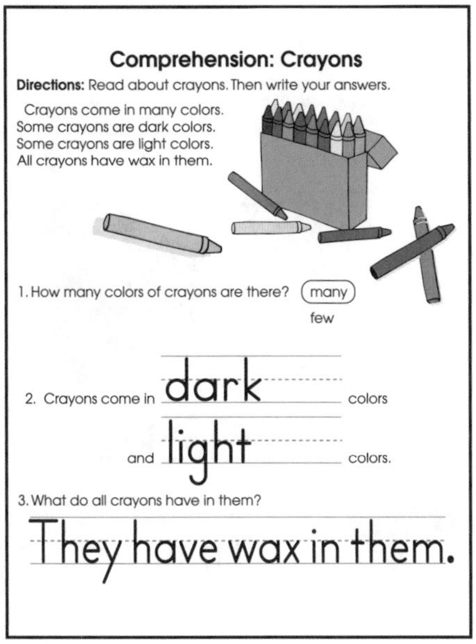

Comprehension: Crayons

Directions: Read about crayons. Then write your answers.

Crayons come in many colors.
Some crayons are dark colors.
Some crayons are light colors.
All crayons have wax in them.

1. How many colors of crayons are there? (many) few

2. Crayons come in dark colors and light colors.

3. What do all crayons have in them?

They have wax in them.

Page 92

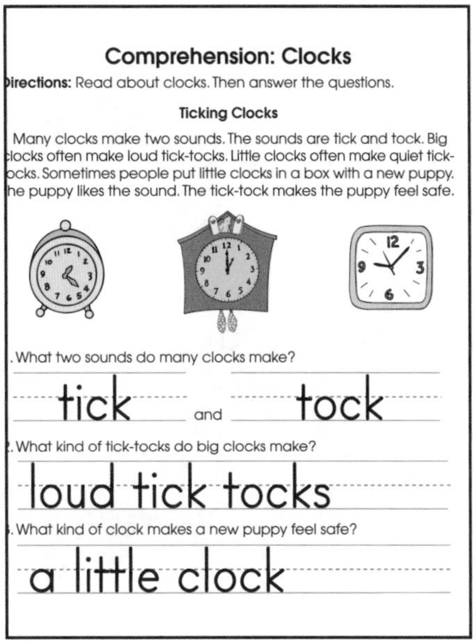

Comprehension: Clocks

irections: Read about clocks. Then answer the questions.

Ticking Clocks

Many clocks make two sounds. The sounds are tick and tock. Big locks often make loud tick-tocks. Little clocks often make quiet tick-ocks. Sometimes people put little clocks in a box with a new puppy. he puppy likes the sound. The tick-tock makes the puppy feel safe.

. What two sounds do many clocks make?

tick and tock

. What kind of tick-tocks do big clocks make?

loud tick tocks

. What kind of clock makes a new puppy feel safe?

a little clock

Page 93

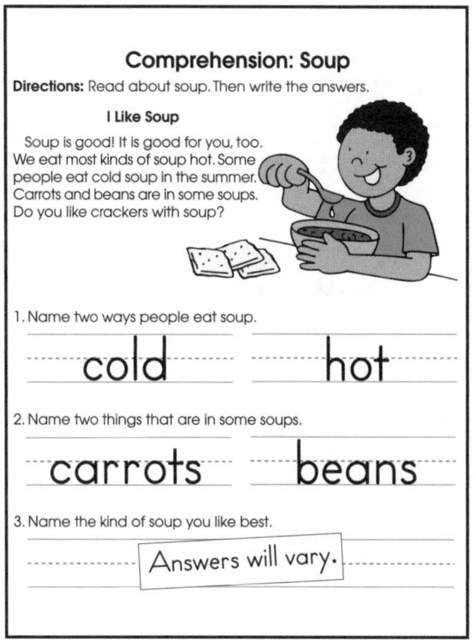

Comprehension: Soup

Directions: Read about soup. Then write the answers.

I Like Soup

Soup is good! It is good for you, too. We eat most kinds of soup hot. Some people eat cold soup in the summer. Carrots and beans are in some soups. Do you like crackers with soup?

1. Name two ways people eat soup.

cold hot

2. Name two things that are in some soups.

carrots beans

3. Name the kind of soup you like best.

Answers will vary.

Page 94

Comprehension: The Teddy Bear Song

Do you know the Teddy Bear Song? It is very old!

Directions: Read the Teddy Bear Song. Then answer the questions.

Teddy bear, teddy bear, turn around.
Teddy bear, teddy bear, touch the ground.
Teddy bear, teddy bear, climb upstairs.
Teddy bear, teddy bear, say your prayers.
Teddy bear, teddy bear, turn out the light.
Teddy bear, teddy bear, say, "Good night!"

1. What is the first thing the teddy bear does?

He turns around.

2. What is the last thing the teddy bear does?

He says, "Good night!"

3. What would you name a teddy bear?

Answers will vary.

Page 95

Sequencing: Put Teddy Bear to Bed

Directions: Read the song about the teddy bear again. Write a number in each box to show the order of the story.

3 4 1 2

Page 96

Comprehension: A New Teddy Bear Song

Directions: Write words to make a new teddy bear song. Act out your new song with your teddy bear as you read it.

Answers will vary.

Teddy bear, teddy bear, turn ______.

Teddy bear, teddy bear, touch the ______.

Teddy bear, teddy bear, climb ______.

Teddy bear, teddy bear, turn out ______.

Teddy bear, teddy bear, say, ______.

Page 97

Sequencing: Petting a Cat

Directions: Read the story. Then write the answers.

Do you like cats? I do. To pet a cat, move slowly. Hold out your hand. The cat will come to you. Then pet its head. Do not grab a cat! It will run away.

To pet a cat . . .

1. Move slowly.
2. Hold out your hand.
3. The cat will come to you.
4. Pet the cat's head.
5. Do not grab a cat!

Page 98

Comprehension: Cats

Directions: Read the story about cats again. Then write the answers.

1. What is a good title for the story?
   Answers will vary.
2. The story tells you how to pet a cat.
3. What part of your body should you pet a cat with?
   your hand
4. Why should you move slowly to pet a cat?
   Answers will vary.
5. Why do you think a cat will run away if you grab it?
   Answers will vary.

Page 99

Comprehension: Cats

Directions: Look at the pictures and read about four cats. Then write the correct name beside each cat.

Fluffy, Blackie and Tiger are playing. Tom is sleeping. Blackie has spots. Tiger has stripes.

Fluffy

Tiger

Blackie

Tom

Page 100

Same and Different: Cats

Directions: Compare the picture of the cats on page 149 to this picture. Write a word from the box to tell what is different about each cat.

purple ball	green bow	blue brush	red collar

1. Tom is wearing a red collar.
2. Blackie has a blue brush.
3. Fluffy is wearing a green bow.
4. Tiger has a purple ball.

Page 101

Comprehension: Tigers

Directions: Read about tigers. Then write the answers.

Tigers sleep during the day. They hunt at night. Tigers eat meat. They hunt deer. They like to eat wild pigs. If they cannot find meat, tigers will eat fish.

1. When do tigers sleep?
   during the day
2. Name two things tigers eat. Answers may include:
   meat, deer, wild pigs or fish
3. When do tigers hunt? at night

Page 102

Following Directions: Tiger Puzzle

Directions: Read the story about tigers again. Then complete the puzzle.

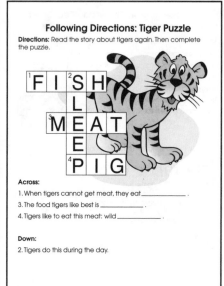

Across:

1. When tigers cannot get meat, they eat ______.
3. The food tigers like best is ______.
4. Tigers like to eat this meat: wild ______.

Down:

2. Tigers do this during the day.

Page 103

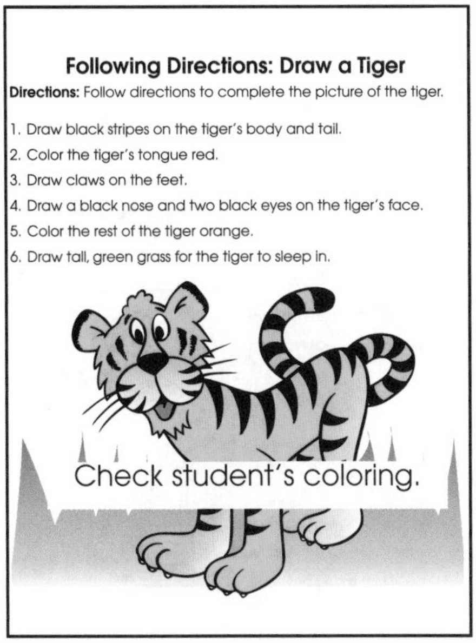

Following Directions: Draw a Tiger

Directions: Follow directions to complete the picture of the tiger.

1. Draw black stripes on the tiger's body and tail.
2. Color the tiger's tongue red.
3. Draw claws on the feet.
4. Draw a black nose and two black eyes on the tiger's face.
5. Color the rest of the tiger orange.
6. Draw tall, green grass for the tiger to sleep in.

Check student's coloring.

Page 104

Comprehension: Write a Party Invitation

Directions: Read about the party. Then complete the invitation.

The party will be at Dog's house. The party will start at 1:00 P.M. It will last 2 hours. Write your birthday for the date of the party.

Party Invitation

Where: Dog's house

Date: Answers will vary.

Time It Begins: 1:00 P.M.

Time It Ends: 3:00 P.M.

Answers will vary.

Directions: On the last line, write something else about the party.

Page 105

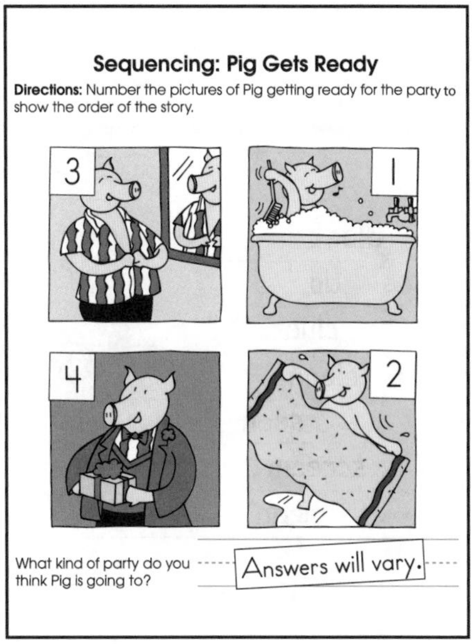

Sequencing: Pig Gets Ready

Directions: Number the pictures of Pig getting ready for the party to show the order of the story.

What kind of party do you think Pig is going to? Answers will vary.

Page 106

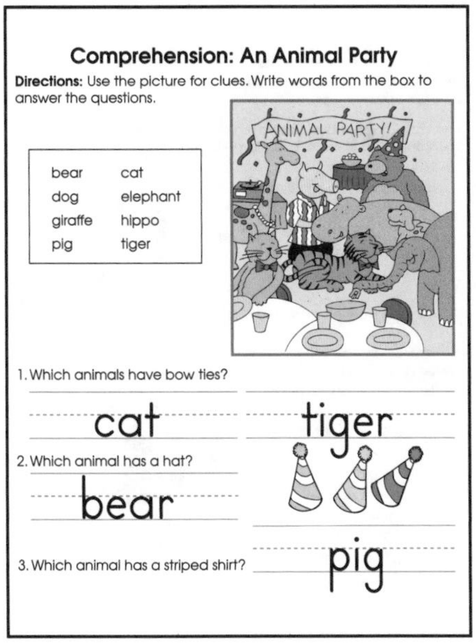

Comprehension: An Animal Party

Directions: Use the picture for clues. Write words from the box to answer the questions.

bear	cat
dog	elephant
giraffe	hippo
pig	tiger

1. Which animals have bow ties? cat tiger
2. Which animal has a hat? bear
3. Which animal has a striped shirt? pig

Page 107

Classifying: Party Items

Directions: Draw a □ around objects that are food for the party. Draw a △ around the party guests. Draw a ○ around the objects used for fun at the party.

Page 108

Comprehension: Rhymes

Directions: Read about words that rhyme. Then circle the answers.

Words that rhyme have the same end sounds. "Wing" and "sing" rhyme. "Boy" and "toy" rhyme. "Dime" and "time" rhyme. Can you think of other words that rhyme?

1. Words that rhyme have the same (end sounds.) end letters.
2. "Time" rhymes with "tree." ("dime.")

Directions: Write one rhyme for each word.

wing Answers will vary. boy

dime pink

Page 109

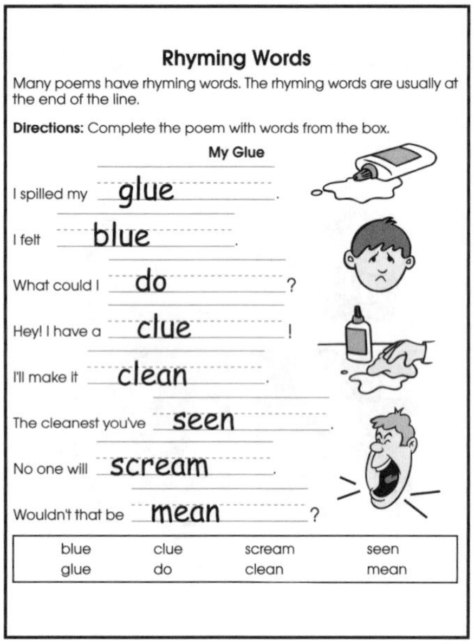

Rhyming Words

Many poems have rhyming words. The rhyming words are usually at the end of the line.

Directions: Complete the poem with words from the box.

My Glue

I spilled my glue.
I felt blue.
What could I do?
Hey! I have a clue!
I'll make it clean.
The cleanest you've seen.
No one will scream.
Wouldn't that be mean?

blue	clue	scream	seen
glue	do	clean	mean

Page 110

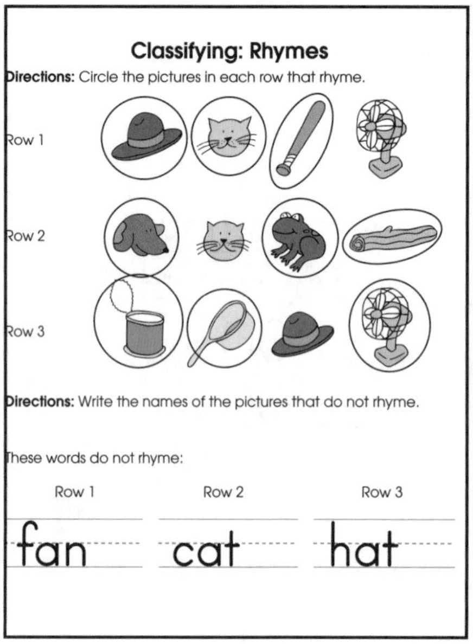

Classifying: Rhymes

Directions: Circle the pictures in each row that rhyme.

Row 1

Row 2

Row 3

Directions: Write the names of the pictures that do not rhyme.

These words do not rhyme:

Row 1	Row 2	Row 3
fan	cat	hat

Page 111

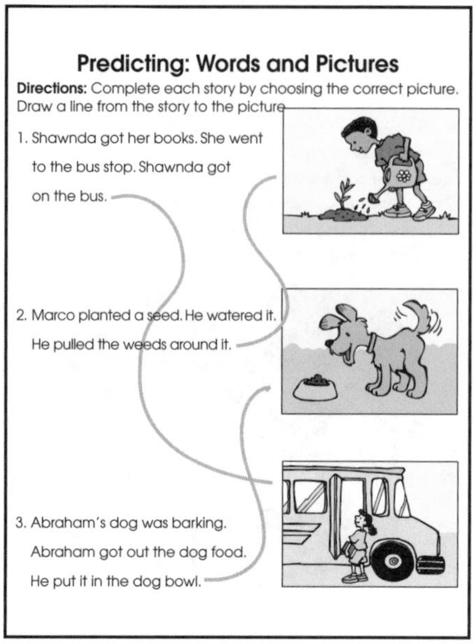

Predicting: Words and Pictures

Directions: Complete each story by choosing the correct picture. Draw a line from the story to the picture.

1. Shawnda got her books. She went to the bus stop. Shawnda got on the bus.
2. Marco planted a seed. He watered it. He pulled the weeds around it.
3. Abraham's dog was barking. Abraham got out the dog food. He put it in the dog bowl.

Page 112

Predicting: Story Ending

Directions: Read the story. Draw a picture in the last box to complete the story.

That's my ball. I got it first.

1 2 3 4

Pictures will vary.

It's mine!

Page 113

Predicting: Story Ending

Directions: Read the story. Draw a picture in the last box to complete the story.

Marco likes to paint. He likes to help his dad.

1 2 3 4

Pictures will vary.

He is tired when he's finished.

Page 114

Predicting: Story Ending

Directions: Read each story. Circle the sentence that tells how the story will end.

Ann was riding her bike. She saw a dog in the park. She stopped to pet it. Ann left to go home.

The dog went swimming.

The dog followed Ann.

The dog went home with a cat.

Antonio went to a baseball game. A baseball player hit a ball toward him. He reached out his hands.

The player caught the ball.

The ball bounced on a car.

Antonio caught the ball.

Answer Key

Page 115

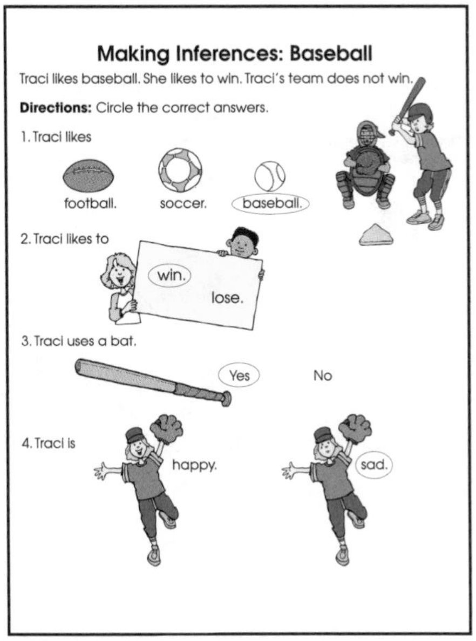

Making Inferences: Baseball

Traci likes baseball. She likes to win. Traci's team does not win.

Directions: Circle the correct answers.

1. Traci likes

football. soccer. baseball.

2. Traci likes to

win. lose.

3. Traci uses a bat.

Yes No

4. Traci is

happy. sad.

Page 116

Making Inferences: The Stars

Lynn looks at the stars. She sings a song about them. She makes a wish on them. The stars help Lynn sleep.

Directions: Circle the correct answers.

1. Lynn likes the

moon. sun. stars.

2. What song do you think she sings?

Row, Row, Row Your Boat

Twinkle, Twinkle Little Star

Happy Birthday to You

3. What does Lynn "make" on the stars?

a wish a spaceship lunch

Page 117

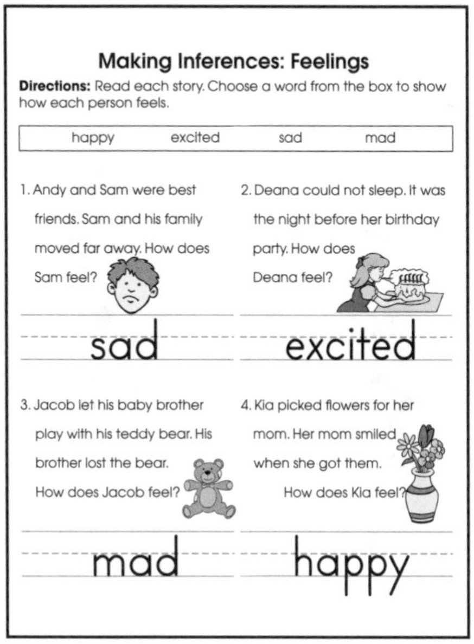

Making Inferences: Feelings

Directions: Read each story. Choose a word from the box to show how each person feels.

happy excited sad mad

1. Andy and Sam were best friends. Sam and his family moved far away. How does Sam feel?

sad

2. Deana could not sleep. It was the night before her birthday party. How does Deana feel?

excited

3. Jacob let his baby brother play with his teddy bear. His brother lost the bear. How does Jacob feel?

mad

4. Kia picked flowers for her mom. Her mom smiled when she got them. How does Kia feel?

happy

Page 118

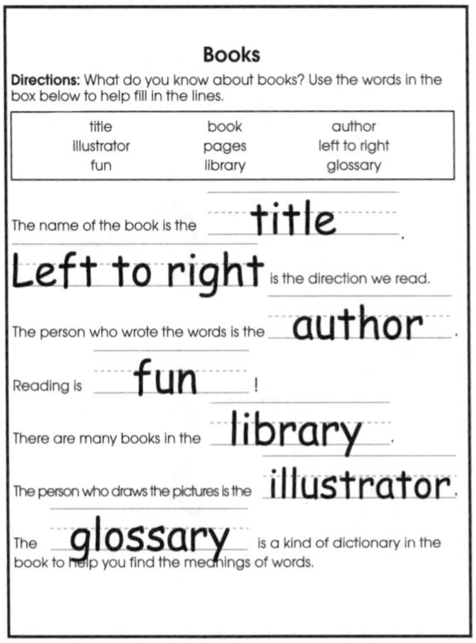

Books

Directions: What do you know about books? Use the words in the box below to help fill in the lines.

title	book	author
illustrator	pages	left to right
fun	library	glossary

The name of the book is the title.

Left to right is the direction we read.

The person who wrote the words is the author.

Reading is fun!

There are many books in the library.

The person who draws the pictures is the illustrator.

The glossary is a kind of dictionary in the book to help you find the meanings of words.

Page 120

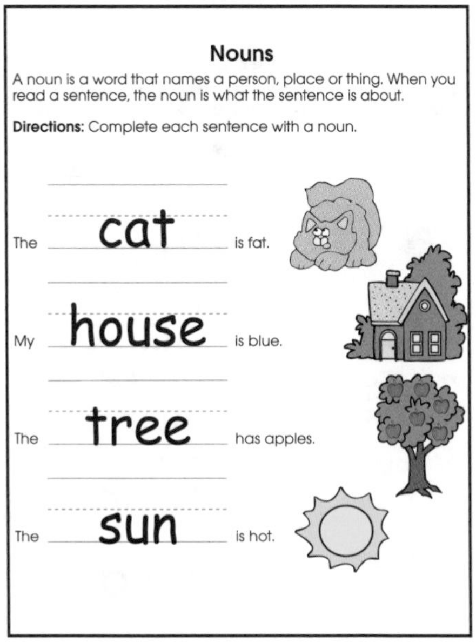

Nouns

A noun is a word that names a person, place or thing. When you read a sentence, the noun is what the sentence is about.

Directions: Complete each sentence with a noun.

The cat is fat.

My house is blue.

The tree has apples.

The sun is hot.

Page 121

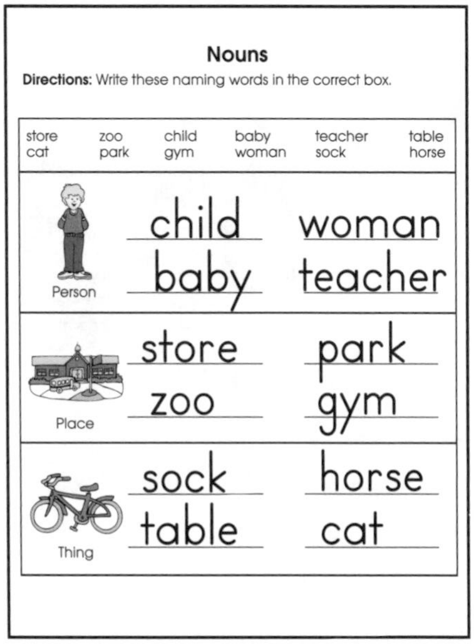

Nouns

Directions: Write these naming words in the correct box.

store cat zoo park child gym baby woman teacher sock table horse

Person	child, baby	woman, teacher
Place	store, zoo	park, gym
Thing	sock, table	horse, cat

Page 122

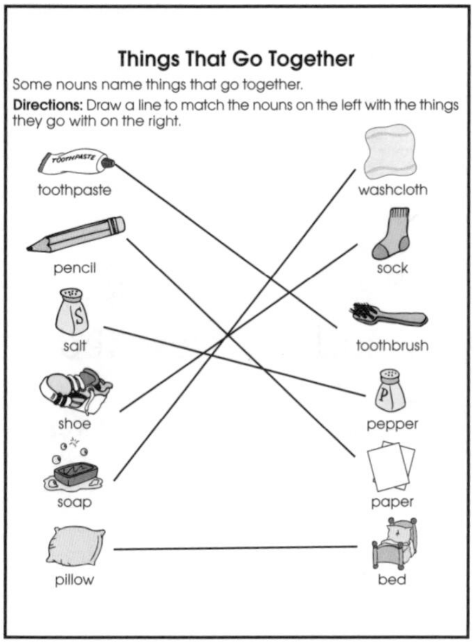

Things That Go Together

Some nouns name things that go together.

Directions: Draw a line to match the nouns on the left with the things they go with on the right.

Page 123

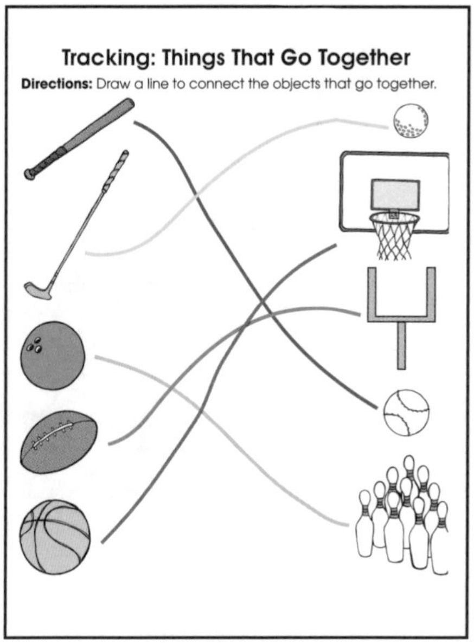

Tracking: Things That Go Together

Directions: Draw a line to connect the objects that go together.

Page 124

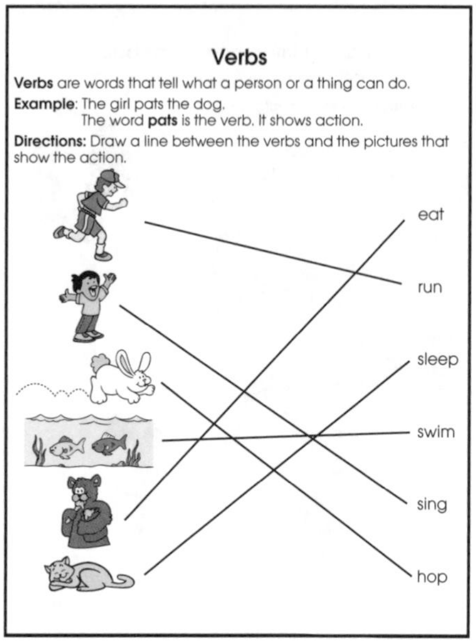

Verbs

Verbs are words that tell what a person or a thing can do.

Example: The girl pats the dog.
The word **pats** is the verb. It shows action.

Directions: Draw a line between the verbs and the pictures that show the action.

Page 125

Verbs

Directions:
Look at the picture and read the words. Write an action word in each sentence below.

1. The two boys like to talk together.
2. The children kick the soccer ball.
3. Some children like to swing on the swing.
4. The girl can run very fast.
5. The teacher rings the bell.

Page 126

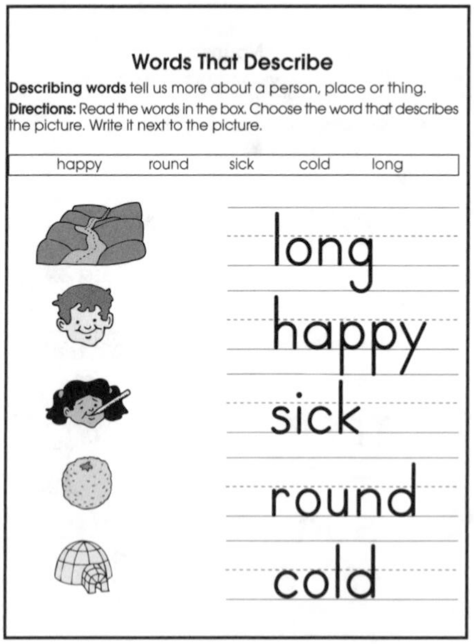

Words That Describe

Describing words tell us more about a person, place or thing.

Directions: Read the words in the box. Choose the word that describes the picture. Write it next to the picture.

happy round sick cold long

Page 127

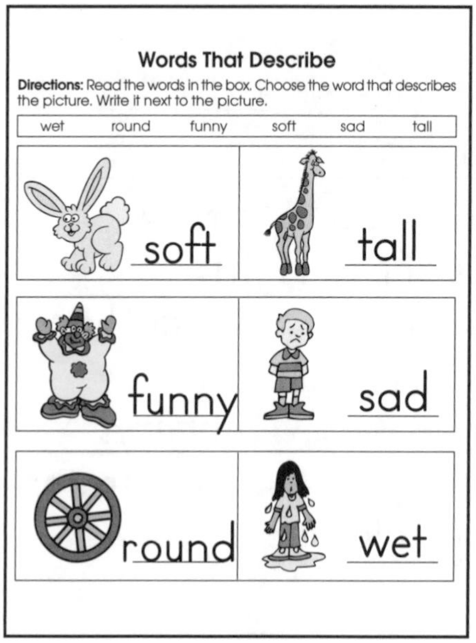

Words That Describe

Directions: Read the words in the box. Choose the word that describes the picture. Write it next to the picture.

wet round funny soft sad tall

Answer Key

Page 128

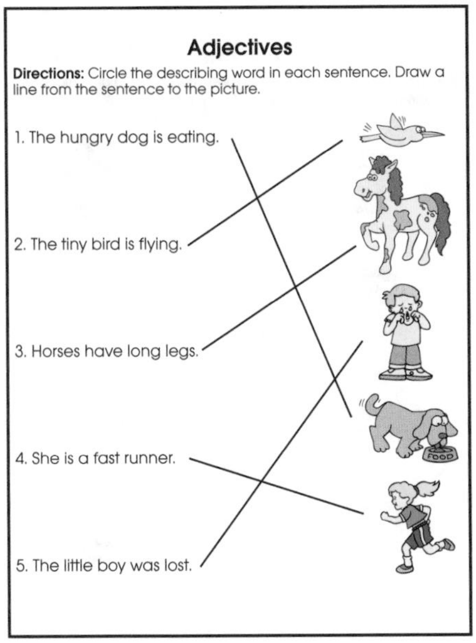

Adjectives

Directions: Circle the describing word in each sentence. Draw a line from the sentence to the picture.

1. The hungry dog is eating.
2. The tiny bird is flying.
3. Horses have long legs.
4. She is a fast runner.
5. The little boy was lost.

Page 129

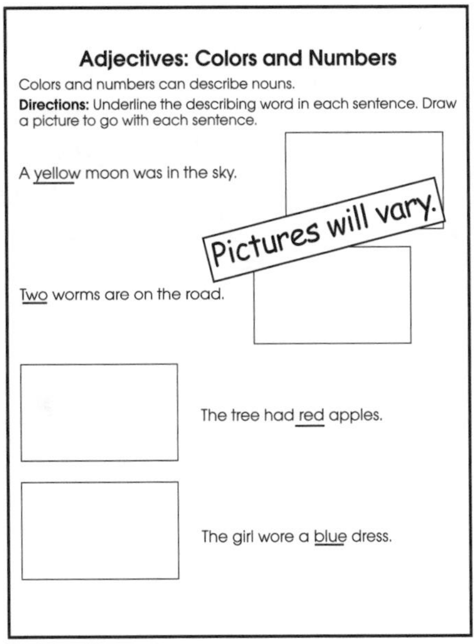

Adjectives: Colors and Numbers

Colors and numbers can describe nouns.

Directions: Underline the describing word in each sentence. Draw a picture to go with each sentence.

A yellow moon was in the sky.

Two worms are on the road.

The tree had red apples.

The girl wore a blue dress.

Page 130

Comparative Adjectives

Directions: Look at each group of pictures. Write 1, 2 or 3 under the picture to show where it should be.

Example:

tallest 3	tall 1	taller 2
small 1	smallest 3	smaller 2
biggest 3	big 1	bigger 2
wider 2	wide 1	widest 3

Page 131

Comparative Adjectives

Directions: Look at the pictures in each row. Write 1, 2 or 3 under the picture to show where it should be.

shortest 3	shorter 2	short 1
longest 3	longer 2	long 1
happy 1	happier 2	happiest 3
hotter 2	hot 1	hottest 3

Page 132

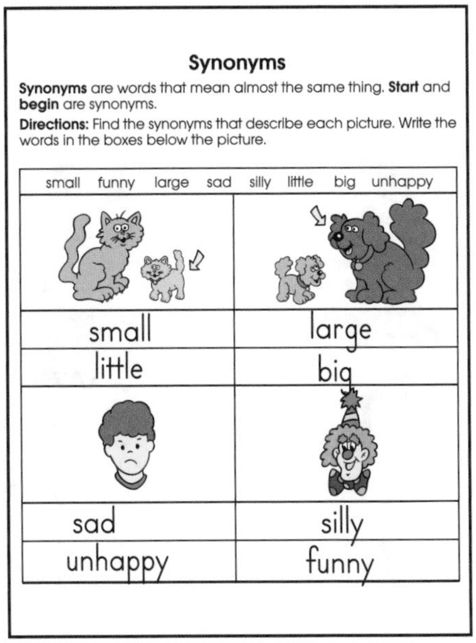

Synonyms

Synonyms are words that mean almost the same thing. **Start** and **begin** are synonyms.

Directions: Find the synonyms that describe each picture. Write the words in the boxes below the picture.

small funny large sad silly little big unhappy

small	large
little	big
sad	silly
unhappy	funny

Page 133

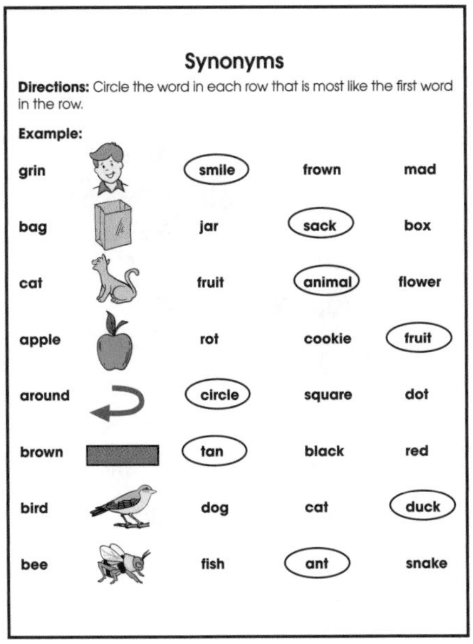

Synonyms

Directions: Circle the word in each row that is most like the first word in the row.

Example:

grin	smile	frown	mad
bag	jar	sack	box
cat	fruit	animal	flower
apple	rot	cookie	fruit
around	circle	square	dot
brown	tan	black	red
bird	dog	cat	duck
bee	fish	ant	snake

Answer Key

Page 134

Synonyms

Directions: Read each sentence and look at the underlined word. Circle the word that means the same thing. Write the new words.

1. The boy was mad.	happy	(angry)	pup
2. The dog is brown.	(pup)	cat	rat
3. I like to scream.	soar	mad	(shout)
4. The bird can fly.	(soar)	jog	warm
5. The girl can run.	sleep	(jog)	shout
6. I am hot.	(warm)	cold	soar

angry pup shout

soar jog warm

Page 135

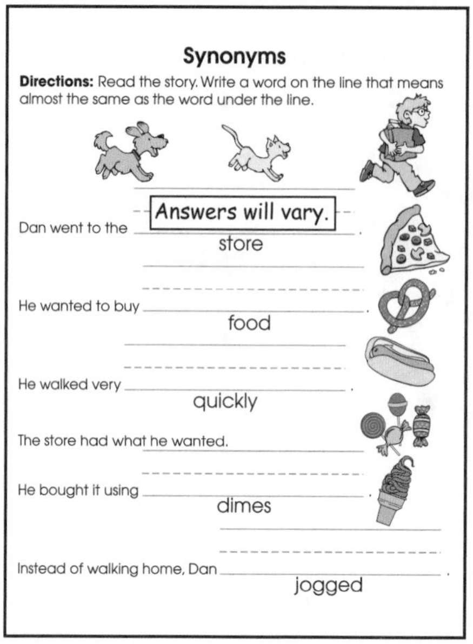

Synonyms

Directions: Read the story. Write a word on the line that means almost the same as the word under the line.

Answers will vary.

Dan went to the ______ . store

He wanted to buy ______ . food

He walked very ______ . quickly

The store had what he wanted.

He bought it using ______ . dimes

Instead of walking home, Dan ______ . jogged

Page 136

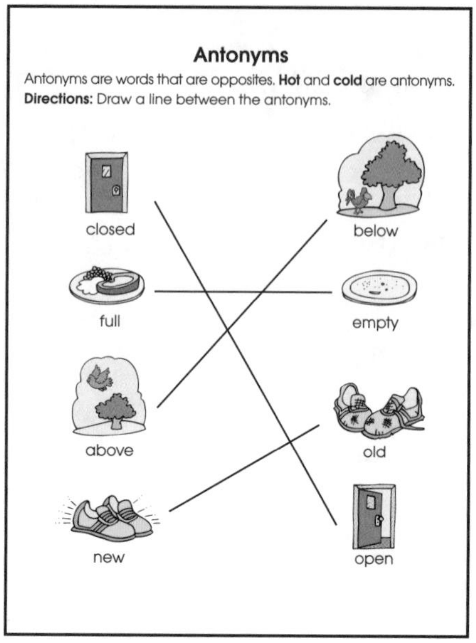

Antonyms

Antonyms are words that are opposites. **Hot** and **cold** are antonyms.

Directions: Draw a line between the antonyms.

Page 137

Antonyms

Directions: Draw lines to connect the words that are opposites.

Page 138

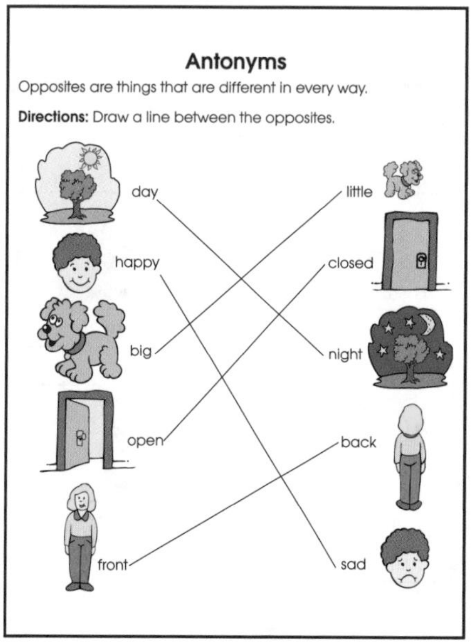

Antonyms

Opposites are things that are different in every way.

Directions: Draw a line between the opposites.

Page 139

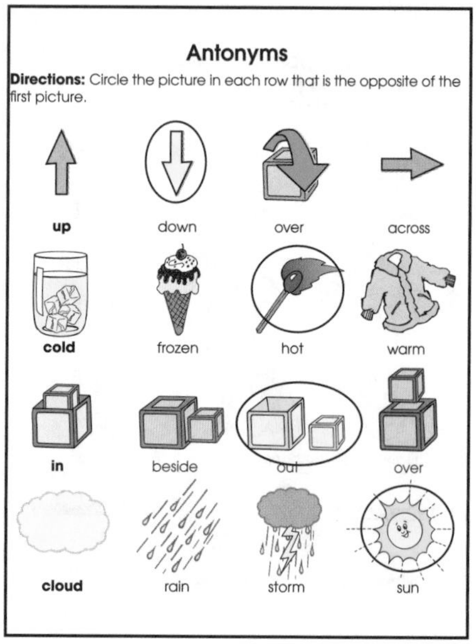

Antonyms

Directions: Circle the picture in each row that is the opposite of the first picture.

Answer Key

Page 140

Antonyms

Directions: Read each clue. Write the answers in the puzzle.

Across:
1. Opposite of low
2. Opposite of no
4. Opposite of empty
6. Opposite of loose

Down:
1. Opposite of light
3. Opposite of dangerous
5. Opposite of right

Page 141

Homophones

Homophones are words that **sound** the same but are spelled differently and mean something different. **Blew** and **blue** are homophones.

Directions: Look at the word pairs. Choose the word that describes the picture. Write the word on the line next to the picture.

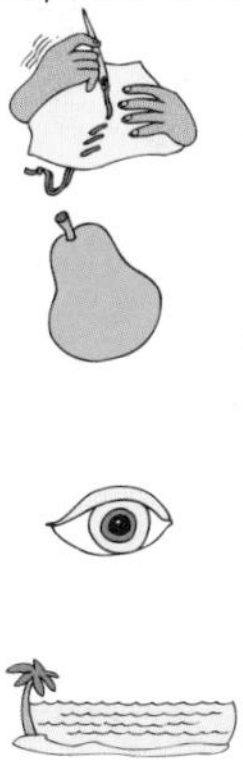

1. sew so sew
2. pair pear pear
3. eye I eye
4. see sea sea

Page 142

Homophones

Directions: Read each sentence. Underline the two words that sound the same but are spelled differently and mean something different.

1. Tom ate eight grapes.
2. Becky read Little Red Riding Hood.
3. I went to buy two dolls.
4. Five blue feathers blew in the wind.
5. Would you get wood for the fire?

Page 143

Sentences

Sentences begin with capital letters.

Directions: Read the sentences and write them below. Begin each sentence with a capital letter.

Example: the cat is fat.

The cat is fat.

my dog is big.

My dog is big.

the boy is sad.

The boy is sad.

bikes are fun!

Bikes are fun!

dad can bake.

Dad can bake.

Page 144

Word Order

If you change the order of the words in a sentence, you can change the meaning of the sentence.

Directions: Read the sentences. Draw a circle around the sentence that describes the picture.

Example:

The fox jumped over the dogs.
The dogs jumped over the fox.

1. The cat watched the bird.
The bird watched the cat.

2. The girl looked at the boy.
The boy looked at the girl.

3. The turtle ran past the rabbit.
The rabbit ran past the turtle.

Page 145

Word Order

Directions: Look at the picture. Put the words in order. Write the sentences on the lines below.

1. We made lemonade. some
2. good. It was
3. We the sold lemonade.
4. cost It five cents.
5. fun. We had

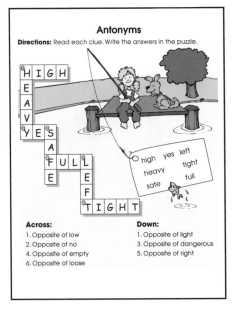

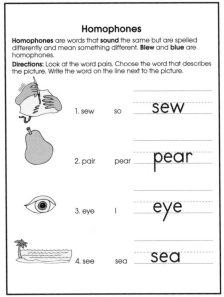

1. We made some lemonade.
2. It was good.
3. We sold the lemonade.
4. It cost five cents.
5. We had fun.

Answer Key

Page 146

Telling Sentences

Directions: Read the sentences and write them below. Begin each sentence with a capital letter. End each sentence with a period.

1. most children like pets
2. some children like dogs
3. some children like cats
4. some children like snakes
5. some children like all animals

1. Most children like pets.
2. Some children like dogs.
3. Some children like cats.
4. Some children like snakes.
5. Some children like all animals.

Page 147

Telling Sentences

Directions: Read the sentences and write them below. Begin each sentence with a capital letter. End each sentence with a period.

1. i like to go to the store with Mom
2. we go on Friday
3. i get to push the cart
4. i get to buy the cookies
5. i like to help Mom

1. I like to go to the store with Mom.
2. We go on Friday.
3. I get to push the cart.
4. I get to buy the cookies.
5. I like to help Mom.

Page 148

Asking Sentences

Directions: Write the first word of each asking sentence. Be sure to begin each question with a capital letter. End each question with a question mark.

1. Do you like the zoo? **do**
2. How much does it cost? **how**
3. Can you feed the ducks? **can**
4. Will you see the monkeys? **will**
5. What time will you eat lunch? **what**

Page 149

Asking Sentences

Directions: Read the asking sentences. Write the sentences below. Begin each sentence with a capital letter. End each sentence with a question mark.

1. what game will we play
2. do you like to read
3. how old are you
4. who is your best friend
5. can you tie your shoes

1. What game will we play?
2. Do you like to read?
3. How old are you?
4. Who is your best friend?
5. Can you tie your shoes?

Page 150

Periods and Question Marks

Directions: Put a period or a question mark at the end of each sentence below.

1. Do you like parades?
2. The clowns lead the parade.
3. Can you hear the band?
4. The balloons are big.
5. Can you see the horses?

Page 151

Is and Are

We use **is** in sentences about one person or one thing. We use **are** in sentences about more than one person or thing.

Example: The dog **is** barking.
The dogs **are** barking.

Directions: Write **is** or **are** in the sentences below.

1. Jim is playing baseball.

2. Fred and Sam are good friends.

3. Cupcakes are my favorite treat.

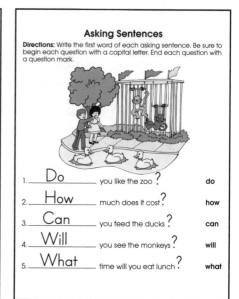

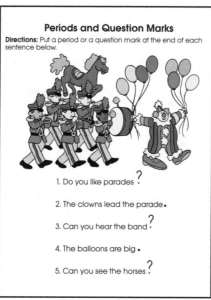

4. Lisa is a good soccer player.

Page 152

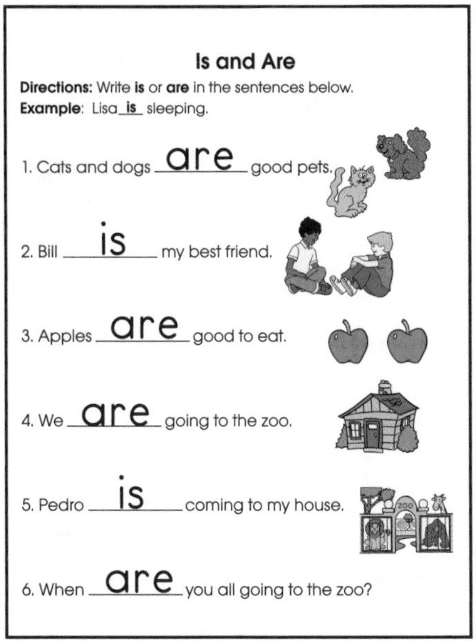

Is and Are

Directions: Write **is** or **are** in the sentences below.

Example: Lisa _is_ sleeping.

1. Cats and dogs __are__ good pets.
2. Bill __is__ my best friend.
3. Apples __are__ good to eat.
4. We __are__ going to the zoo.
5. Pedro __is__ coming to my house.
6. When __are__ you all going to the zoo?

Page 154

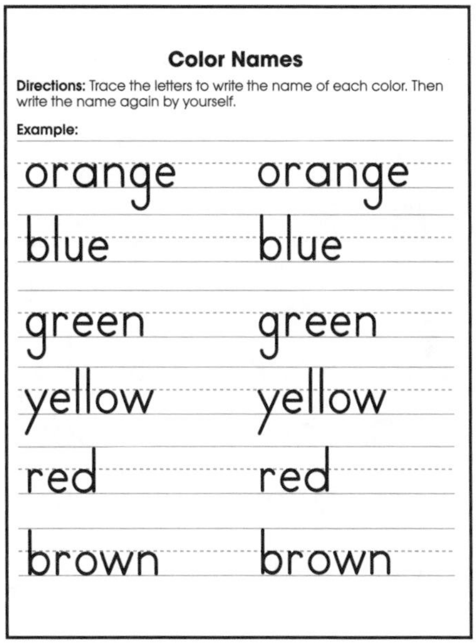

Color Names

Directions: Trace the letters to write the name of each color. Then write the name again by yourself.

Example:

orange orange
blue blue
green green
yellow yellow
red red
brown brown

Page 155

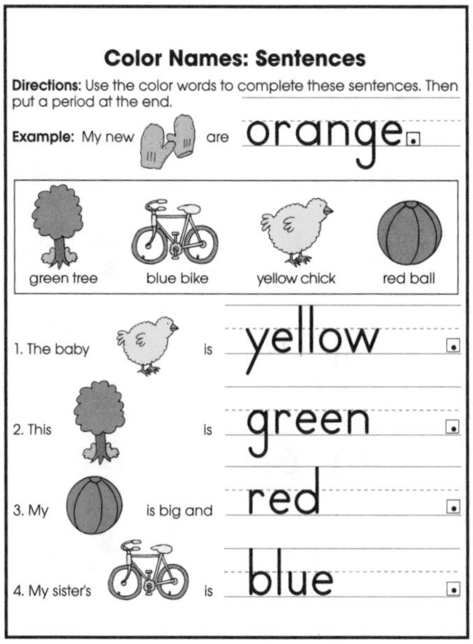

Color Names: Sentences

Directions: Use the color words to complete these sentences. Then put a period at the end.

Example: My new mittens are orange.

green tree | blue bike | yellow chick | red ball

1. The baby chick is yellow.
2. This tree is green.
3. My ball is big and red.
4. My sister's bike is blue.

Page 156

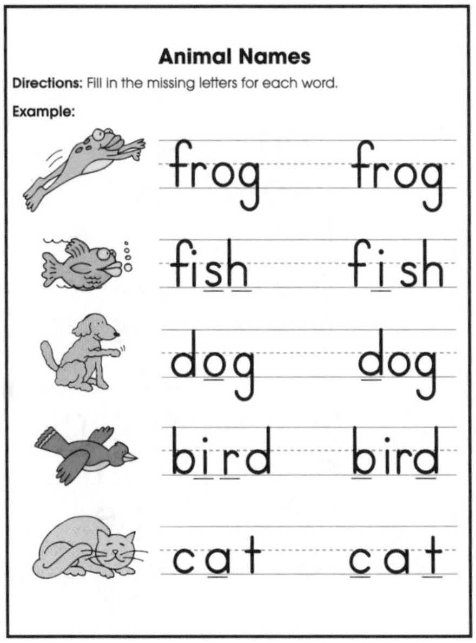

Animal Names

Directions: Fill in the missing letters for each word.

Example:

frog frog
fish fish
dog dog
bird bird
cat cat

Page 157

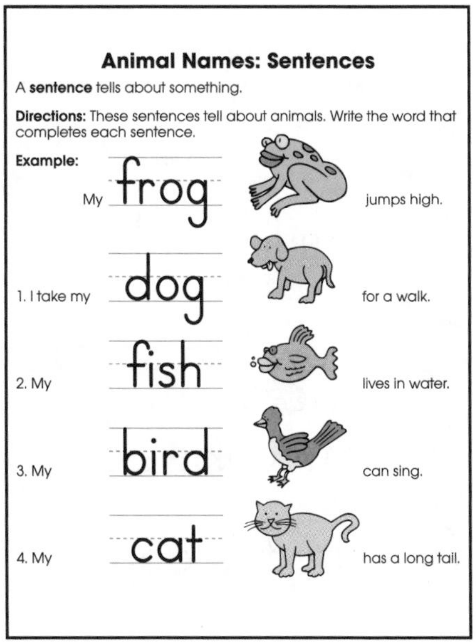

Animal Names: Sentences

A **sentence** tells about something.

Directions: These sentences tell about animals. Write the word that completes each sentence.

Example: My frog jumps high.

1. I take my dog for a walk.
2. My fish lives in water.
3. My bird can sing.
4. My cat has a long tail.

Page 158

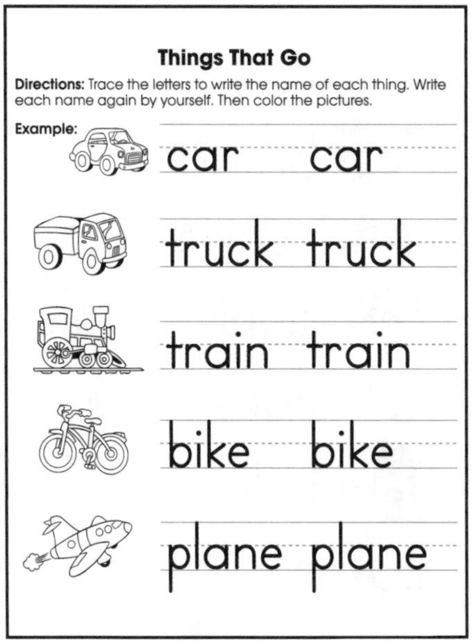

Things That Go

Directions: Trace the letters to write the name of each thing. Write each name again by yourself. Then color the pictures.

Example:

car car
truck truck
train train
bike bike
plane plane

Answer Key

Page 159

Things That Go: Sentences

Directions: These sentences tell about things that go. Write the word that completes each sentence.

Example:

The car is in the garage.

1. The truck was at the farm.
2. My bike had a flat tire.
3. The plane flew high.
4. The train went fast.

Page 160

Clothing Words

Directions: Trace the letters to write the name of each clothing word. Then write each name again by yourself.

Example:

shirt shirt
pants pants
jacket jacket
socks socks
shoes shoes
dress dress
hat hat

Page 161

Clothing Words: Sentences

Directions: Some of these sentences tell a whole idea. Others have something missing. If something is missing, draw a line to the word that completes the sentence. Put a period at the end of each sentence.

Example:

She is wearing a polka-dot — dress.

1. The baseball player wore a — hat.
2. His pants were torn.
3. The socks had — holes.
4. The jacket had blue buttons.
5. The shoes were brown.

Page 162

Food Names

Directions: Trace the letters to write the name of each food word. Write each name again by yourself. Then color the pictures.

Example:

bread bread
cookie cookie
apple apple
cake cake
milk milk
egg egg

Page 163

Food Names: Asking Sentences

An **asking sentence** asks a question. Asking sentences end with a question mark.

Directions: Write each sentence on the line. Begin each sentence with a capital letter. Put a period at the end of the telling sentences and a question mark at the end of the asking sentences.

Example: do you like cake

Do you like cake?

1. the cow has spots

The cow has spots.

2. is that cookie good

Is that cookie good?

3. she ate the apple

She ate the apple.

Page 164

Number Words

Directions: Trace the letters to write the name of each number. Write the numbers again by yourself. Then color the number pictures.

Example: Colors will vary.

1 one one
2 two two
3 three three
4 four four
5 five five
6 six six
7 seven seven
8 eight eight
9 nine nine
10 ten ten

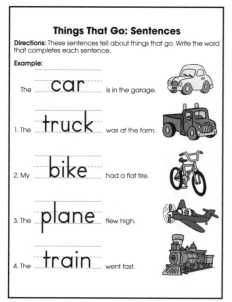

Answer Key

Page 165

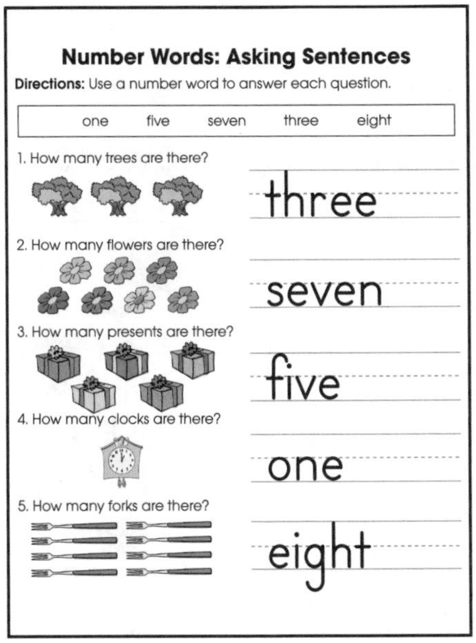

Number Words: Asking Sentences

Directions: Use a number word to answer each question.

one five seven three eight

1. How many trees are there? three
2. How many flowers are there? seven
3. How many presents are there? five
4. How many clocks are there? one
5. How many forks are there? eight

Page 166

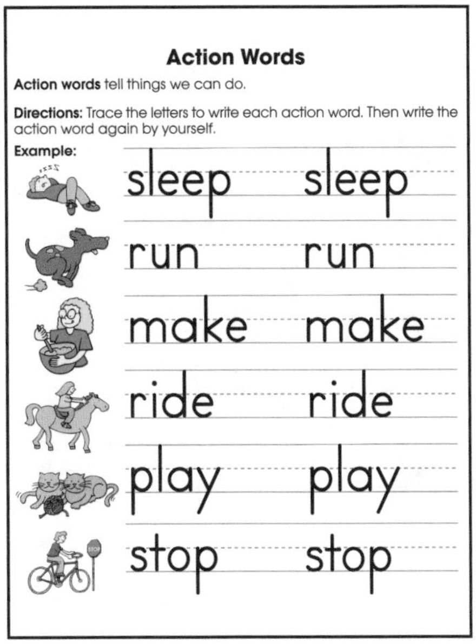

Action Words

Action words tell things we can do.

Directions: Trace the letters to write each action word. Then write the action word again by yourself.

Example:

sleep sleep

run run

make make

ride ride

play play

stop stop

Page 167

Action Words: More Than One

To show more than one of something, add **s** to the end of the word.

Example: one cat two cats

Directions: In each sentence, add **s** to show more than one. Then write the action word that completes each sentence.

sit jump stop ride

Example: The frog s sleep in the sun.

1. The boy s sit on the fence.
2. The car s stop at the sign.
3. The girl s swim in the water.
4. The dog s sit in the wagon.

Page 168

Action Words: Asking Sentences

Directions: Write an asking sentence about each picture. Begin each sentence with **can**. Add an action word. Begin each asking sentence with a capital letter and end it with a question mark.

Example:
I with you can

Can I sit with you?

she can

Can she cook?

with you can I

Can I play with you?

can she fast

Can she run fast?

Page 169

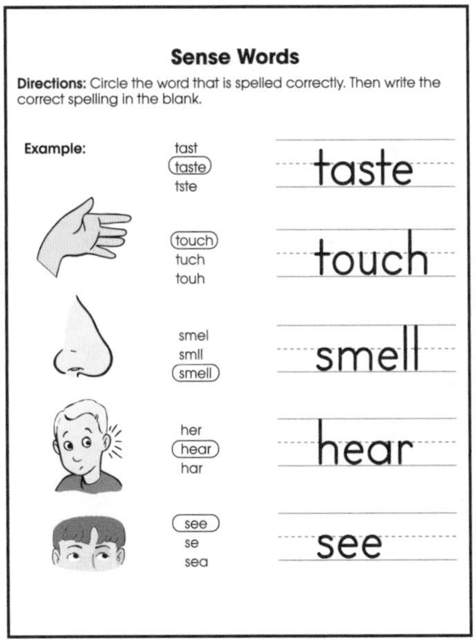

Sense Words

Directions: Circle the word that is spelled correctly. Then write the correct spelling in the blank.

Example: tast (taste) tste — taste

(touch) tuch touh — touch

smel smll (smell) — smell

her (hear) har — hear

(see) se sea — see

Page 170

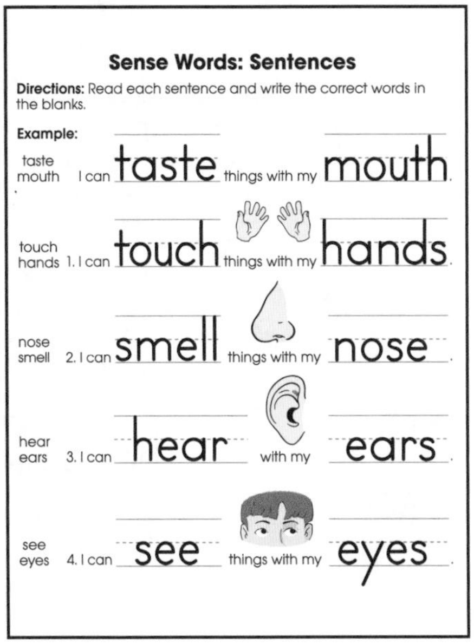

Sense Words: Sentences

Directions: Read each sentence and write the correct words in the blanks.

Example: taste mouth — I can taste things with my mouth.

touch hands — 1. I can touch things with my hands.

nose smell — 2. I can smell things with my nose.

hear ears — 3. I can hear with my ears.

see eyes — 4. I can see things with my eyes.

Page 171

My World

Directions: Fill in the missing letters for each word.

tree tree
grass grass
flower flower
pond pond
sand sand
sky sky

Page 172

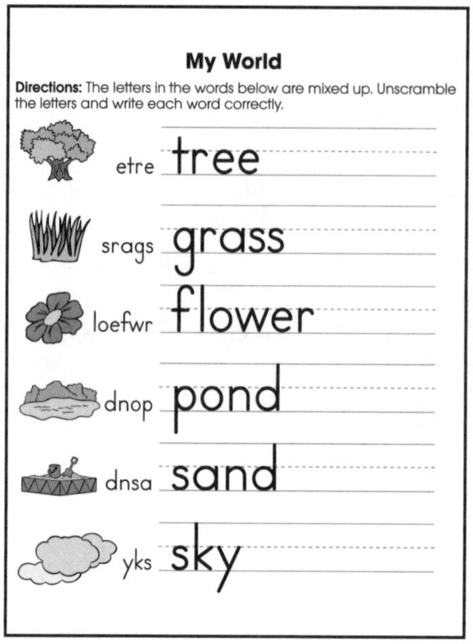

My World

Directions: The letters in the words below are mixed up. Unscramble the letters and write each word correctly.

etre tree
srags grass
loefwr flower
dnop pond
dnsa sand
yks sky

Page 173

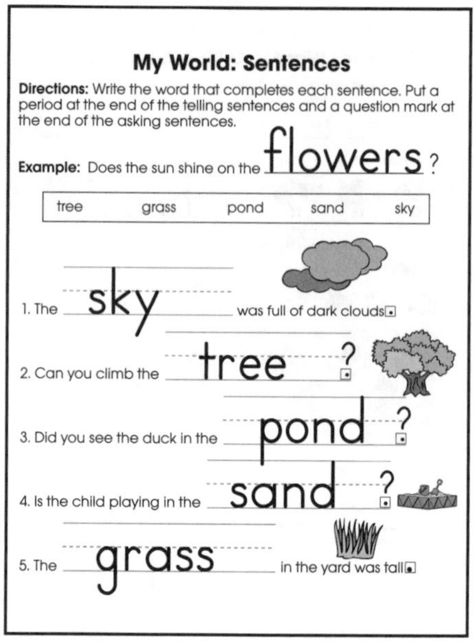

My World: Sentences

Directions: Write the word that completes each sentence. Put a period at the end of the telling sentences and a question mark at the end of the asking sentences.

Example: Does the sun shine on the flowers?

tree grass pond sand sky

1. The sky was full of dark clouds.
2. Can you climb the tree?
3. Did you see the duck in the pond?
4. Is the child playing in the sand?
5. The grass in the yard was tall.

Page 174

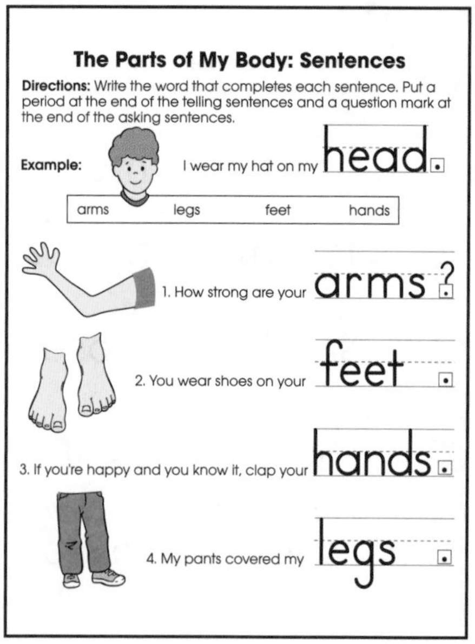

The Parts of My Body: Sentences

Directions: Write the word that completes each sentence. Put a period at the end of the telling sentences and a question mark at the end of the asking sentences.

Example: I wear my hat on my head.

arms legs feet hands

1. How strong are your arms?
2. You wear shoes on your feet.
3. If you're happy and you know it, clap your hands.
4. My pants covered my legs.

Page 175

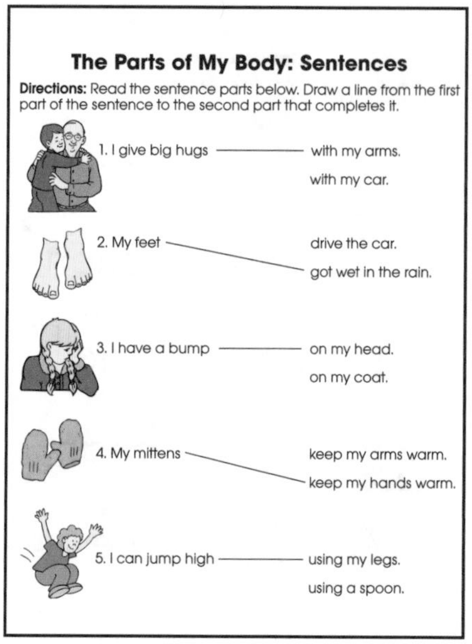

The Parts of My Body: Sentences

Directions: Read the sentence parts below. Draw a line from the first part of the sentence to the second part that completes it.

1. I give big hugs — with my arms. / with my car.
2. My feet — drive the car. / got wet in the rain.
3. I have a bump — on my head. / on my coat.
4. My mittens — keep my arms warm. / keep my hands warm.
5. I can jump high — using my legs. / using a spoon.

Page 176

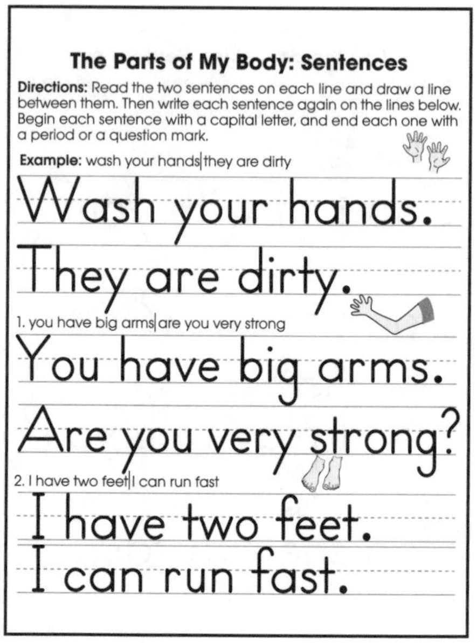

The Parts of My Body: Sentences

Directions: Read the two sentences on each line and draw a line between them. Then write each sentence again on the lines below. Begin each sentence with a capital letter, and end each one with a period or a question mark.

Example: wash your hands|they are dirty

Wash your hands.
They are dirty.

1. you have big arms|are you very strong

You have big arms.
Are you very strong?

2. I have two feet|I can run fast

I have two feet.
I can run fast.

Page 178

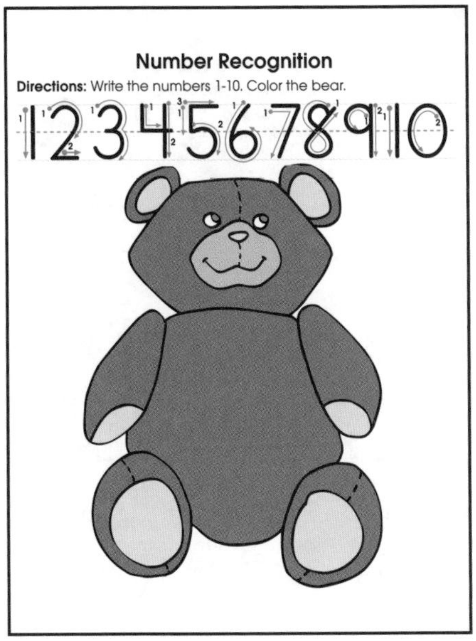
Number Recognition

Directions: Write the numbers 1-10. Color the bear.

1 2 3 4 5 6 7 8 9 10

Page 179

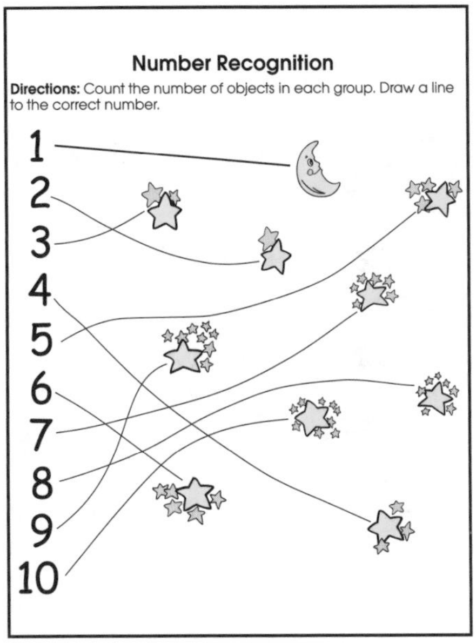
Number Recognition

Directions: Count the number of objects in each group. Draw a line to the correct number.

1 2 3 4 5 6 7 8 9 10

Page 180

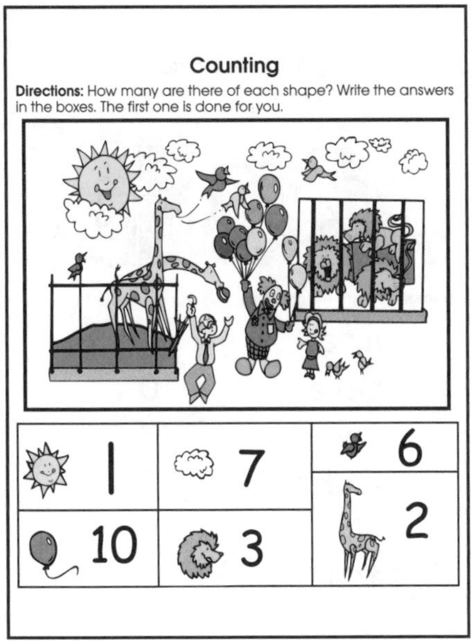
Counting

Directions: How many are there of each shape? Write the answers in the boxes. The first one is done for you.

1	7	6
10	3	2

Page 181

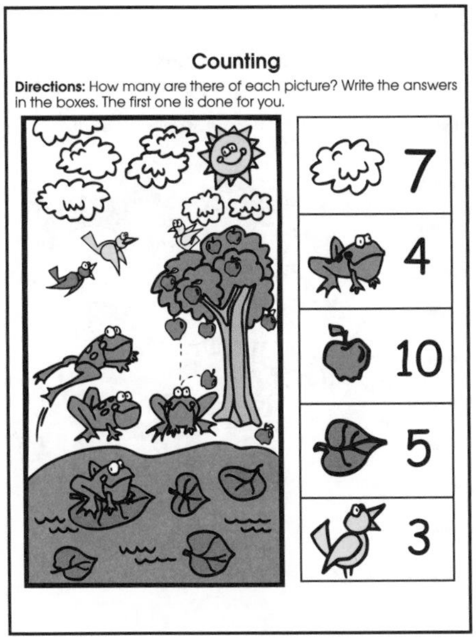
Counting

Directions: How many are there of each picture? Write the answers in the boxes. The first one is done for you.

7

4

10

5

3

Page 182

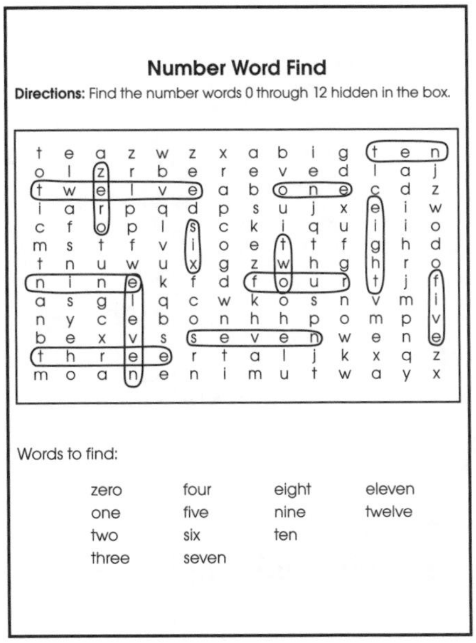
Number Word Find

Directions: Find the number words 0 through 12 hidden in the box.

t	e	a	z	w	z	x	a	b	i	g	t	e	n
o	l	z	r	b	e	r	e	v	e	d	l	a	j
t	w	e	l	v	e	a	b	o	n	e	c	d	z
i	a	r	p	q	d	p	s	u	j	x	e	i	w
c	f	o	p	l	s	c	k	i	q	u	i	i	o
m	s	t	f	v	i	o	e	t	t	f	g	h	d
t	n	u	w	u	x	g	z	w	h	g	h	r	o
n	i	n	e	k	f	d	f	o	u	r	t	j	f
a	s	g	l	q	c	w	k	o	s	n	v	m	i
n	y	c	e	b	o	n	h	h	p	o	m	p	v
b	e	x	v	s	s	e	v	e	n	w	e	n	e
t	h	r	e	e	r	t	a	l	j	k	x	q	z
m	o	a	n	e	n	i	m	u	t	w	a	y	x

Words to find:

zero	four	eight	eleven
one	five	nine	twelve
two	six	ten	
three	seven		

Page 183

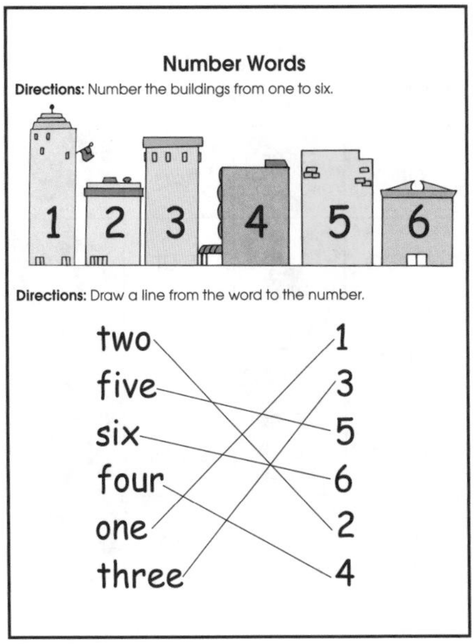
Number Words

Directions: Number the buildings from one to six.

1 2 3 4 5 6

Directions: Draw a line from the word to the number.

two	1
five	3
six	5
four	6
one	2
three	4

Answer Key

Page 184

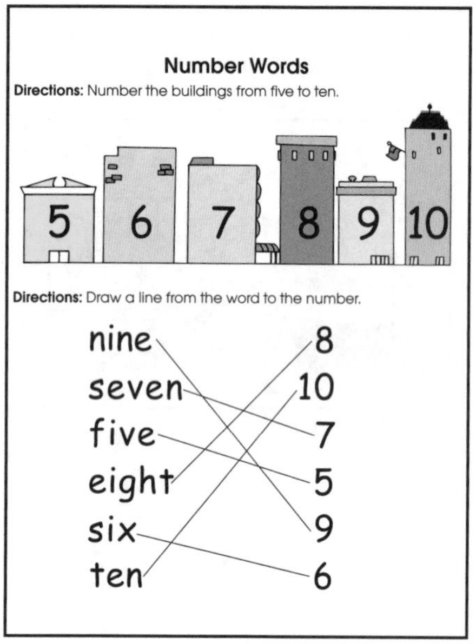

Number Words

Directions: Number the buildings from five to ten.

5 6 7 8 9 10

Directions: Draw a line from the word to the number.

nine	8
seven	10
five	7
eight	5
six	9
ten	6

Page 185

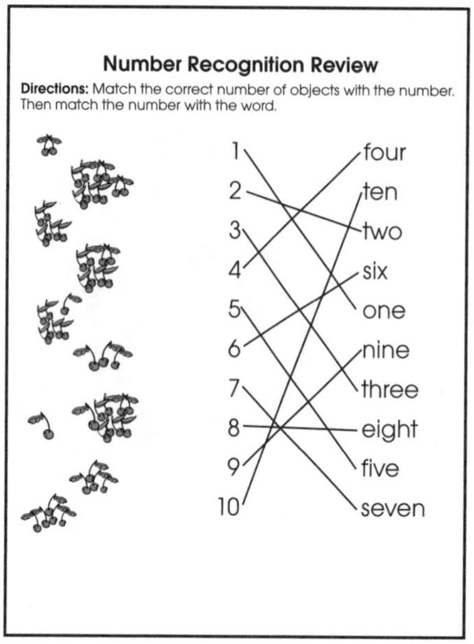

Number Recognition Review

Directions: Match the correct number of objects with the number. Then match the number with the word.

1	four
2	ten
3	two
4	six
5	one
6	nine
7	three
8	eight
9	five
10	seven

Page 186

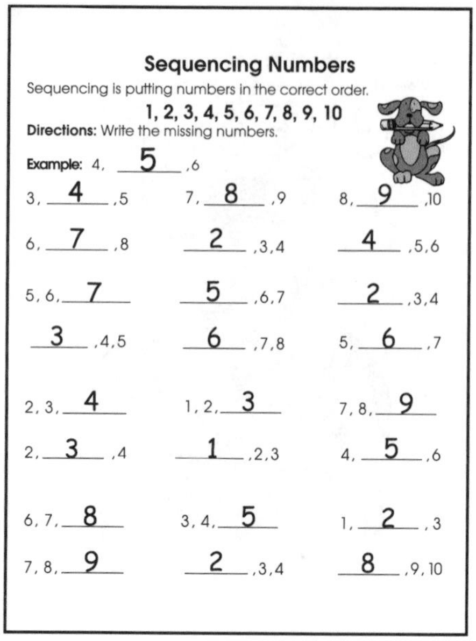

Sequencing Numbers

Sequencing is putting numbers in the correct order.

1, 2, 3, 4, 5, 6, 7, 8, 9, 10

Directions: Write the missing numbers.

Example: 4, 5, 6

3, 4, 5	7, 8, 9	8, 9, 10
6, 7, 8	2, 3, 4	4, 5, 6
5, 6, 7	5, 6, 7	2, 3, 4
3, 4, 5	6, 7, 8	5, 6, 7
2, 3, 4	1, 2, 3	7, 8, 9
2, 3, 4	1, 2, 3	4, 5, 6
6, 7, 8	3, 4, 5	1, 2, 3
7, 8, 9	2, 3, 4	8, 9, 10

Page 187

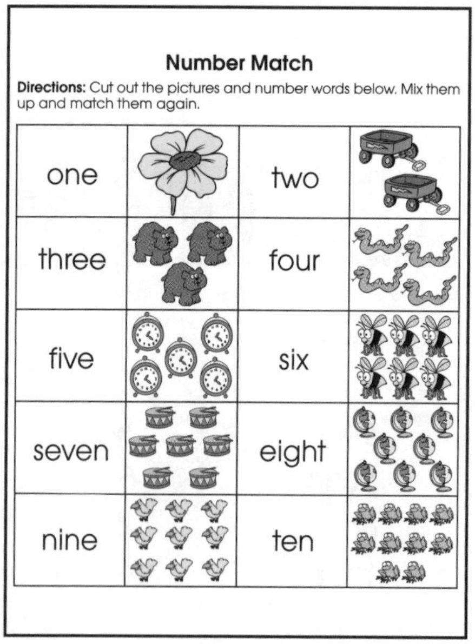

Number Match

Directions: Cut out the pictures and number words below. Mix them up and match them again.

one		two	
three		four	
five		six	
seven		eight	
nine		ten	

Page 189

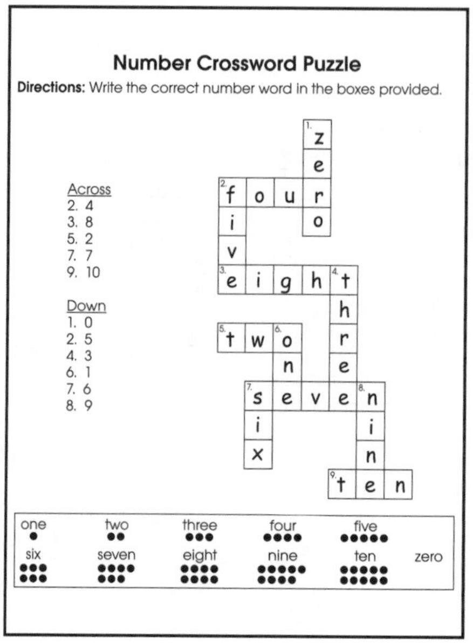

Number Crossword Puzzle

Directions: Write the correct number word in the boxes provided.

Across
2. 4
3. 8
5. 2
7. 7
9. 10

Down
1. 0
2. 5
4. 3
6. 1
7. 6
8. 9

one two three four five six seven eight nine ten zero

Page 190

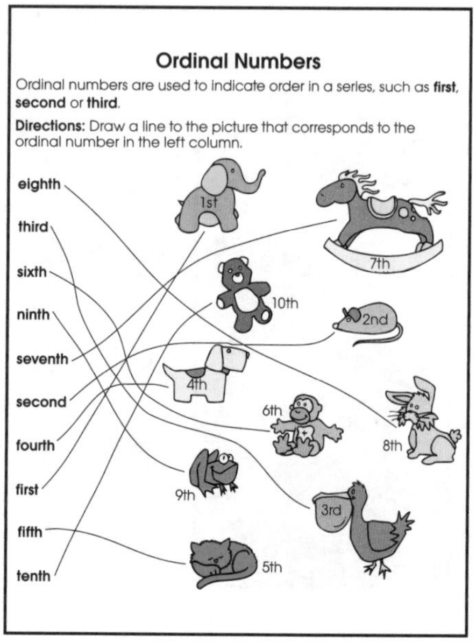

Ordinal Numbers

Ordinal numbers are used to indicate order in a series, such as **first**, **second** or **third**.

Directions: Draw a line to the picture that corresponds to the ordinal number in the left column.

Answer Key

Page 191

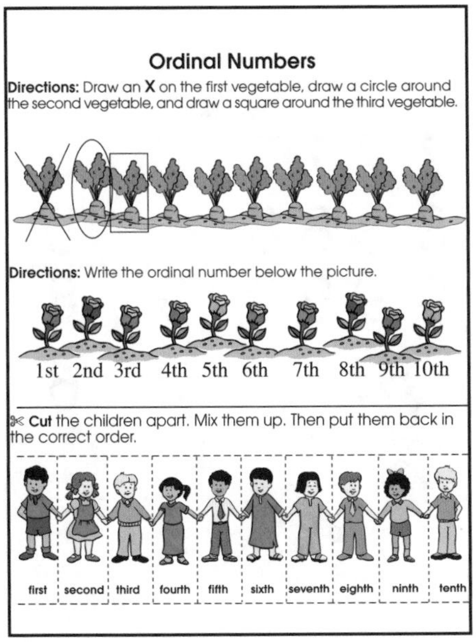

Ordinal Numbers

Directions: Draw an **X** on the first vegetable, draw a circle around the second vegetable, and draw a square around the third vegetable.

Directions: Write the ordinal number below the picture.

1st 2nd 3rd 4th 5th 6th 7th 8th 9th 10th

✂ **Cut** the children apart. Mix them up. Then put them back in the correct order.

first second third fourth fifth sixth seventh eighth ninth tenth

Page 193

Sequencing: Standing in Line

Directions: These children are waiting to see a movie. Look at them and follow the instructions.

1. Color the person who is first in line yellow.
2. Color the person who is last in line brown.
3. Color the person who is second in line pink.
4. Circle the person who is at the end of the line.

Page 194

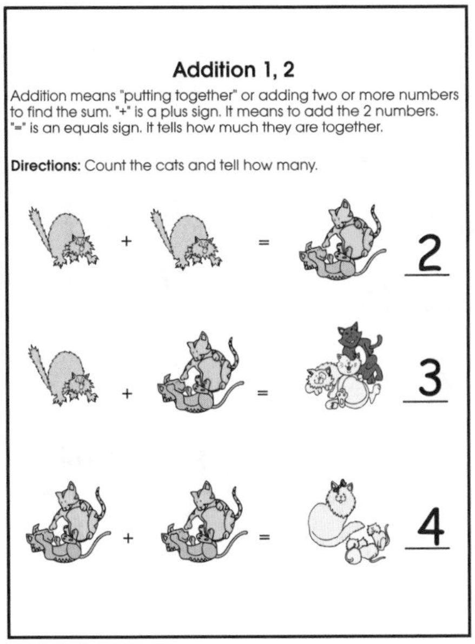

Addition 1, 2

Addition means "putting together" or adding two or more numbers to find the sum. "+" is a plus sign. It means to add the 2 numbers. "=" is an equals sign. It tells how much they are together.

Directions: Count the cats and tell how many.

+ = 2

+ = 3

+ = 4

Page 195

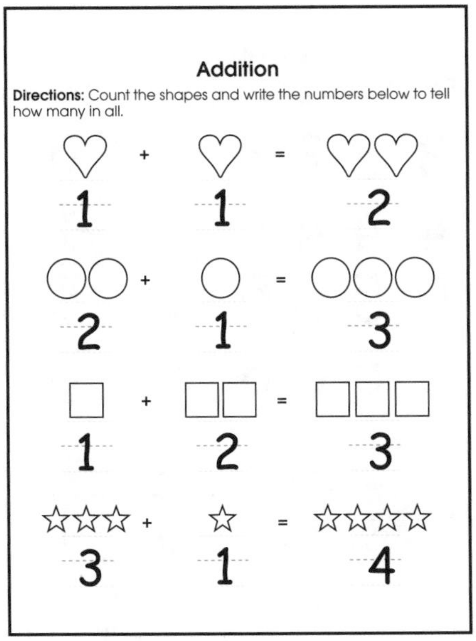

Addition

Directions: Count the shapes and write the numbers below to tell how many in all.

1 + 1 = 2

2 + 1 = 3

1 + 2 = 3

3 + 1 = 4

Page 196

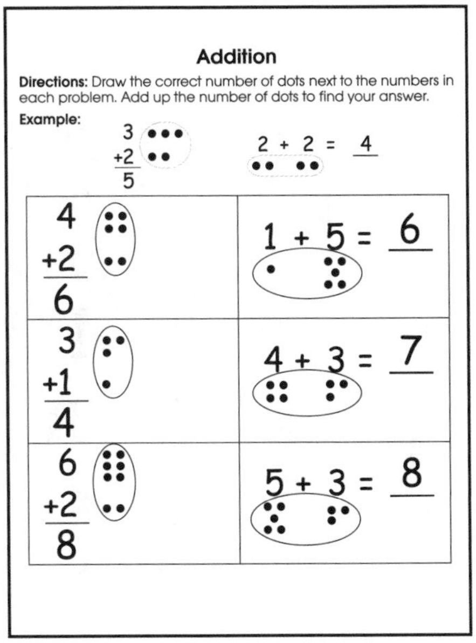

Addition

Directions: Draw the correct number of dots next to the numbers in each problem. Add up the number of dots to find your answer.

Example: 3 + 2 = 5   2 + 2 = 4

4 + 2 = 6	1 + 5 = 6
3 + 1 = 4	4 + 3 = 7
6 + 2 = 8	5 + 3 = 8

Page 197

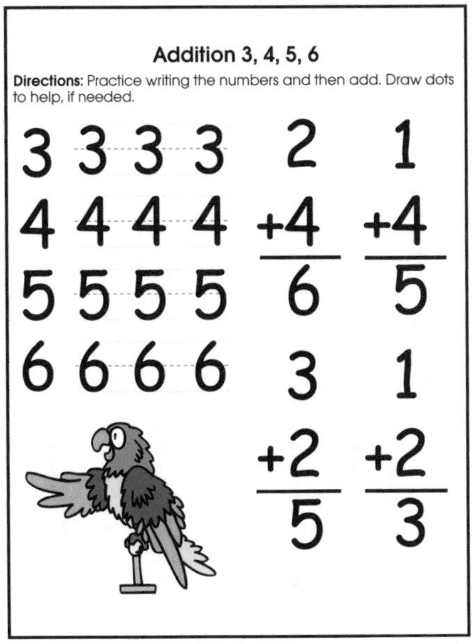

Addition 3, 4, 5, 6

Directions: Practice writing the numbers and then add. Draw dots to help, if needed.

3 3 3 3

4 4 4 4

5 5 5 5

6 6 6 6

2 + 4 = 6   1 + 4 = 5

3 + 2 = 5   1 + 2 = 3

Answer Key

Page 198

Addition 4, 5, 6, 7

Directions: Practice writing the numbers and then add. Draw dots to help, if needed.

4 4 4 4
5 5 5 5
6 6 6 6
7 7 7 7

$2 + 5 = 7$ $3 + 1 = 4$

$4 + 1 = 5$ $2 + 4 = 6$

Page 199

Addition 6, 7, 8

Directions: Practice writing the numbers and then add. Draw dots to help, if needed.

6 6 6 6
7 7 7 7
8 8 8 8

$3 + 4 = 7$ $5 + 1 = 6$

$2 + 6 = 8$ $4 + 4 = 8$

Page 200

Addition 7, 8, 9

Directions: Practice writing the numbers and then add. Draw dots to help, if needed.

7 7 7 7
8 8 8 8
9 9 9 9

$8 + 1 = 9$ $3 + 5 = 8$

$2 + 7 = 9$ $6 + 1 = 7$

Page 201

Addition Table

Directions: Add across and down with a friend. Fill in the spaces.

+	0	1	2	3	4	5
0	0	1	2	3	4	5
1	1	2	3	4	5	6
2	2	3	4	5	6	7
3	3	4	5	6	7	8
4	4	5	6	7	8	9
5	5	6	7	8	9	10

Do you notice any number patterns in the Addition Table?

Page 202

Subtraction 1, 2, 3

Subtraction means "taking away" or subtracting one number from another. "–" is a minus sign. It means to subtract the second number from the first.

Directions: Practice writing the numbers and then subtract. Draw dots and cross them out, if needed.

1 1 1 1
2 2 2 2
3 3 3 3

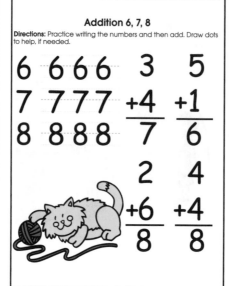

$3 - 1 = 2$ $4 - 3 = 1$

$2 - 1 = 1$ $3 - 2 = 1$

Page 203

Subtraction 3, 4, 5, 6

Directions: Practice writing the numbers and then subtract. Draw dots and cross them out, if needed.

3 3 3 3
4 4 4 4
5 5 5 5
6 6 6 6

$5 - 2 = 3$ $6 - 1 = 5$

$6 - 3 = 3$ $5 - 1 = 4$

Answer Key

Page 204

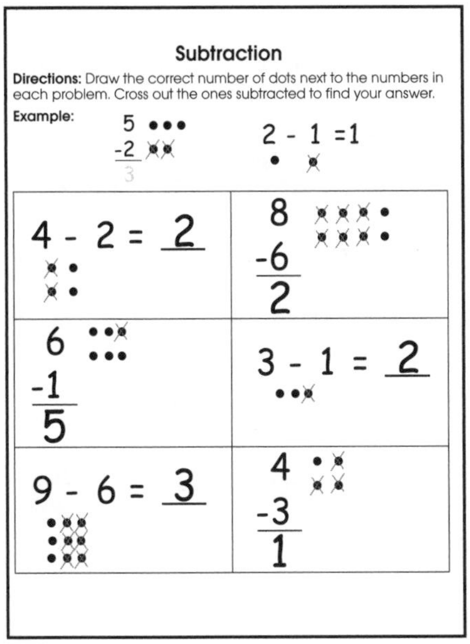

Subtraction

Directions: Draw the correct number of dots next to the numbers in each problem. Cross out the ones subtracted to find your answer.

Example: 5 − 2 = 3   2 − 1 = 1

4 − 2 = 2	8 − 6 = 2
6 − 1 = 5	3 − 1 = 2
9 − 6 = 3	4 − 3 = 1

Page 205

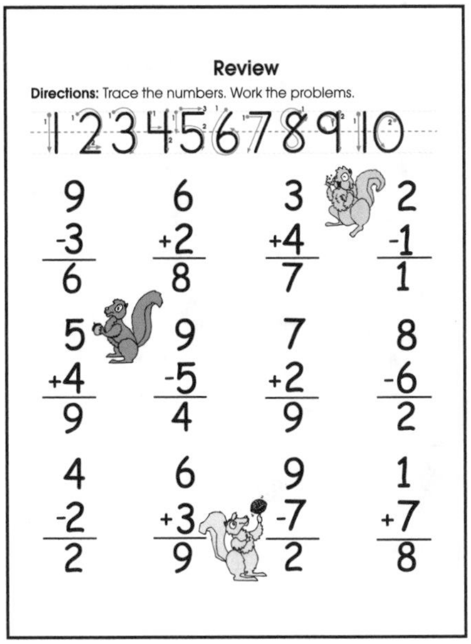

Review

Directions: Trace the numbers. Work the problems.

1 2 3 4 5 6 7 8 9 10

9 − 3 = 6	6 + 2 = 8	3 + 4 = 7	2 − 1 = 1
5 + 4 = 9	9 − 5 = 4	7 + 2 = 9	8 − 6 = 2
4 − 2 = 2	6 + 3 = 9	9 − 7 = 2	1 + 7 = 8

Page 206

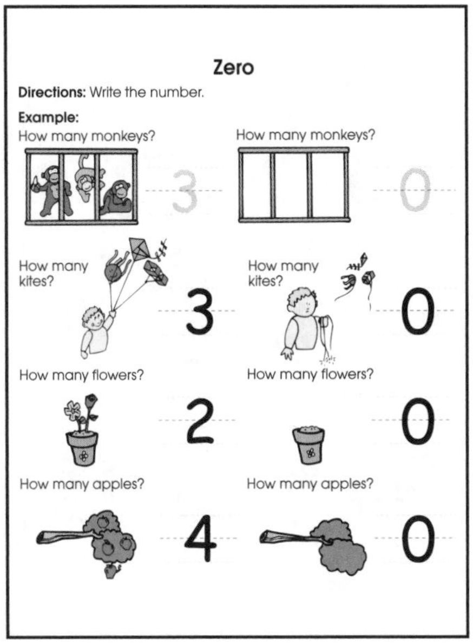

Zero

Directions: Write the number.

Example:
How many monkeys? 3 How many monkeys? 0

How many kites? 3 How many kites? 0

How many flowers? 2 How many flowers? 0

How many apples? 4 How many apples? 0

Page 207

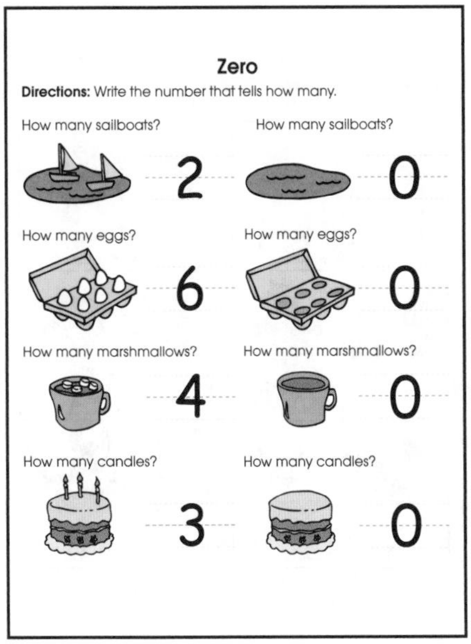

Zero

Directions: Write the number that tells how many.

How many sailboats? 2 How many sailboats? 0

How many eggs? 6 How many eggs? 0

How many marshmallows? 4 How many marshmallows? 0

How many candles? 3 How many candles? 0

Page 208

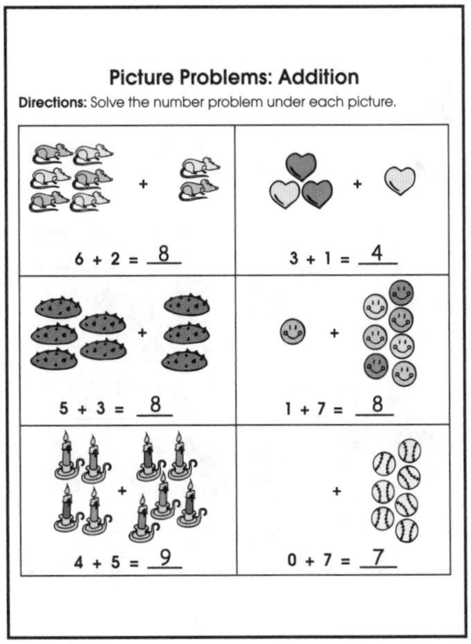

Picture Problems: Addition

Directions: Solve the number problem under each picture.

6 + 2 = 8	3 + 1 = 4
5 + 3 = 8	1 + 7 = 8
4 + 5 = 9	0 + 7 = 7

Page 209

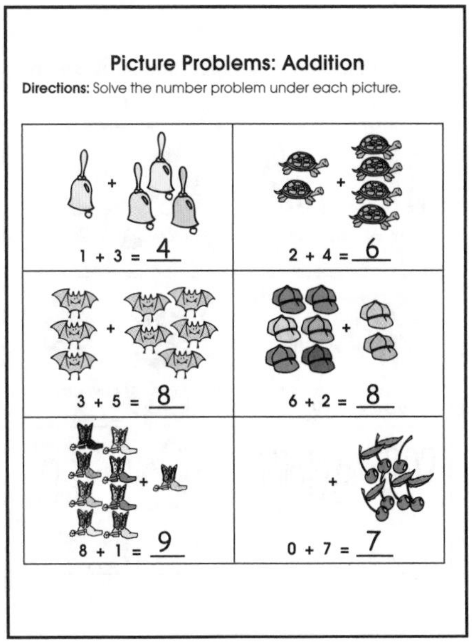

Picture Problems: Addition

Directions: Solve the number problem under each picture.

1 + 3 = 4	2 + 4 = 6
3 + 5 = 8	6 + 2 = 8
8 + 1 = 9	0 + 7 = 7

Answer Key

Page 210

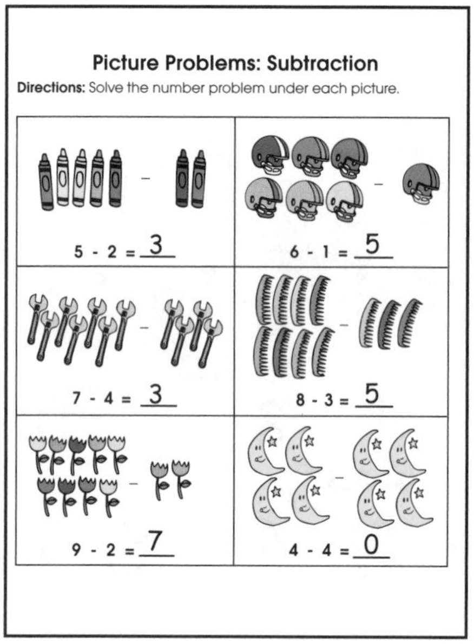

Picture Problems: Subtraction

Directions: Solve the number problem under each picture.

5 - 2 = 3	6 - 1 = 5
7 - 4 = 3	8 - 3 = 5
9 - 2 = 7	4 - 4 = 0

Page 211

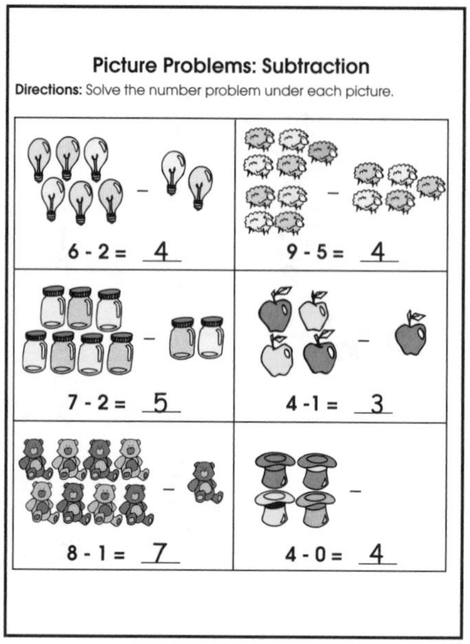

Picture Problems: Subtraction

Directions: Solve the number problem under each picture.

6 - 2 = 4	9 - 5 = 4
7 - 2 = 5	4 - 1 = 3
8 - 1 = 7	4 - 0 = 4

Page 212

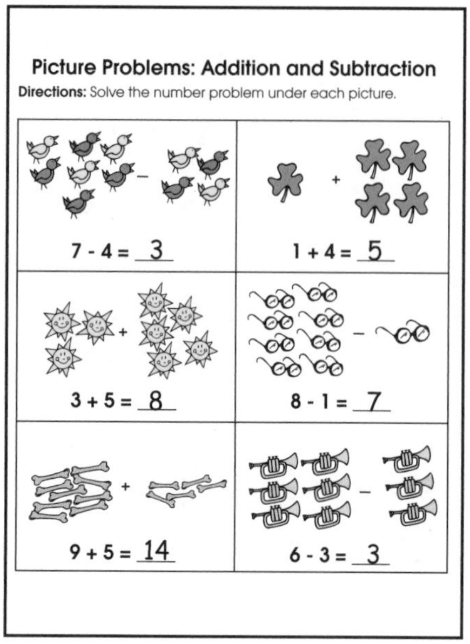

Picture Problems: Addition and Subtraction

Directions: Solve the number problem under each picture.

7 - 4 = 3	1 + 4 = 5
3 + 5 = 8	8 - 1 = 7
9 + 5 = 14	6 - 3 = 3

Page 213

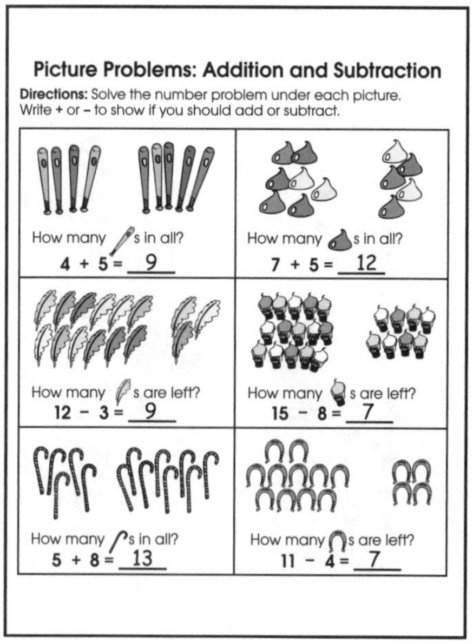

Picture Problems: Addition and Subtraction

Directions: Solve the number problem under each picture. Write + or – to show if you should add or subtract.

How many s in all? 4 + 5 = 9	How many s in all? 7 + 5 = 12
How many s are left? 12 – 3 = 9	How many s are left? 15 – 8 = 7
How many s in all? 5 + 8 = 13	How many s are left? 11 – 4 = 7

Page 214

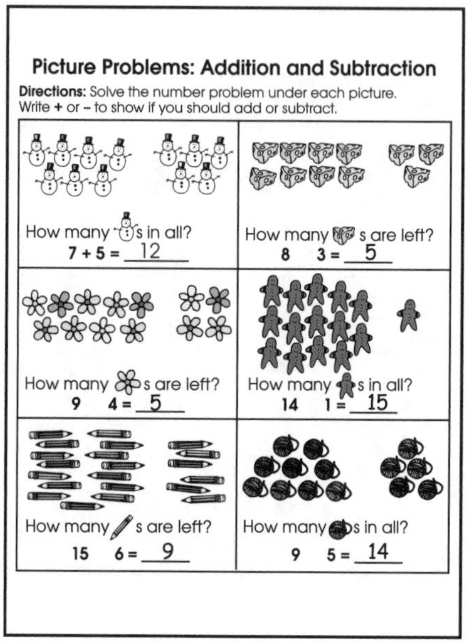

Picture Problems: Addition and Subtraction

Directions: Solve the number problem under each picture. Write + or – to show if you should add or subtract.

How many s in all? 7 + 5 = 12	How many s are left? 8 3 = 5
How many s are left? 9 4 = 5	How many s in all? 14 1 = 15
How many s are left? 15 6 = 9	How many s in all? 9 5 = 14

Page 215

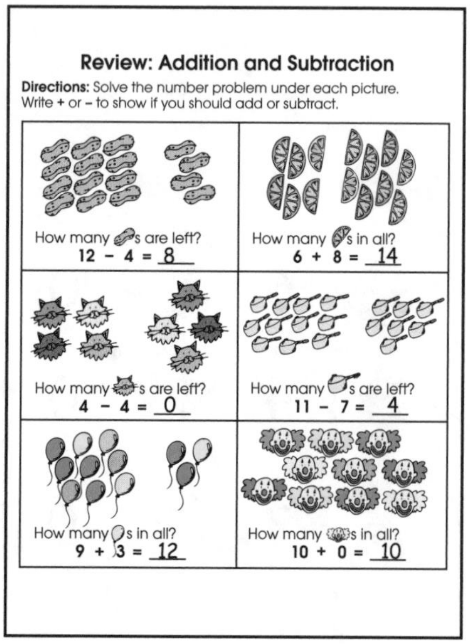

Review: Addition and Subtraction

Directions: Solve the number problem under each picture. Write + or – to show if you should add or subtract.

How many s are left? 12 – 4 = 8	How many s in all? 6 + 8 = 14
How many s are left? 4 – 4 = 0	How many s are left? 11 – 7 = 4
How many s in all? 9 + 3 = 12	How many s in all? 10 + 0 = 10

Answer Key

Page 216

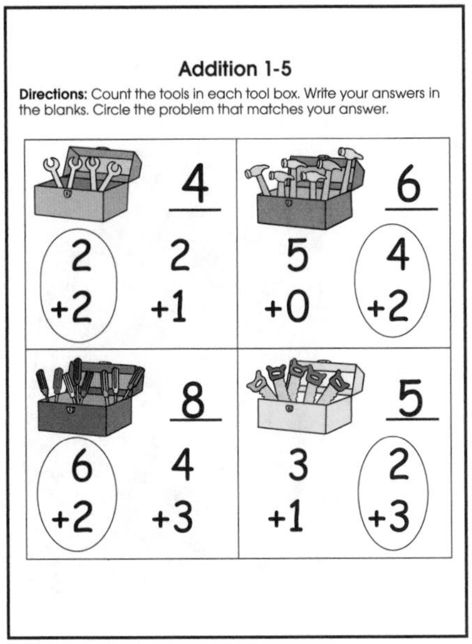

Addition 1-5

Directions: Count the tools in each tool box. Write your answers in the blanks. Circle the problem that matches your answer.

4: 2 +2 (circled), 2 +1

6: 5 +0, 4 +2 (circled)

8: 6 +2 (circled), 4 +3

5: 3 +1, 2 +3 (circled)

Page 217

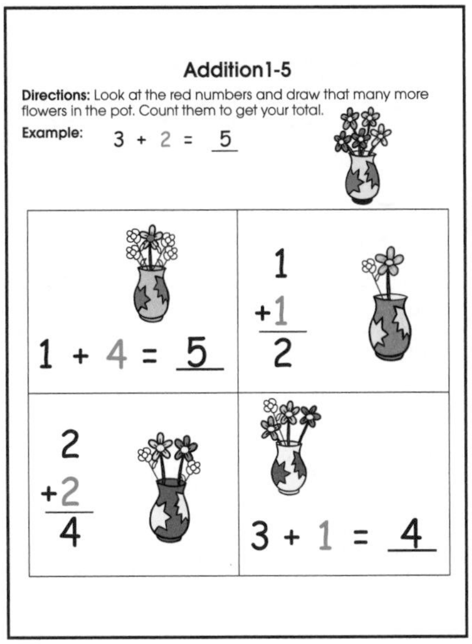

Addition1-5

Directions: Look at the red numbers and draw that many more flowers in the pot. Count them to get your total.

Example: 3 + 2 = 5

1 + 4 = 5

1 +1 = 2

2 +2 = 4

3 + 1 = 4

Page 218

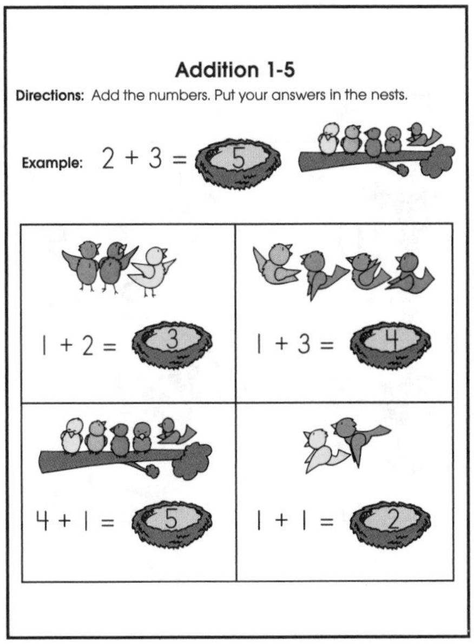

Addition 1-5

Directions: Add the numbers. Put your answers in the nests.

Example: 2 + 3 = 5

1 + 2 = 3

1 + 3 = 4

4 + 1 = 5

1 + 1 = 2

Page 219

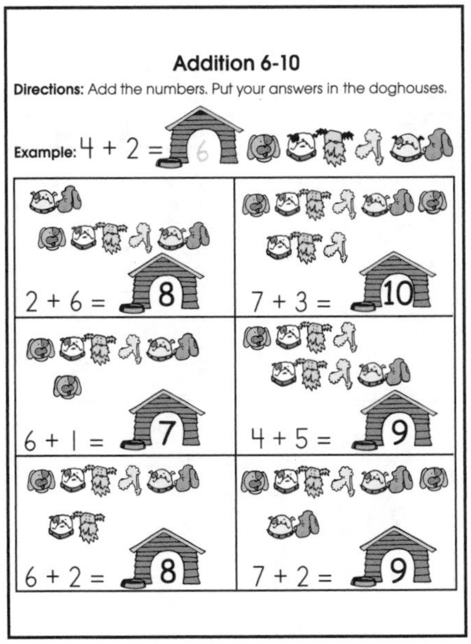

Addition 6-10

Directions: Add the numbers. Put your answers in the doghouses.

Example: 4 + 2 = 6

2 + 6 = 8

7 + 3 = 10

6 + 1 = 7

4 + 5 = 9

6 + 2 = 8

7 + 2 = 9

Page 220

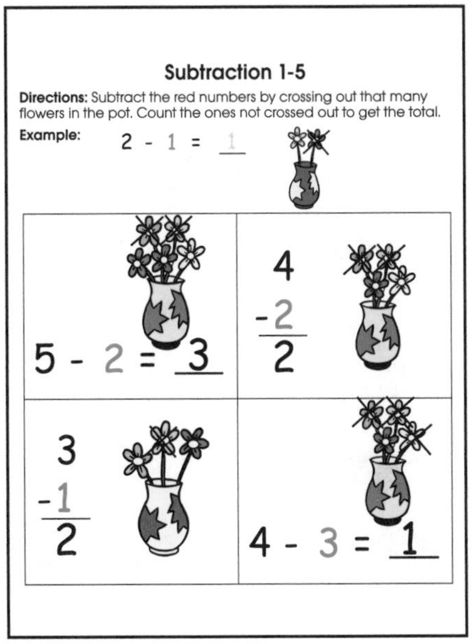

Subtraction 1-5

Directions: Subtract the red numbers by crossing out that many flowers in the pot. Count the ones not crossed out to get the total.

Example: 2 - 1 = 1

5 - 2 = 3

4 -2 = 2

3 -1 = 2

4 - 3 = 1

Page 221

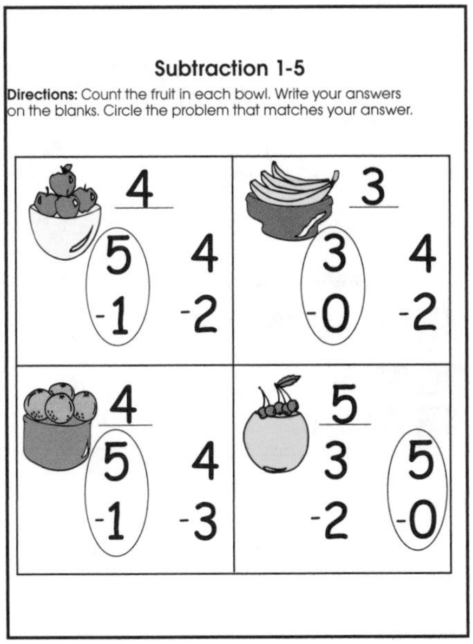

Subtraction 1-5

Directions: Count the fruit in each bowl. Write your answers on the blanks. Circle the problem that matches your answer.

4: 5 -1 (circled), 4 -2

3: 3 -0 (circled), 4 -2

4: 5 -1 (circled), 4 -3

5: 3 -2, 5 -0 (circled)

Answer Key

Page 222

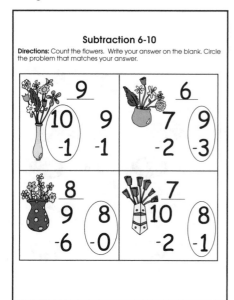

Subtraction 6-10

Directions: Count the flowers. Write your answer on the blank. Circle the problem that matches your answer.

9 — (10 - 1) circled, 9 - 1	6 — 7 - 2, (9 - 3) circled
8 — 9 - 6, (8 - 0) circled	7 — 10 - 2, (8 - 1) circled

Page 223

Addition and Subtraction

Directions: Solve the problems. Remember, addition means "putting together" or adding two or more numbers to find the sum. Subtraction means "taking away" or subtracting one number from another.

1 + 3 = 4 4 - 3 = 1 4 + 5 = 9

6 + 1 = 7 7 - 2 = 5 8 - 4 = 4

9 - 1 = 8 10 - 3 = 7

5 - 2 = 3 6 + 3 = 9

8 + 2 = 10 5 + 5 = 10

Page 224

Addition and Subtraction

Remember, addition means "putting together" or adding two or more numbers to find the sum. Subtraction means "take away" or subtracting one number from another.

Directions: Solve the problems. From your answers, use the code to color the quilt.

Color:
6 = blue
7 = yellow
8 = green
9 = red
10 = orange

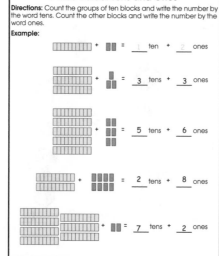

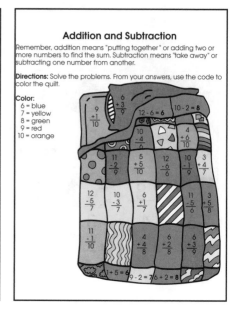

Page 225

Place Value: Tens and Ones

The place value of a digit, or numeral, is shown by where it is in the number. For example, in the number **23**, **2** has the place value of **tens**, and **3** is ones.

Directions: Count the groups of ten crayons and write the number by the word **tens**. Count the other crayons and write the number by the word **ones**.

Example: + = 1 ten + 1 one

+ = 2 tens + 3 ones

+ = 4 tens + 8 ones

+ = 7 tens + 2 ones

6 tens + 3 ones = 63 5 tens + 1 one = 51

3 tens + 8 ones = 38 9 tens + 7 ones = 97

4 tens + 5 ones = 45 2 tens + 8 ones = 28

Page 226

Place Value: Tens and Ones

Directions: Count the groups of ten blocks and write the number by the word tens. Count the other blocks and write the number by the word ones.

Example:

+ = 1 ten + 2 ones

+ = 3 tens + 3 ones

+ = 5 tens + 6 ones

+ = 2 tens + 8 ones

+ = 7 tens + 2 ones

Page 227

Place Value: Tens and Ones

Directions: Write the answers in the correct spaces.

	tens	ones		
3 tens, 2 ones	3	2	=	32
3 tens, 7 ones	3	7	=	37
9 tens, 1 one	9	1	=	91
5 tens, 6 ones	5	6	=	56
6 tens, 5 ones	6	5	=	65
6 tens, 8 ones	6	8	=	68
2 tens, 8 ones	2	8	=	28
4 tens, 9 ones	4	9	=	49
1 ten, 4 ones	1	4	=	14
8 tens, 2 ones	8	2	=	82
4 tens, 2 ones	4	2	=	42

28 = 2 tens, 8 ones
64 = 6 tens, 4 ones
56 = 5 tens, 6 ones
72 = 7 tens, 2 ones
38 = 3 tens, 8 ones
17 = 1 ten, 7 ones
63 = 6 tens, 3 ones
12 = 1 ten, 2 ones

Answer Key

Page 228

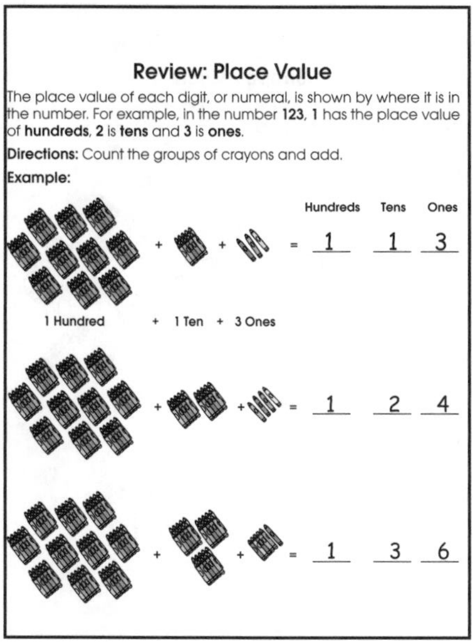

Review: Place Value

The place value of each digit, or numeral, is shown by where it is in the number. For example, in the number **123**, **1** has the place value of **hundreds**, **2** is **tens** and **3** is **ones**.

Directions: Count the groups of crayons and add.

Example:

	Hundreds	Tens	Ones
1 Hundred + 1 Ten + 3 Ones =	1	1	3
=	1	2	4
=	1	3	6

Page 229

Counting by Fives

Directions: Count by fives to draw the path to the playground.

Page 230

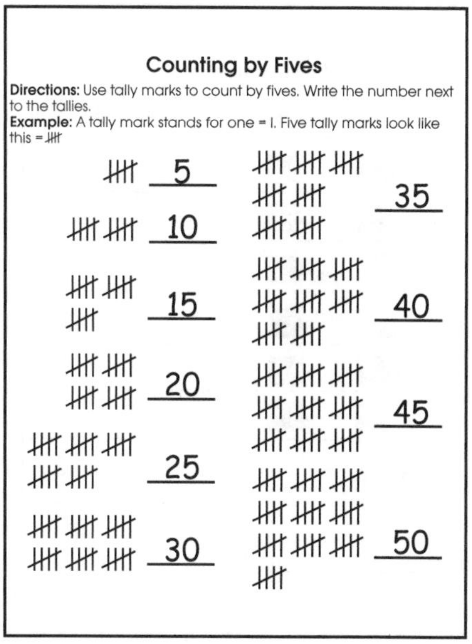

Counting by Fives

Directions: Use tally marks to count by fives. Write the number next to the tallies.

Example: A tally mark stands for one = I. Five tally marks look like this = ||||

5, 10, 15, 20, 25, 30, 35, 40, 45, 50

Page 231

Counting by Tens

Directions: Count in order by tens to draw the path the boy takes to the store.

Page 232

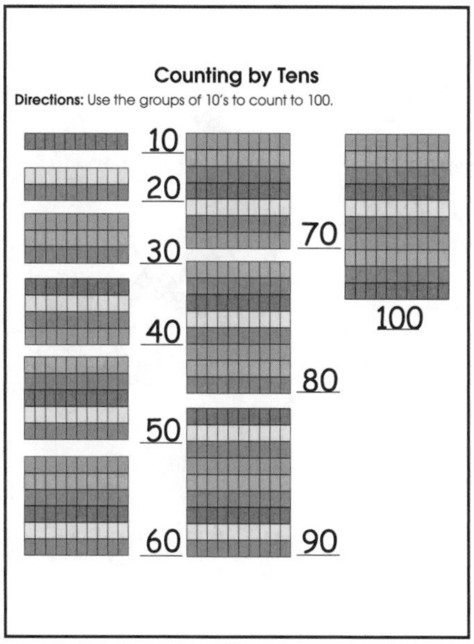

Counting by Tens

Directions: Use the groups of 10's to count to 100.

10, 20, 30, 40, 50, 60, 70, 80, 90, 100

Page 233

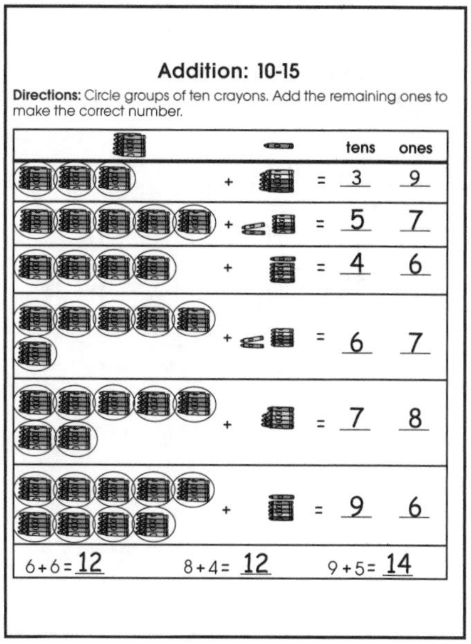

Addition: 10-15

Directions: Circle groups of ten crayons. Add the remaining ones to make the correct number.

		tens	ones
+	=	3	9
+	=	5	7
+	=	4	6
+	=	6	7
+	=	7	8
+	=	9	6

6+6= 12 8+4= 12 9+5= 14

Answer Key

Page 234

Subtraction: 10-15

Directions: Count the crayons in each group. Put an **X** through the number of crayons being subtracted. How many are left?

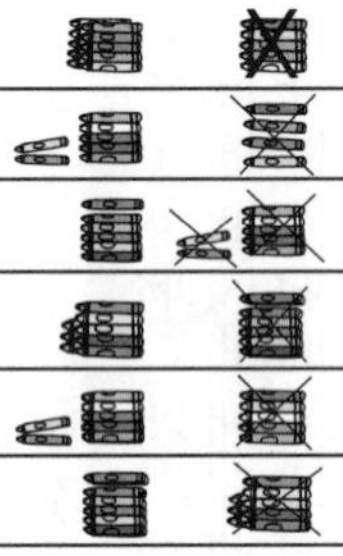

	-	5	=	10
	-	4	=	7
	-	7	=	6
	-	6	=	8
	-	5	=	7
	-	8	=	6

13 - 8 = 5	11 - 5 = 6	12 - 9 = 3
14 - 7 = 7	10 - 7 = 3	13 - 3 = 10
15 - 9 = 6	11 - 8 = 3	12 - 10 = 2

Page 235

Shapes: Square

A square is a figure with four corners and four sides of the same length. This is a square □.

Directions: Find the squares and circle them.

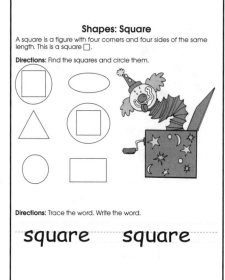

Directions: Trace the word. Write the word.

square square

Page 236

Shapes: Circle

A circle is a figure that is round. This is a circle ○.

Directions: Find the circles and put a square around them.

Directions: Trace the word. Write the word.

circle circle

Page 237

Shapes: Square and Circle

Directions: Practice drawing squares. Trace the samples and make four of your own.

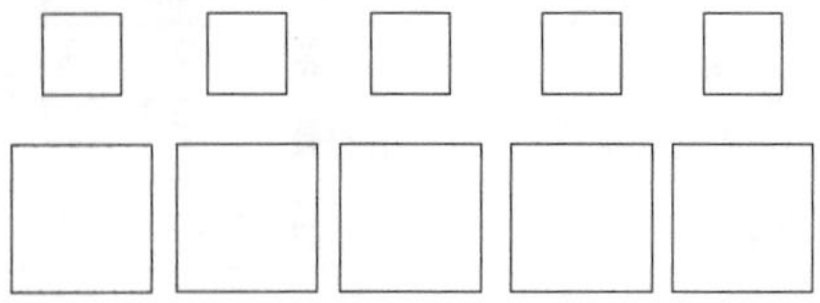

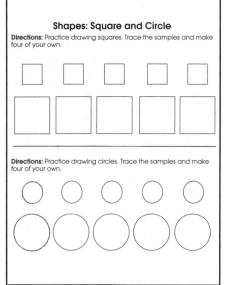

Directions: Practice drawing circles. Trace the samples and make four of your own.

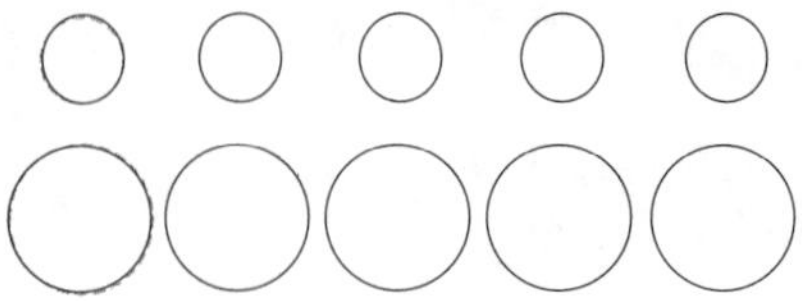

Page 238

Shapes: Triangle

A triangle is a figure with three corners and three sides. This is a triangle △.

Directions: Find the triangles and put a circle around them.

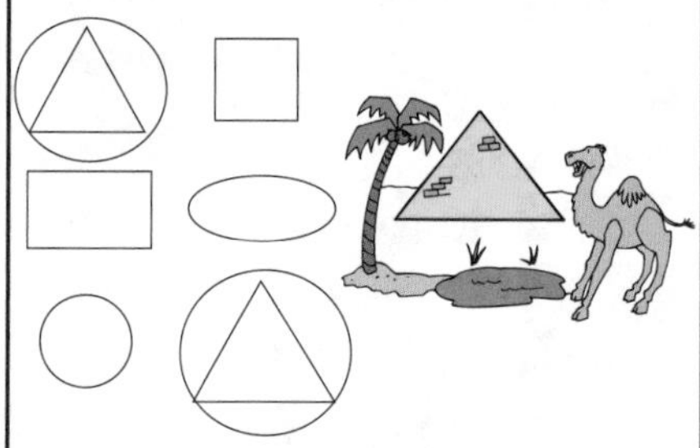

Directions: Trace the word. Write the word.

triangle triangle

Page 239

Shapes: Rectangle

A rectangle is a figure with four corners and four sides. Sides opposite each other are the same length. This is a rectangle ▭.

Directions: Find the rectangles and put a circle around them.

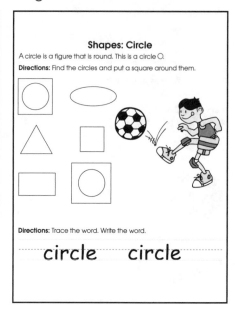

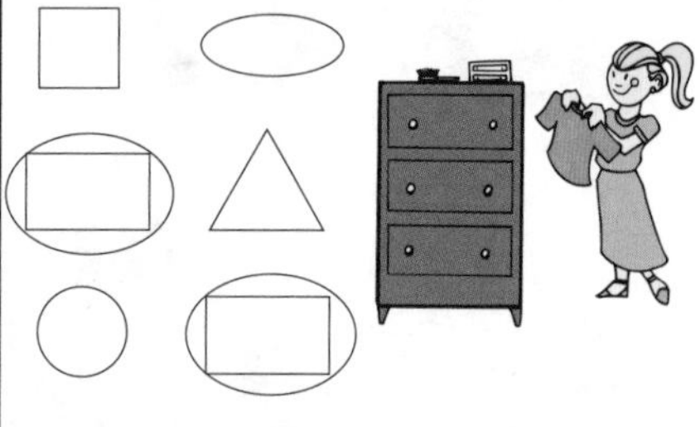

Directions: Trace the word. Write the word.

rectangle rectangle

Answer Key

Page 240

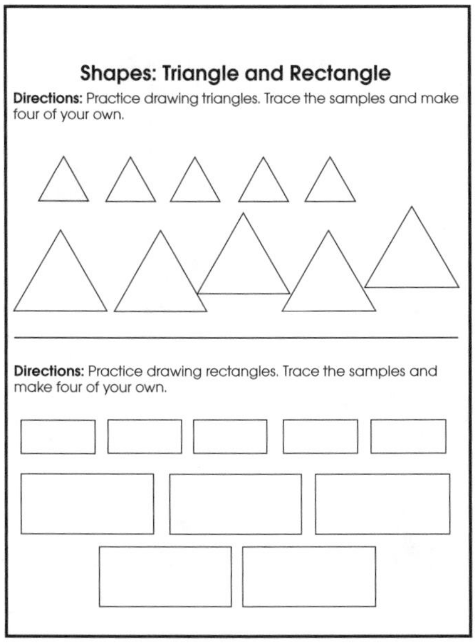

Shapes: Triangle and Rectangle

Directions: Practice drawing triangles. Trace the samples and make four of your own.

Directions: Practice drawing rectangles. Trace the samples and make four of your own.

Page 241

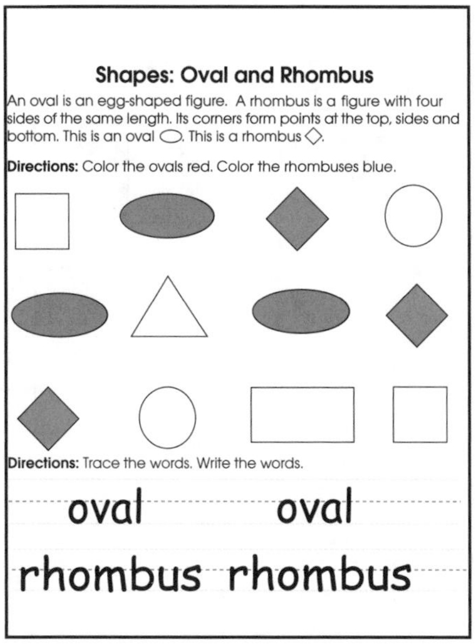

Shapes: Oval and Rhombus

An oval is an egg-shaped figure. A rhombus is a figure with four sides of the same length. Its corners form points at the top, sides and bottom. This is an oval ⬭. This is a rhombus ◇.

Directions: Color the ovals red. Color the rhombuses blue.

Directions: Trace the words. Write the words.

oval oval

rhombus rhombus

Page 242

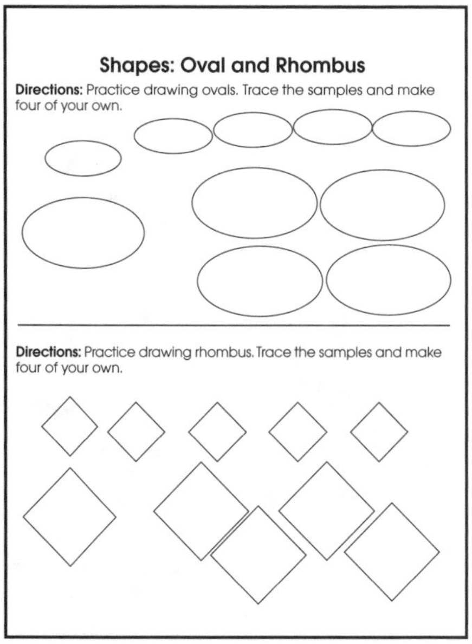

Shapes: Oval and Rhombus

Directions: Practice drawing ovals. Trace the samples and make four of your own.

Directions: Practice drawing rhombus. Trace the samples and make four of your own.

Page 243

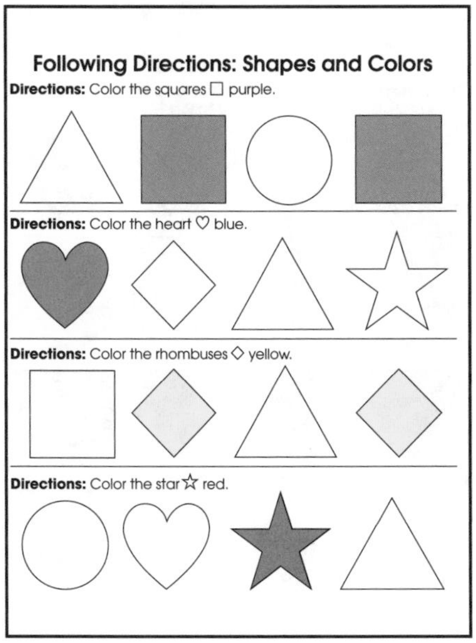

Following Directions: Shapes and Colors

Directions: Color the squares □ purple.

Directions: Color the heart ♡ blue.

Directions: Color the rhombuses ◇ yellow.

Directions: Color the star ☆ red.

Page 244

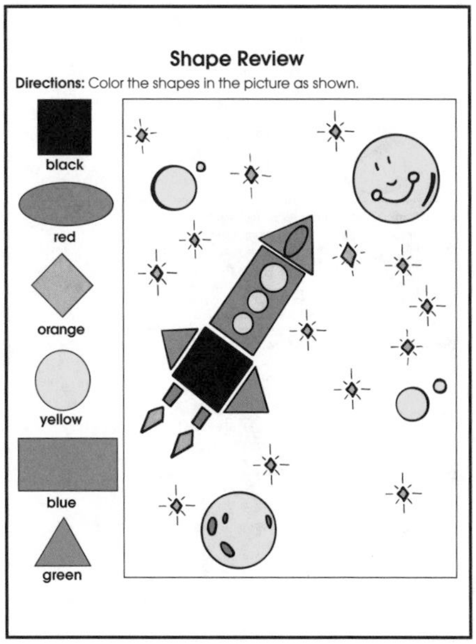

Shape Review

Directions: Color the shapes in the picture as shown.

Page 245

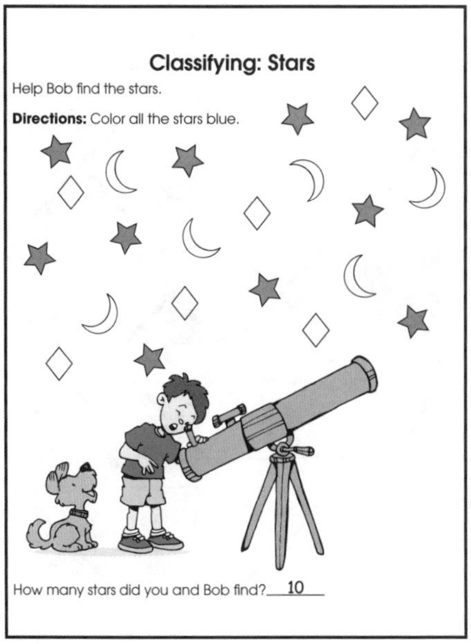

Classifying: Stars

Help Bob find the stars.

Directions: Color all the stars blue.

How many stars did you and Bob find? 10

Answer Key

Page 246

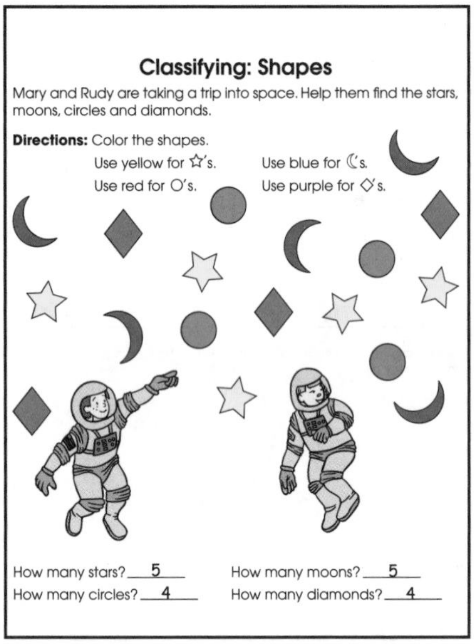
Classifying: Shapes

Mary and Rudy are taking a trip into space. Help them find the stars, moons, circles and diamonds.

Directions: Color the shapes.
Use yellow for ☆'s. Use blue for ☾'s.
Use red for ○'s. Use purple for ◇'s.

How many stars? 5 How many moons? 5
How many circles? 4 How many diamonds? 4

Page 247

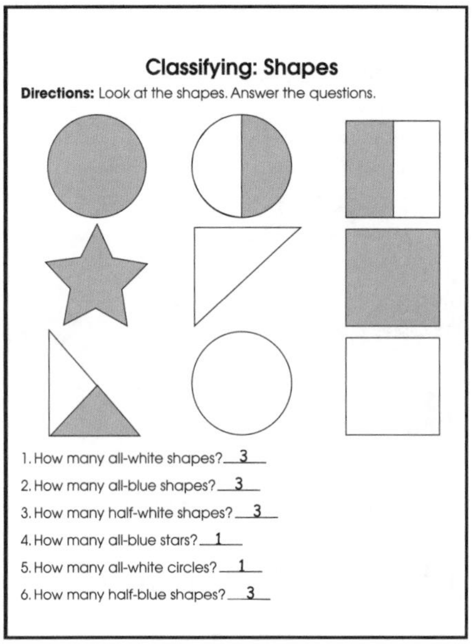
Classifying: Shapes

Directions: Look at the shapes. Answer the questions.

1. How many all-white shapes? 3
2. How many all-blue shapes? 3
3. How many half-white shapes? 3
4. How many all-blue stars? 1
5. How many all-white circles? 1
6. How many half-blue shapes? 3

Page 248

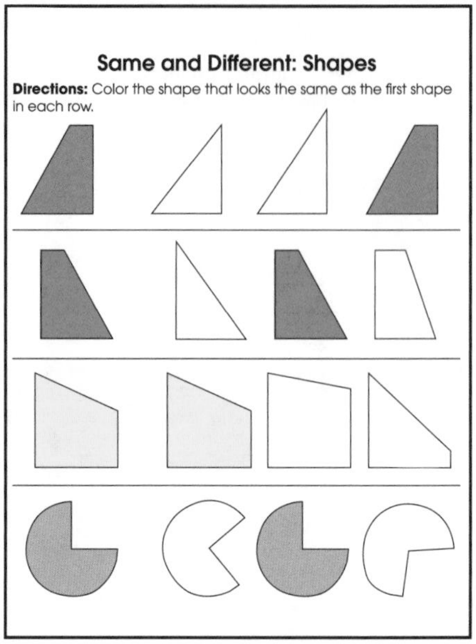
Same and Different: Shapes

Directions: Color the shape that looks the same as the first shape in each row.

Page 249

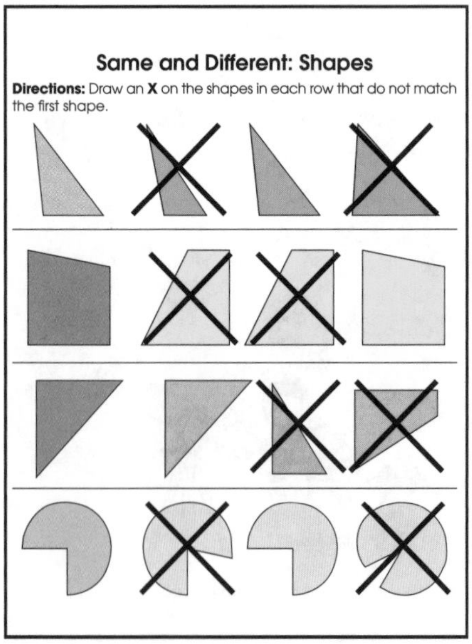
Same and Different: Shapes

Directions: Draw an **X** on the shapes in each row that do not match the first shape.

Page 250

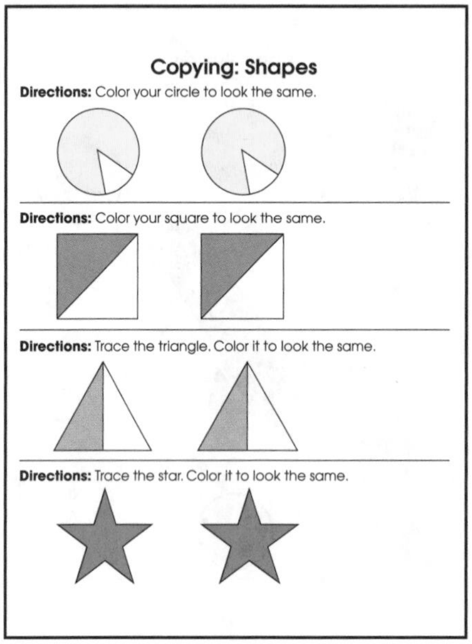
Copying: Shapes

Directions: Color your circle to look the same.

Directions: Color your square to look the same.

Directions: Trace the triangle. Color it to look the same.

Directions: Trace the star. Color it to look the same.

Page 251

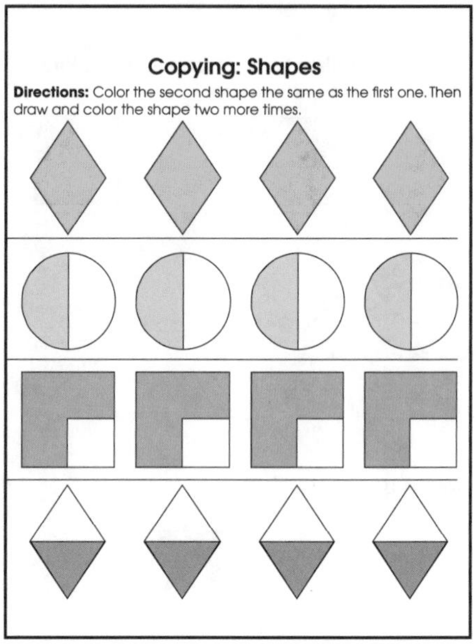
Copying: Shapes

Directions: Color the second shape the same as the first one. Then draw and color the shape two more times.

Answer Key

Page 252

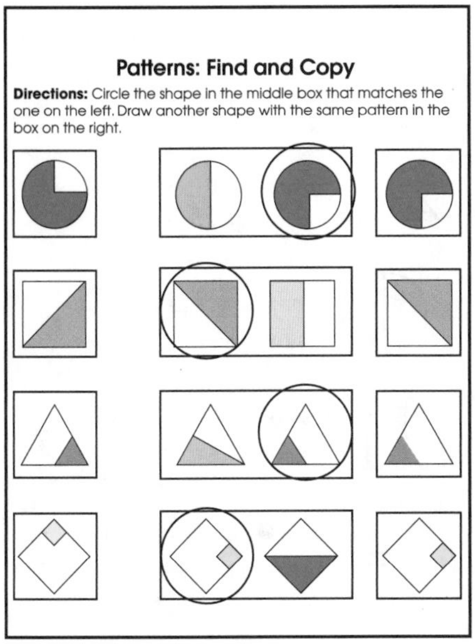

Patterns: Find and Copy

Directions: Circle the shape in the middle box that matches the one on the left. Draw another shape with the same pattern in the box on the right.

Page 253

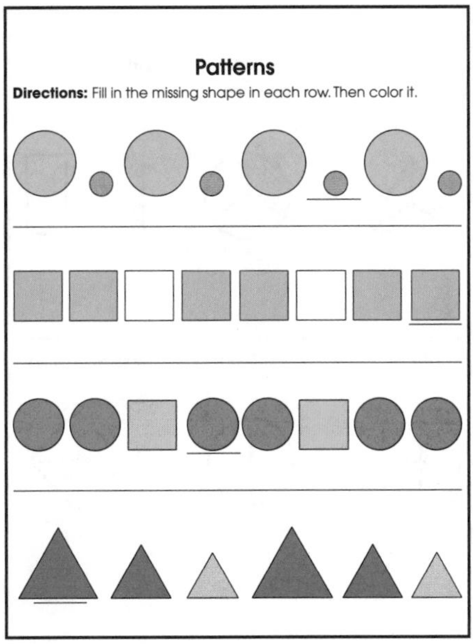

Patterns

Directions: Fill in the missing shape in each row. Then color it.

Page 254

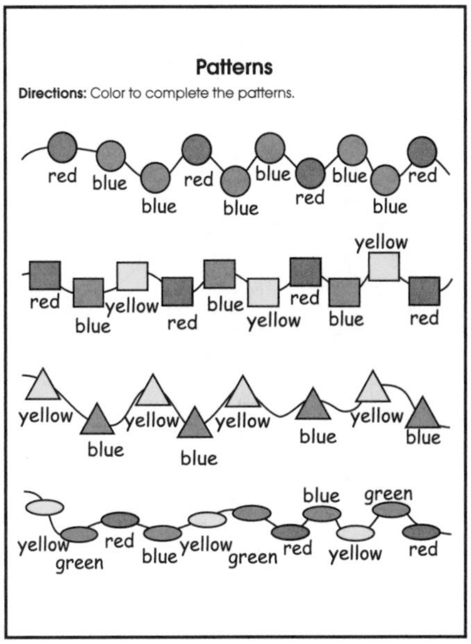

Patterns

Directions: Color to complete the patterns.

Page 255

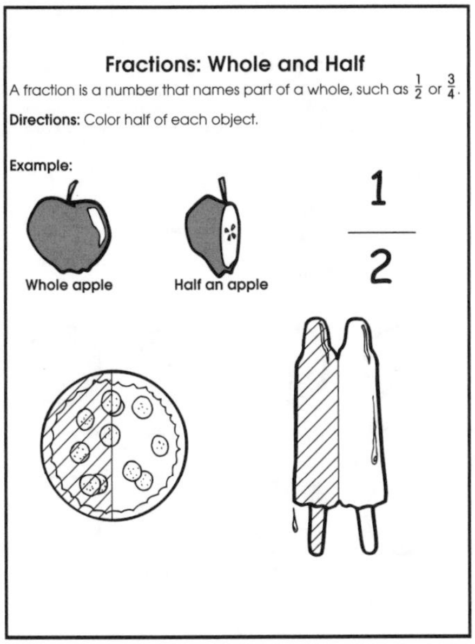

Fractions: Whole and Half

A fraction is a number that names part of a whole, such as $\frac{1}{2}$ or $\frac{3}{4}$.

Directions: Color half of each object.

Page 256

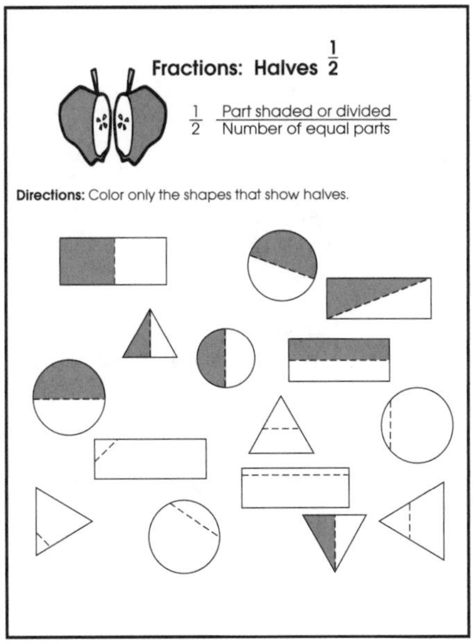

Fractions: Halves $\frac{1}{2}$

$\frac{1}{2}$ $\frac{\text{Part shaded or divided}}{\text{Number of equal parts}}$

Directions: Color only the shapes that show halves.

Page 257

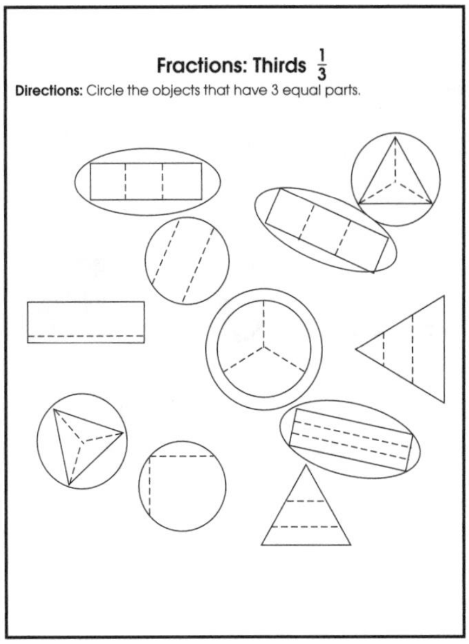

Fractions: Thirds $\frac{1}{3}$

Directions: Circle the objects that have 3 equal parts.

Answer Key

Page 258

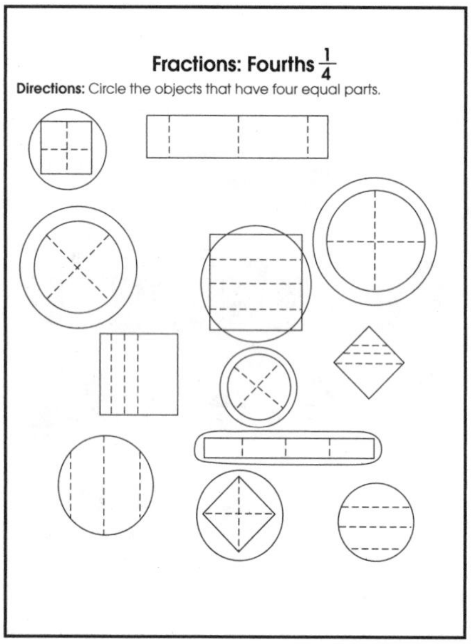

Fractions: Fourths $\frac{1}{4}$

Directions: Circle the objects that have four equal parts.

Page 259

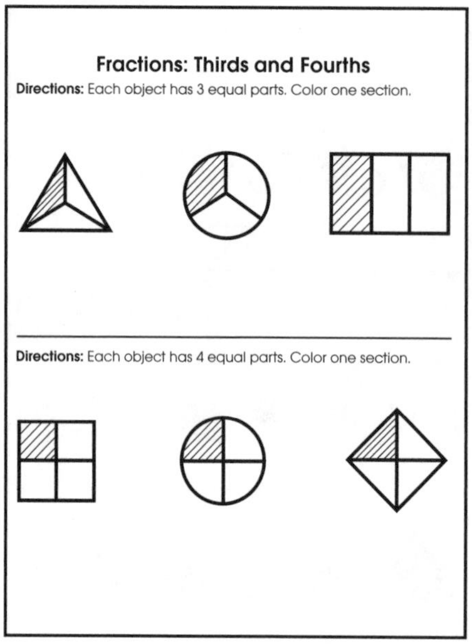

Fractions: Thirds and Fourths

Directions: Each object has 3 equal parts. Color one section.

Directions: Each object has 4 equal parts. Color one section.

Page 260

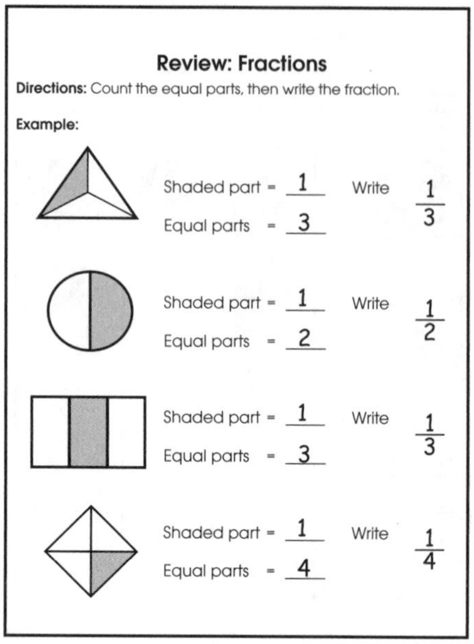

Review: Fractions

Directions: Count the equal parts, then write the fraction.

Example:

Shaded part = 1 Equal parts = 3 Write $\frac{1}{3}$

Shaded part = 1 Equal parts = 2 Write $\frac{1}{2}$

Shaded part = 1 Equal parts = 3 Write $\frac{1}{3}$

Shaded part = 1 Equal parts = 4 Write $\frac{1}{4}$

Page 261

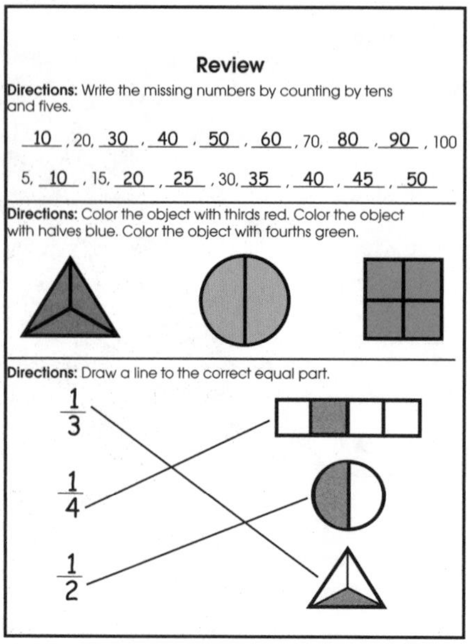

Review

Directions: Write the missing numbers by counting by tens and fives.

10, 20, 30, 40, 50, 60, 70, 80, 90, 100

5, 10, 15, 20, 25, 30, 35, 40, 45, 50

Directions: Color the object with thirds red. Color the object with halves blue. Color the object with fourths green.

Directions: Draw a line to the correct equal part.

Page 262

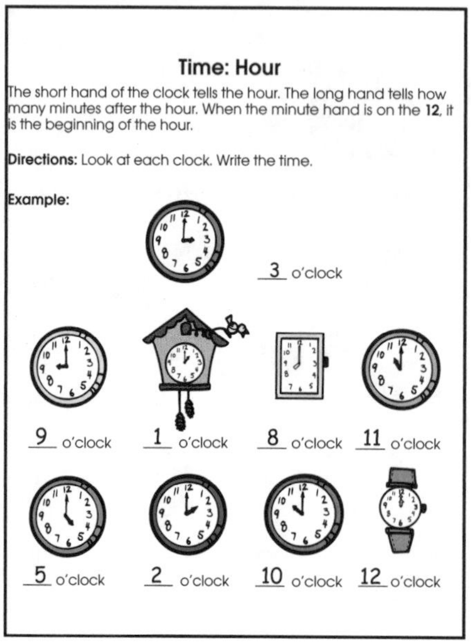

Time: Hour

The short hand of the clock tells the hour. The long hand tells how many minutes after the hour. When the minute hand is on the **12**, it is the beginning of the hour.

Directions: Look at each clock. Write the time.

Example: 3 o'clock

9 o'clock | 1 o'clock | 8 o'clock | 11 o'clock

5 o'clock | 2 o'clock | 10 o'clock | 12 o'clock

Page 263

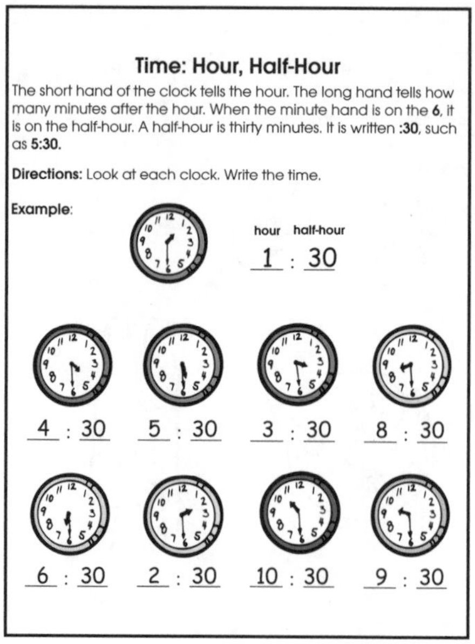

Time: Hour, Half-Hour

The short hand of the clock tells the hour. The long hand tells how many minutes after the hour. When the minute hand is on the **6**, it is on the half-hour. A half-hour is thirty minutes. It is written **:30**, such as **5:30**.

Directions: Look at each clock. Write the time.

Example: hour half-hour 1 : 30

4 : 30 | 5 : 30 | 3 : 30 | 8 : 30

6 : 30 | 2 : 30 | 10 : 30 | 9 : 30

Page 264

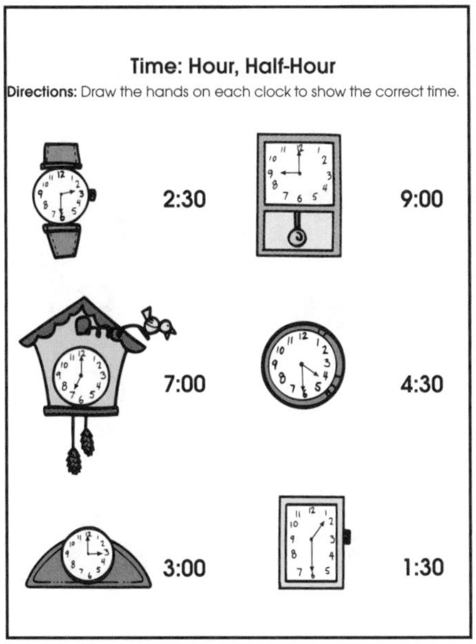

Time: Hour, Half-Hour

Directions: Draw the hands on each clock to show the correct time.

2:30 9:00

7:00 4:30

3:00 1:30

Page 265

Time: Counting by Fives

Directions: Fill in the numbers on the clock face. Count by fives around the clock.

There are 60 minutes in one hour.

Page 266

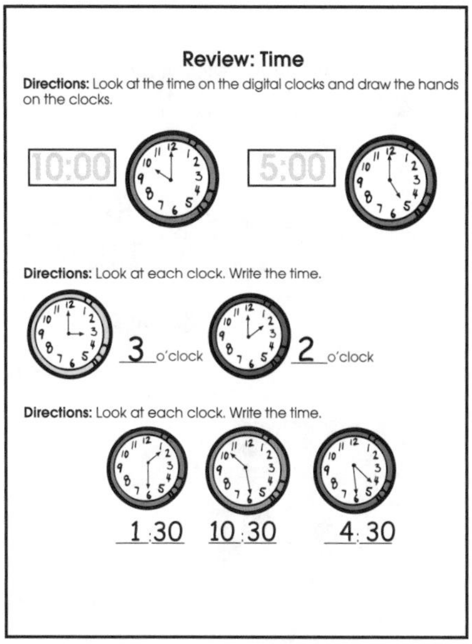

Review: Time

Directions: Look at the time on the digital clocks and draw the hands on the clocks.

Directions: Look at each clock. Write the time.

3 o'clock 2 o'clock

Directions: Look at each clock. Write the time.

1:30 10:30 4:30

Page 267

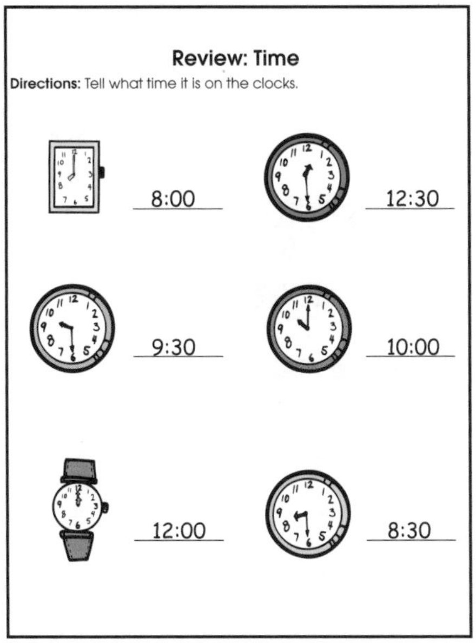

Review: Time

Directions: Tell what time it is on the clocks.

8:00 12:30

9:30 10:00

12:00 8:30

Page 268

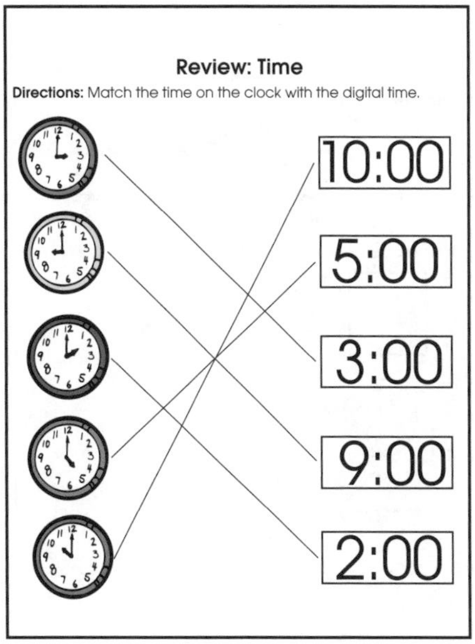

Review: Time

Directions: Match the time on the clock with the digital time.

Page 269

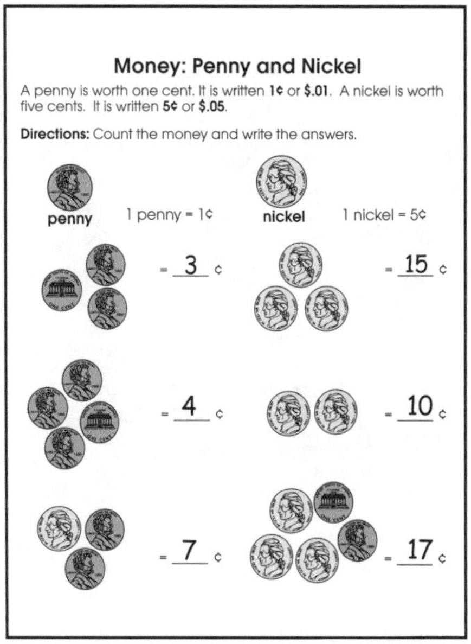

Money: Penny and Nickel

A penny is worth one cent. It is written **1¢** or **$.01**. A nickel is worth five cents. It is written **5¢** or **$.05**.

Directions: Count the money and write the answers.

= 3 ¢ = 15 ¢

= 4 ¢ = 10 ¢

= 7 ¢ = 17 ¢

Answer Key

Page 270

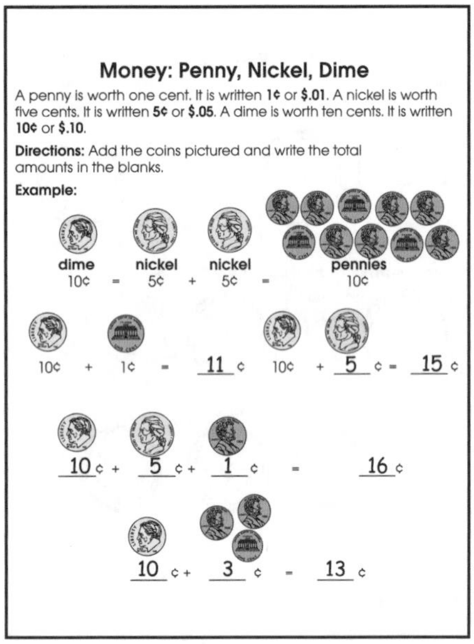
Money: Penny, Nickel, Dime

A penny is worth one cent. It is written **1¢** or **$.01**. A nickel is worth five cents. It is written **5¢** or **$.05**. A dime is worth ten cents. It is written **10¢** or **$.10**.

Directions: Add the coins pictured and write the total amounts in the blanks.

Example:

dime 10¢ = nickel 5¢ + nickel 5¢ = pennies 10¢

10¢ + 1¢ = 11 ¢   10¢ + 5 ¢ = 15 ¢

10 ¢ + 5 ¢ + 1 ¢ = 16 ¢

10 ¢ + 3 ¢ = 13 ¢

Page 271

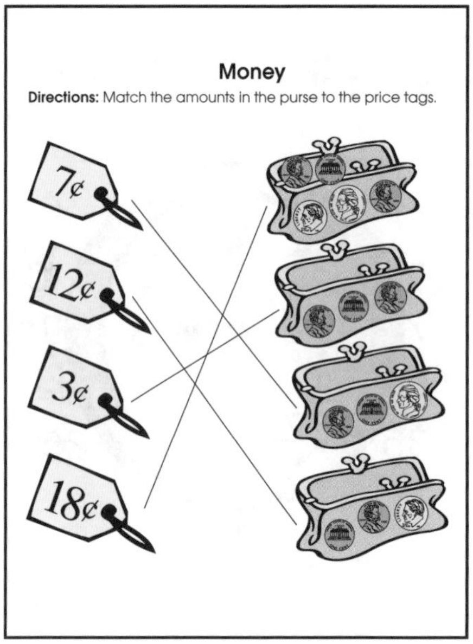
Money

Directions: Match the amounts in the purse to the price tags.

Page 272

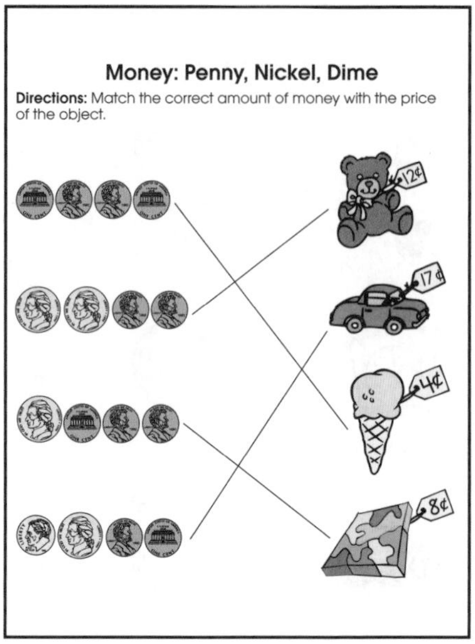
Money: Penny, Nickel, Dime

Directions: Match the correct amount of money with the price of the object.

Page 273

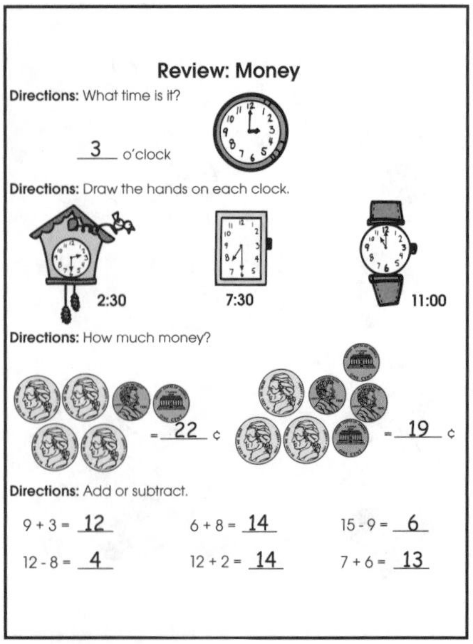
Review: Money

Directions: What time is it?

3 o'clock

Directions: Draw the hands on each clock.

2:30   7:30   11:00

Directions: How much money?

= 22 ¢   = 19 ¢

Directions: Add or subtract.

9 + 3 = 12   6 + 8 = 14   15 - 9 = 6

12 - 8 = 4   12 + 2 = 14   7 + 6 = 13

Page 274

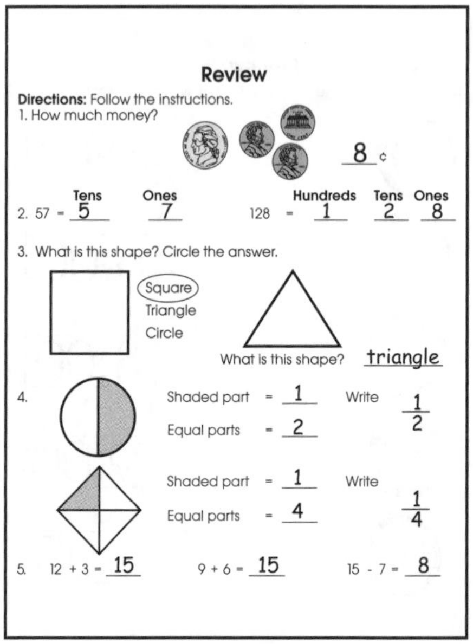
Review

Directions: Follow the instructions.

1. How much money? 8 ¢

2. 57 = 5 Tens 7 Ones   128 = 1 Hundreds 2 Tens 8 Ones

3. What is this shape? Circle the answer.

(Square) Triangle Circle

What is this shape? triangle

4. Shaded part = 1, Equal parts = 2, Write $\frac{1}{2}$

Shaded part = 1, Equal parts = 4, Write $\frac{1}{4}$

5. 12 + 3 = 15   9 + 6 = 15   15 - 7 = 8

Page 275

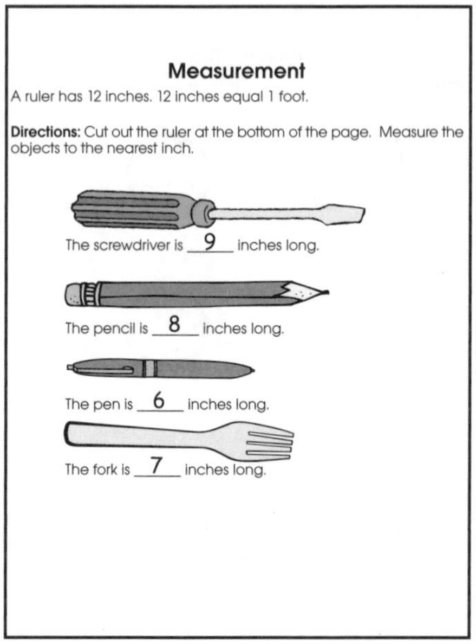
Measurement

A ruler has 12 inches. 12 inches equal 1 foot.

Directions: Cut out the ruler at the bottom of the page. Measure the objects to the nearest inch.

The screwdriver is 9 inches long.

The pencil is 8 inches long.

The pen is 6 inches long.

The fork is 7 inches long.